The Work of the Industrial Film Maker

LIBRARY OF FILM AND TELEVISION PRACTICE

THE WORK OF THE FILM DIRECTOR
A. J. Reynertson

THE WORK OF THE SCIENCE FILM MAKER
Alex Strasser

THE WORK OF THE INDUSTRIAL FILM MAKER
John Burder

THE WORK OF THE TELEVISION JOURNALIST
Robert Tyrrell

THE WORK OF THE MOTION PICTURE CAMERAMAN
Freddie Young and Paul Petzold

The Work of the Industrial Film Maker

JOHN BURDER

COMMUNICATION ARTS BOOKS
Hastings House, Publishers
New York, N.Y. 10016

Library of Congress Cataloging in Publication Data
Burder, John.
The work of the industrial film maker.
(Library of film and television practice)
1. Cinematography, Industrial. I. Title.
TR894.B87 778.5'38'6 73–635
ISBN 0–8038–8053–7

Printed in Great Britain by Fletcher & Son Ltd, Norwich and bound by Richard Clay (The Chaucer Press) Ltd., Bungay, Suffolk

Contents

FOREWORD 9

1 WHY FILM? 11

The audience for industrial films 11
Why a sponsor should make a film 13
Aim and audience 17
Selling products and services 18
Selling delivery dates 20
Film as an economy measure 21
Recruiting films 23
Training 24
General training films 24
Morale and safety 25
Prestige and promotion 28
Investment and result 30
Sponsors' success and failure 32

2 PRELIMINARY PLANNING 34

Unit at work 35
Internal units 36
Equipment for internal units 39
Decision making for the sponsor 40
On behalf of the sponsors 41
On behalf of the film production company 41
Premises for an internal unit 42
Inter-departmental liaison 45
Staffing an internal unit 47
Sub-contracting 50
Sub-contracting post-production work 51
Is an internal unit worthwhile? 53

3 PRE-PRODUCTION STAGE   57

The brief   57
The budget   59
Commission for a script   61
Outline script   62
Covering sales points   68
"Scientific" sequence   72
"Production" sequence   74
Producer–sponsor relationship   78
Specialised subjects   78
The script approved   86
Producer-Initiated films   86
Joint sponsorship   87
The Fire Script   89
Film budgets   92
Technical costs   93
Insurance   94
Artistes and technicians   94
Film stock   96
Detailed shooting script   98
Indicating camera movements   98
Film grammar   99
Shooting schedule   101
The location   101
Call sheets   105
Stock shots   107
Planning saves time   108

4 FILM STOCK AND EQUIPMENT   110

Colour or black and white?   110
Stock costs   111
Negative and reversal stock   112
How light level works   113
Film types   115
Printing: enlarging and reduction   119
Film storage   120
Integral tripack films   121
Lengths and windings   123
Choice of camera   123
Camera sound systems   125
Viewfinder systems   126
Lens characteristics   127
Automatic exposure control   129
Advantages of TTL meter   135

Format and the future 135
Eclair 16 camera 136
Bolex 16 137
Lighting equipment 139
Incandescent light 140

5 IN PRODUCTION 145

Setting up 145
Lighting for day or night 148
Rehearsals 149
Other factors in rehearsal 150
Shooting without sound 153
Location work 153
Poor lighting conditions 154
Control over monochrome film 156
Directing 158
Continuity 160
Continuity of action 164
Shooting without a script 165
Shooting synchronised dialogue 166
Importance of pace 168
Value of close-ups 169
Shooting record 169
Slow motion 170
Stop motion 172
Keep it simple 174
Subject and camera movement 174
Panning and zooming 174
Sound recording 175
The cast 176
Factual scenes 177
Planned character scenes 180
Dialogue scenes 180
Prompting 181
VIP visits 182
Equipment security 184
Checking of equipment 184
Rushes and daily routine 186
Identifying and ordering rush prints 186

6 POST PRODUCTION 188

Graded prints 189
Production of cutting copies 190
Initial editing stages 191

The editor and his job   191
Equipment for editor   193
Editing machine   193
Synchroniser   195
Editing   196
Breaking down rushes   197
First assembly   197
Tape and cement joins   198
Matching action cuts   198
Making a fine cut   201
Cutting moving shots   202
Opticals   203
Marking and ordering opticals   204
A and B roll   205
Opticals from single roll   206
Cutting pace   207
Cutting speech and dialogue scenes   207
Cutting to music   207
"Commentary over" final version   208
Pre-recorded commentary   210
Choice of commentator   212
Effects tracks   213
Ordering library sounds   214
Laying effects tracks   214
Preparing a dubbing cue sheet   219
Preparation for foreign versions   220
Rock and roll dubbing   221
Negative cutting   222
Checkerboard cutting   223
Soundtrack for printing   223
Answer print   225
Duplicate master   227

7   USING INDUSTRIAL FILMS   230

Cinema   231
Television   231
Film library   232
Sponsor distribution   234
Mobile shows   236
Company cinema   240
Equipment for company cinema theatre   241
Previews   243

GLOSSARY   247
INDEX   252

Foreword

AN INDUSTRIAL film can prove a first class investment if it is properly planned, competently produced and efficiently used. Many potential sponsors are unaware of what film can achieve and many established sponsors know little of film production techniques. Some seem to believe that films grow on trees! This book explores industrial film achievements, opportunities and production techniques.

I would like to thank the many organisations and individuals who have kindly provided information and equipment to test. My research has been carried out in the UK, the USA and Germany and it would be impossible to list all those who have been kind enough to help. I am particularly indepted to Sorel Films and my partner Alistair Cameron. The encouragement of Mrs Burder and the efficiency of Valerie Jones and Margaret Sylvester in translating my mis-typed manuscript are both gratefully acknowledged.

An industrial film can sell, train, convince, explain and instruct. It can be a complete waste of money. It can also be a good investment. This book attempts to explain how, and why.

JOHN BURDER

Why Film?

"WHY SHOULD WE make a film? We haven't even got a projector."
Those words, spoken by the sales manager of a company producing
laminated plastics, were my first introduction to the world of industrial
film. They have been echoed many times. Many potential film sponsors
are completely ignorant of the facts about industrial films. And many
who do commission productions have little idea how a sponsored film
is made. Nevertheless they need to be told if not persuaded, and nothing
could be closer to a film sponsor's interests than a good working
knowledge not only of how such films are made but how they can be
used to the greatest advantage. This book explores the different production processes and explains how films are made and how they can
be used.

The question the sales manager asked is one which should be
answered. Why make a film at all? Is a sponsored film a worthwhile
investment? If you are thinking of making a film you must first consider these questions. You must ensure that the film you plan to produce will be seen by an audience. And the audience must be of the
right kind. There are many kinds of audience and a number of ways
of reaching them.

The audience for industrial films

Many sponsored films are distributed by film libraries. Sponsors
provide copies of their productions and a film library lists the titles and
a synopsis in a catalogue which is sent to organisations and individuals
with access to film projection equipment. The films are usually made
available without charge. Borrowers are asked to complete a viewing
report sheet listing the number of people in the audience.

When prints have been screened they are returned to the library and
examined for damage. A comprehensive insurance scheme compensates

for prints lost in transit. At the end of each month the sponsor receives a report from the library telling him who has seen his film. Details of bookings can sometimes be notified in advance. To pay for this complete service, the library makes a small charge each time a copy of a film is seen by an audience. Library prints are screened on average once every ten days. Charges are not usually high and represent a good investment. The sponsor also has to supply and pay for all the prints used.

In the UK alone, over 17 million people see films booked from libraries each year. Most countries have libraries distributing 16-mm films and by using the Inforfilm organisation, international library distribution can be arranged. There are other ways too in which an industrial film can reach an audience.

Well-made industrial films should have no difficulty reaching an audience. Library distribution offers an excellent way of reaching a mass or a selective audience and there are also other outlets. Many companies take space at exhibitions. There is normally a limit to what can be shown on an exhibition stand, but film removes this limit. On one film it is possible to show far more than most exhibition stands allow an exhibitor to present on site. A projector and a back projection screen can be fitted into 3 square feet. One film can show a complete range of equipment. It can outline a service or demonstrate all the capabilities of a factory. It can show everything a sponsor wants to show. And there are other outlets too. A sponsor can organise his own mobile showings, booking halls on a national or regional basis. Showings can be advertised in the press or guests can be invited or local organisations offered a free show. Many clubs and societies welcome a film show. It makes a change from the normal sort of weekly or monthly meeting. Film shows are different, and they are remembered. Some sponsors plan and present their own shows. Others arrange for local photographic dealers to look after the technical side while they themselves concentrate on arranging an audience and introducing the programme. Shows must, of course, be efficiently presented—a poor quality show will be remembered for all the wrong reasons.

Television is another outlet to be considered. In the UK, few industrial films are shown on television but in the USA there is a wider distribution network. British television programmes are presented by the BBC and the independent television companies. But the BBC is a non-commercial network—it does not show commercials and is not allowed to advertise in any way. The ITV companies make their money by selling advertising time for the presentation of commercials. So none of the major networks is really interested in showing sponsored industrial films, though the BBC do use a few films for trade test transmission. In the USA there are over 800 stations and with more outlet there is a greater shortage of programme material. Industrial films are sometimes used as filler or standby material, and a few are included in scheduled transmissions. For television presentation, an industrial film must be completely unbiased. It must not promote a product or a service in any obvious way, for if it does, a network will only present it if the sponsor buys time on a commercial promotion basis. Films for television should set out to interest and entertain a general audience and if they succeed in meeting these two requirements they may be used by some television stations. Comparatively few sponsored films are shown on television, but it is another outlet, and for films that are not hard selling, it is well worth remembering.

Some films are never intended for general showing, but are only made for internal company use. Many training and work study films are made for showing to staff, and film used within a company can often earn its keep. There are, however, a few sponsors who make general interest films and insist on handling their own distribution. The films sit on shelves waiting for people to write in and ask for them.

Few sponsors have the experience, time or equipment to handle a general distribution. It is better to entrust the work to a distributor with the equipment and staff to do the work properly. Even specialised films made for internal company use need care and maintenance.

One of the most interesting and profitable ways of using a sponsored film is by presenting it on one of the portable self-contained projectors now on the market. Three projectors are in general use. The Videotronic, the Fairchild and a machine made by Technicolor have all been designed for industrial and educational purposes. They are completely unlike any conventional film projector, for they are self contained with their own built-in screens, picture and sound systems. They all use super 8-mm film and are cassette-loading. No technical skill is needed to operate them. You simply put the machine on a desk, open the screen, slot in a cassette and show the film. Cassette projectors are relatively new, and they have opened up an entirely new audience for the industrial film. People who do not have the time or the inclination to visit a cinema can now see a film without moving from their desks.

Why a sponsor should make a film

Now to answer the sales manager's question "Why should we make a film?" A film can, of course, serve many purposes. It can advertise. It can recruit staff and train them and can analyse working techniques. It can keep overseas customers informed and show them a factory they might otherwise not see. It can show a complete range of products—far more than any window, brochure or display. It can present a company image and show the company and its products in detail. It can outline a proposition and back it up with evidence. It can ask a question and provide the right answer. It can outline a service and illustrate economy, efficiency and speed. If the company sells, it can present a case in the way it should be presented, to potential customers all over the world.

What kind of product can best be promoted by using film? This is a difficult question to answer, for there is almost no subject which cannot be presented. I have seen many sales promotional films dealing with subjects ranging from a complete missile defence system to a bottle of wine. For 20 minutes one film tried to sell me a holiday in Spain. The next film I saw told me why I should only buy a particular brand of fertiliser! They were different films, and different products, with one aim in common—to sell. Pictures of Spanish beaches, showing people on holiday enjoying themselves, have been dropped through my letter box before. Reams of holiday brochures, issued by every country able to offer a few weeks of sun annually, arrive each year in the middle of winter. The brochures are all beautifully illustrated. They show the hotels, sun and sea, but they cannot show atmosphere. Film can capture atmosphere. It can take Spain in midsummer to an audience of potential customers sitting in a dreary hall in Birmingham on a December afternoon. It is an effective sales weapon and, to those selling holidays, a very important one.

Selling fork lift trucks is another case. You can show a fork lift truck in an illustrated brochure. The text can explain that it has been designed to work in all conditions. But on film you can show the equipment in use. You can show how easy it is to operate and how well it works, and the soundtrack can amplify the sales promotional points. The efficiency, the quality, the saving, the advantages—advantages which anyone seeing the film will be more ready to believe.

Fork lift trucks are normally bought by people used to taking decisions. A bottle of wine can be bought by a managing director or a messenger, yet a film can still increase sales. In making the film, different tactics must be used. Quality may the right point to emphasise. But there are other sales points—which film can explore. The Charles Kinloch Company sponsored a film about wines. It set out to show that wines sold in shops and supermarkets can be enjoyed by everyone, and no special skill or knowledge is required to drink or appreciate wines bought off the shelf. The film sold wines by selling simplicity. It said wine was there to enjoy without worrying too much about traditional drinking practices and old established techniques. To the ordinary beer drinker it said "You don't have to sniff a glass of wine or look in rapture to enjoy it!" Another film, also about wine, but sponsored by another company, emphasised age and quality. Both films sold wine.

and both were successful. They were aimed at different audiences, used different techniques and increased sales.

Companies producing non-portable products can often use film advantageously. A product can be shown in operation and it can be explored in the way the promoting company thinks best. Some time ago I was approached by the marketing director of an engineering group. His company produced cranes. They made many different types which sold well all over the world. The company had several overseas factories and sales figures were good. Yet, the marketing director was worried because sales were largely confined to a number of old established designs. New cranes, with improved performance but revolutionary appearance, only sold slowly. The market was sceptical. Photographs and technical specifications had been sent to customers all over the world but there were still more orders for the older, known models. As production capacity had been increased to deal with anticipated new demand, the directors were anxious to increase orders for the new equipment. They turned to film.

Specifications on paper are often very impressive. They are particularly impressive if the papers are in the right hands. Unfortunately, often they are not, and performance figures are misunderstood. Facts about new cranes designed to work reliably in hot and cold climates may be remarkable, especially to someone with the time and knowledge to read and understand the figures. But on film, equipment and conditions can both be shown. The cranes can be seen unloading whale meat on the edge of the Arctic, and loading containers in an Australian summer. For our film a detailed script was produced. It set out to show what the equipment could do. Savings in time, space and cost were all explored and the script was planned for international use. The requirements of many different potential customers had to be considered. Problems and solutions had to be presented in a manner interesting enough for world-wide use. The soundtrack, too, was carefully planned. Apart from the sound effects needed to give a feeling of pace, the film used comments made by customers already using the cranes shown on the screen. Each comment made a different sales point. In 15 minutes, the film visited four continents and showed six types of crane working in totally different surroundings doing different jobs. Seven companies explained why they had bought equipment and what it had achieved for them. And the cranes were all seen in use. And that is more than any briefcase stuffed with photographs can achieve. Facts, presented in an interesting and convincing manner.

The crane film was made for international use. There is nothing unusual about that. Many industrial films are produced in one language and distributed in others. The producers of the crane film made an English language version first and then translated the sound into seven different languages. The film proved a success and within a year production capacity was again being increased. Why did it succeed, and what are the ingredients of this kind of success?

The film only showed what the company wanted to sell. It presented its case in a clear, factual and interesting manner. These points are vital, though they are not the only points needed to ensure success. Before a script is finalised you must explore distribution outlets. The producers of the crane film realised there was no point in making a film if they could not ensure that the right people would see it. They checked, and made certain that copies sent to overseas factories would be used. Videotronic projectors were added to the production budget. And overseas film libraries were contacted and asked if they could arrange a selective distribution to industrial customers. Before the film was shot, the sponsors had a good idea of how it would be used and how many copies they would need. Planned distribution is an important ingredient of success.

There are many products which, like cranes, cannot be carried in a briefcase. Film can put this matter right. The portable cassette projectors I have mentioned can be carried like a briefcase. No company executive likes his office being turned upside down and few, if any, will tolerate the equipment needed for a conventional film showing. They will not wait while a room is blacked out, a screen set up and a projector placed on a stand at the correct projection distance. But they will often watch a cassette-type machine, placed on their desks. You need no screen and no extra equipment. The whole outfit can be carried like a briefcase. It is compact, portable and new enough to make people want to see it in operation. These machines open up an entirely new audience for the sponsored industrial film. They can put sponsors in touch with top management or with an architect on site. They can show a man in a country house three different types of swimming pool, and explain how they could be assembled on his lawn. They can show the chief engineer on a production line a new piece of machinery. They can show things which cannot be carried in a briefcase, to people who could place orders. One film cassette, slotted into a portable projector, can present a product or service and convince a potential customer that he needs it.

We have so far considered the part which industrial films can play in promoting sales of products of a general industrial nature. Some applications are more specialised. The films we have discussed were made for showing to the general public in some instances and to company management in others. These are typical audiences for an industrial film. Some films are designed to appeal to everyone, but specialised subjects benefit too. Urine testing is perhaps not everyone's idea of subject matter for a film! A London laboratory sponsored a film for showing to medical audiences and it has now been successfully shown for over ten years. It has become a valued work of reference dealing with a very specialised subject. Film can deal with many specialised subjects, but every film must be designed for the audiences who will see it. There are many specialised audiences ready to screen well-informed films. Guest Keen & Nettlefold, one of Britain's large industrial groups, has a company making flue linings. They are specialised products and GKN sponsored a film for showing to building trade audiences. The film showed that their flue lining was light and easy to install. It was designed to interest those in the building trade and it was used by GKN representatives at area meetings and given a profitable specialised distribution to a selected number of library customers.

Aim and audience

Films for specialised audiences need special treatment. It is difficult to make one film which is suitable for showing both to trade audiences and to the general public.

Films for trade showing are frequently concerned with increasing profits, cutting costs and improving efficiency. General audiences are more interested in quality, cost and application. If a product promotional film is to be made for trade audiences it will require one kind of script, emphasising one set of advantages. If the same product is to be filmed for general showing, other advantages will need emphasis, and a different script may have to be produced. Occasionally, the two viewpoints can be reconciled. A general interest film will often interest a trade audience, but if it is not made specifically for trade showing, many opportunities may be lost.

Occasionally, a set of pictures can be made to serve both audiences. The picture can be shown to the trade with one soundtrack, emphasising one set of advantages, while with another soundtrack, emphasising different points, the same picture can be presented to the general public. This system can work well for a few products and services.

A firm making kitchen furniture recently produced a film about a new range of kitchen units designed for easy assembly in the home. When the film was planned, it was made clear that it was only required for showing to the trade. The sales promotion manager decided a film would be a good way of showing his well equipped factory to dealers responsible for selling the units produced. He knew the trade, and knew the points to be given emphasis. He listed them in the film company's brief. The product had to be presented in a way that would show the complete range of unit colours. The advantages to dealers must be emphasised. The saving in storage space, the cut in stock investment costs, immediate delivery, free advertising and display materials and other points all had to be explained. The film production company produced an outline script. Then someone decided the film would also be useful for showing to women's clubs and in schools. A totally different audience was envisaged. The film production company was given another list of points to emphasise. Easy to assemble, low cost, quality finish, easy to clean—all points designed to interest a housewife, and appeal to a potential customer.

It was immediately clear that the two sets of advantages could not be put across satisfactorily at the same time. Some of the trade advantages could be interpreted as disadvantages by an audience of housewives. Greater dealer profit and back-up advertising mean little to a housewife, and can arouse suspicion. The two sales arguments could not be reconciled without losing valuable points in attempting to reach a compromise. Sponsors and producers met and explored the problems. Eventually, two different dialogue scripts were produced to match one edited version of the picture. One soundtrack emphasised one set of advantages whereas the other spoke to a completely different audience. Both achieved their objectives, and the film was produced. When it was edited, one picture version was prepared and two different soundtracks. Copies of the two versions of the film were used for different types of showing.

There are, of course, difficulties in tackling this kind of problem. But the problem must be tackled if a worthwhile film is to result. It is quite useless just making *a* film about *a* product. A film must be made for an audience. Then the product can be presented in the way most likely to appeal to the people who will see the film. Film can sell to public or trade, but two separate films, or versions, may have to be made if both audiences are to be thoroughly exploited.

Selling products and services

Specialised subjects are often only intended for trade audiences. Even apparently boring, non-visual subjects can be presented on film, and sales can often be improved as a result. An international paint company has a division selling a paint mixing system to vehicle refinishers. The system consists of 30 tins of paint and a pair of scales: not the last word in raw materials for a film script! But a film was produced and we shall explore its production in detail later in this book. This film was very successful, because it was designed for showing to audiences in the vehicle refinishing trade. It made no attempt to appeal to everyone but it set out to appeal to potential customers in the refinishing trade. It sold a technical system to a specialised audience and it proved so successful that other films were later produced.

I have already listed several different kinds of product successfully promoted by the effective use of film. I could list enough other examples to fill the remaining pages, for I have yet to find a subject which, with adequate planning, skilful production and carefully planned distribution, cannot be promoted. Literally any subject can be sold on film, though the operation is not quite as simple as it sounds. Anyone can make *a* film, but it is not *a* film which sells. It's a good film, well planned, expertly produced and properly distributed. And not only products can benefit; services have much to gain too.

A product is a tangible item: it can be illustrated in several different ways. Services need more explanation and are harder to illustrate, yet on film these difficulties can often be overcome.

A company running a clean linen service wanted to attract customers among hotels and in industry. They offered a service: clean sheets, towels and linen on a daily basis. It was a good service but a difficult one to sell. Film again proved its value. A script was prepared. It started with a sequence showing the company's laundries with particular emphasis on modern equipment, cleanliness and efficient operation. The following scenes showed van drivers on their daily tour of customers. In a few shots the variety of customers was established without any hard-selling words. We saw, on film, well-known hotels and small boarding houses all linked by a blue van and the company's services. The message was clear: the services were reliable enough to be used by some of the best hotels, and economical enough to be worth while to smaller concerns. The film went on to explore the different requirements of a large factory and a small office. It showed how both needs were met. Emphasis at this point was on towels and further sales points were outlined, and the film ended with a few brief statements from customers. Although the film lasted only ten minutes it showed in detail all the services offered, and the commentary made eighteen sales promotional points. It advanced eighteen reasons why a potential customer should try the service for himself. It showed how that service worked, and demonstrated its advantages.

Selling a service is, as I have mentioned, often a case of selling something which is difficult to illustrate effectively. Consider another example. The sponsors this time were an American company operating a telephone disinfection service. What a service to illustrate! The company had its own marketing policy. At regular intervals, thousands of printed leaflets were sent out. The leaflets showed pictures of girls, in the company uniforms, cleaning telephones. Paragraphs underneath pinpointed the advantages of the service. The leaflets produced results—but, as is so often the case, more were filed in waste-paper baskets than in filing cabinets! After two years using leaflets, followed up by visits from representatives, the company decided to make a film. They were not sure how to go about it so they called in a film consultant and asked him to look into the project with them. He spent several days visiting customers with the girls operating the service. Then he went away and wrote the script. He knew the points he had to put across, and he knew too that they were not adequately covered by the pictures in the booklet. A girl cleaning a telephone may look very nice, but there are convincing financial facts which can be brought into play. And they are facts which, on film, can be clearly illustrated. The facts were simple. Office telephones are used by many people. Germs can collect and spread in a telephone mouthpiece. People staying home through illness cost a company money, and can delay production. Time, productivity and money can be saved if the germ-carrying telephones can be made harmless. These facts provided the basis for the start of the film. The script then went on to show how the service operated without inconveniencing anyone. It ended with a brief résumé of results achieved in places where the service had already been adopted. All good sales points, and easily put across on film.

Selling delivery dates

So film can sell products and services. It can show what you are selling and prove it is worthwhile. And it can prove to a customer that orders placed will be completed on time. Orders sometimes depend on delivery promises. Some time ago a company producing guided missiles negotiated the sale of a complex missile system to an Eastern country. To win the order, equipment had to be delivered and installed at a date noted on the contract. Time was extremely important, and the customer made that very clear. The system was known to be good, and the sales proposition was a sound one presented by people thoroughly well informed about their subject, and equally experienced in sales techniques. Delivery posed the greatest problem, for the equipment had to be set up in the middle of a desert, far away from the English factories where it was to be produced. Could it be delivered on time? It was a key question and every possible argument and fact was produced to convince the customer that delivery would be carried out on the promised date. Details of every mile of the journey from factory to site were worked out and presented with a timetable for installation and testing prior to the completion date. It was a convincing case. One further card was then brought into play.

Two years earlier, the same company had sold another missile system to another Eastern country. Much of the equipment bought was in use in Germany when the deal was signed. The rest was in the United Kingdom. The staff to operate the system had to be recruited and trained. The German equipment had to be dismantled, packed and moved by road to Holland. From there it had to be shipped to the east where it had to rendezvous with other equipment being simultaneously shipped from England. A convoy of thirty lorries then had to be organised to take everything across a desert to the place where it was to be installed. It was a tremendous operation, but it worked. The company was wise enough to film it and the film took six months to complete. Most of it was shot by the company's own film unit. The completed film was first shown to the wives of the people concerned in the operation. That was before the negotiations I have mentioned took place. When the new sale was nearing its climax, the film was re-dubbed in Arabic and flown out with a representative of the company. In 20 minutes it proved that, whatever the hazards, the company could still deliver on time. The contract was signed, thanks to brilliant bargaining, weeks of hard work and an additional aid to prove a crucial point—20 minutes of film.

Film as an economy measure

Film can not only sell but can also save money. A company selling a range of fire alarms and extinguishers used to arrange periodic demonstrations for industrial clients to show how different types of fires could be controlled. These meetings cost money. Staff time was involved and a number of expensive extinguishers were let off and had to be replaced, and considerable expense was involved in preparing suitable hazards. So, they turned to film. There were two main reasons for this decision. They wanted to reduce the cost of demonstrations. And they wanted to reach a wide audience and to educate the public in the use of their products in every kind of emergency.

The film was carefully designed to have a wide appeal. It started with dramatic newsreel shots of fires where extensive damage had been caused. It went on to examine the causes and costs. It was rather like a detective story: the problem was presented but the solution had to be found by the audience in the light of the evidence presented. When the facts had all been outlined, and time allowed for the members of

Film can demonstrate most operational techniques. Live demonstrations of this kind are expensive to stage but, on film, can be given without repeating the costs involved in staging. Picture: Sorel Films.

the audience to draw their own conclusions, the official facts were made known. One fire, causing millions of pounds worth of damage, had started when someone mended a fuse with a nail. Another resulted from a housewife trying to put out a burning frying pan with a bucket of water. There were other examples too, all presented in an interesting factual manner. The film asked the members of the audience a question. What would they do in similar circumstances? This was a neat device for keeping an audience interested, and a good lead into a sequence on fire precautions: smother the flames in the frying pan, don't open all the doors and windows and so on. Simple advice, which the fires themselves had shown was badly needed. Then followed a full-scale presentation of three arranged fires. The audience saw how the fires could be prevented and controlled. The company's fire extinguishers and alarm systems were thoroughly demonstrated. To make the film, three different fires were arranged on a scale far outside the scope of previous industrial demonstrations. By using film, the company could repeat the demonstrations and the message, day after day, year after year, wherever they wished, with only the cost of film postage. In twelve months the cost of the film was recovered by cutting down on demonstrations and the film was seen by thousands of people.

There are many ways in which film can save money and some are more interesting than others. I particularly remember a man who walked into my office on a day when the national newspapers were giving much space to a raid on a company cashier. The cashier had been coshed on his way to the bank, and the attaché case he carried, and lost, contained money and some valuable jewellery owned by an actress. I was beginning to wonder what the man who showed me the newspaper headline had come to see me about and half expected to be offered some second-hand jewels! Instead, he asked me to snatch the small black case he carried. "Try and get it out of my hand," he said. I accepted the challenge, rose from my desk and grabbed the bag from the hand of the man who promptly released it. It immediately locked itself on my hand. The handle of the brief case gripped my hand like a pair of pincers: it was quite impossible for me to let go. But that was not all. Simultaneously, six steel rods, several feet long, shot out from the corners of the case. I was almost impaled. To add to the confusion, a whistle blew shrill blasts from the inside of the case. It was quite an experience.

I am pleased to say that I was very soon released and my office returned to a more normal state of chaos. The man who had provided such a thoughtful demonstration then explained why he had come to see me. His company produced the bag I had just tried to seize. It was designed for use by people taking valuables to places of security and, as I had already learned, it was quite impossible to grab the case and get away. It could be grabbed, but with the rods and whistle, movement was quite impossible, and the pincer grip prevented it being thrown away. It was a neat device, operated by a compressed air cylinder. I will not go into the details of the method of operation, because the important fact is that every time the cycle of events took place, a special compressed air cylinder was used. The cylinders were expensive to replace—too expensive to give repeated demonstrations to every potential customer. Film, you will by now have guessed, helped to save money. One demonstration was suitably dramatised and filmed so that now, by using the film, the equipment can be demonstrated repeatedly anywhere and at any time, without the cost of replacing the cylinders. It cost very little to make a five-minute film to cover this subject. The film has made this product known to numerous customers and it has, of course, saved the cost of giving repeated demonstrations.

Recruiting films

Industrial films do not have to sell or advertise products and services. They can also recruit staff and train them. A film can do much to interest a young audience and film distributors are usually in touch with schools and technical colleges. Careers advisors are always trying to find new material to use and even university appointments boards, who in the older established English universities once seemed to have heard only of the Church and the Army, now use film! What form should a recruiting film take?

In the first world war, military recruiting was greatly influenced by popular opinion. Shows, rallies and public spectacles were arranged, and many people signed up because they felt it was the right thing to do.

Some industrial staff recruiting films try to use similar methods. They present an image of a company and suggest that anyone who knows what he is doing should immediately sign up! This is a stupid approach and one which, fortunately, is nowadays rarely used. Film can certainly recruit staff but a recruitment film must concentrate on facts. People interested in applying for a job want to know what sort of company they are going to join and what prospects it offers its staff. They want to know where they will work, and what they will do, and what facilities the company has to offer.

Recruiting films must be carefully scripted. There are some hilarious examples of what not to do. Many firms try to be too clever and the company is presented as something beyond question, realism being completely disregarded. It pays to concentrate on facts: show the factory and office premises and explain what the company does. Working conditions, canteen and sports facilities can also be shown but

the way in which they are shown must be thoroughly honest. It is useless dressing up a recruiting film. If you lie on the screen, the company
gets the wrong kind of staff who, of course, soon discover the truth.
Keep to the facts and present them in a way potential applicants will
appreciate.

Training

Having recruited the right staff, industrial films can also help to
train them. In the USA, film has been used for training for many years.
Sales training productions have proved their value all over the world
and the American team of Borden and Bussey have helped to train
salesmen in every English-speaking country. Their productions have
many of the elements of a successful training film. They deal with
real situations: situations the people seeing the films recognise and
understand. This is important, for audiences are not stupid, and if they
see that the film tackles problems they know exist, they are more
likely to have faith in the remedies suggested. Realism is important in
any training film. There is one particular film which I have always
found very successful. It's called *Who Killed the Sale*. It presents real
selling situations, and real objections from customers, and suggests
possible solutions. It deals with familiar facts and outlines solutions to
familiar problems. And facts are the currency of success.

If actors are used in a training film realism must be particularly
closely pursued. Situations must ring true. There should always be
plenty of relevant examples and a summary at the end and the film
should be planned to hold the interest of the audience. Few people
like to be told what to do, but if the presentation is interesting you will
have the audience on your side and the message will then be more
readily accepted.

Always avoid dictatorship. The sort of, "You do that because it's
what we want", approach never does any good. Show how, and why,
something is right or wrong, and never dismiss a mistake with "That's
no good." Explain the point.

General training films

Some companies produce their own training films and they can
ensure that every film achieves its purpose. Many less fortunate companies have to rely on other people's productions and a number of such
general training films have been produced. There are series on management and office procedures and films dealing with different aspects of
sales techniques have been made. General training films are often
planned to appeal to as many people as possible. Some companies may

Scenes from *Who Killed The Sale* a first class example of a well made training film. The characters are real, the situations realistic and the message clear. Picture: Rank Short Films Group.

find only part of a film is relevant. When using films for training purposes the company should follow up a showing with a discussion. This is particularly true when a general training film is shown. The points made in the film can then be related to specific company requirements.

Study notes and meeting guides are often issued with films to help a training officer to organise a discussion. Discussion is the important word. If the person who introduces the film follows it up with an uninterrupted lecture, much of the impact may be lost. Film should be allowed to explain itself. When it has run through, reactions can be explored and discussions held on the points made in the film.

Diagrams are sometimes useful in training films, as are special effects. Slow-motion techniques can be used to show how a machine works. Humour in training films can also have its place but it must, in any film, be very carefully used. Nothing is worse than a contrived joke which can easily be anticipated. It is never funny, and does not serve any useful purpose. Facetious commentaries are also a painful bore. Concentrate on facts and consider the point of view of the audience when preparing a script. A training film should never be an excuse for a screened lecture; it should be planned as a film, and not as a talk.

A supermarket chain recently went to great trouble to film the introductory lecture delivered by their chief training officer to all trainees starting a course. The company chairman felt that the film could then be presented in all the company's premises without sending the chief training officer right round the country. It was not a good idea, for the film consisted only of a shot of the Training Officer delivering his lecture. He spoke into the camera lens and for a few minutes was quite interesting. But the interest did not last. The human eye tires quickly and, if interest is to be maintained, the view, or viewpoint, must be constantly changed. If the lecture had been rewritten as a film script it could have been much more successful. The text could have remained the same, but the action might have shown the training officer and the subjects he talked about. The film would then have had more impact, and could have been a great success.

So, industrial film can be used for training. There is no limit to its applications. Major airlines use film to show runways to new aircraft captains. Hospitals use it to train doctors, and companies all over the world use film to train office, sales and technical staff. It can also be used for staff morale and information purposes.

Morale and safety

When a food packaging company decided to move from a London factory to new premises in the country, many staff decided to leave rather than move out of town. The company had a good staff employment record and many of the employees had been with the firm for years. When the company discovered how many were thinking of leaving, they were very concerned, and looked round for a way of making people change their minds. A film proved to be the answer.

The company decided to move out of London because they wanted to expand and in the country it would be possible to build a new factory and enjoy more pleasant working conditions. The staff were not aware of the conditions and considered the country location as if it were in the arctic circle! So the company commissioned a short film. It showed the new factory and the houses available for the staff to live in. The local amenities were explored: new schools, shops, parks and a river. A complete picture of the area was drawn. The film took six weeks to make. Then the company held a party for its staff, and without prior announcement, showed the film. A week later, coaches took the staff down to see the area for themselves. When the London factory closed, 75% of the staff moved with the company.

Films can be particularly useful in promoting industrial safety. Every year, thousands of lives are lost by carelessness and thoughtlessness, on sites and in factories. Responsible bodies have long used film to combat this situation. They sponsor films, and arrange for them to be shown in the right places, to the people who should see them. Producers of industrial safety films are not interested in television audiences or those hogging popcorn in cinema theatres! They want to contact the men working on building sites and on production lines. Safety films must reach these people if they are to prove a success. And audiences have proved accessible and keen. Projectors are set up in staff canteens for lunchtime shows. Mobile projection vans run films outside factory gates at the end of shifts. And special showings for groups of people are regularly organised by safety officers. What are the secrets of a successful safety film?

Sitting in the back row of an audience of construction workers, I found the comments of the audience as interesting as those on the film. The audience was a tough one. No tea and biscuits, or suits and ties. The film show started after lunch and many of the audience had spent some of the lunch hour quenching their thirst. I fully expected to hear some of the sort of comments which sponsors don't really appreciate. I was surprised. There were certainly comments, but they were almost all constructive and appreciative. One comment, made at the very beginning of the film by a man sitting near me, summed up the film's success. "That's me," he said, watching the actor on the screen. "I always do that." The film was a success because it was presented in a realistic way which the construction workers recognised. The characters were so well cast and their scripts so carefully prepared that the workers could see themselves in the characters portrayed. The more someone can identify himself with a person on the screen, the more receptive he is to the message the film is putting across.

Safety films are usually faced with the problem of making people more aware of hazards they already know exist. This requires skill, and it is too easy to make mistakes. Talking down to an audience is always a mistake. It is also easy to forget that the people who will see the finished film may have been doing the job portrayed for years, and they often do not want to be told what to do. So the message must be put across with great tact. Audiences have to be kept on the side of the film, and the best way to do this is to maintain their interest. So, make an interesting safety film and not one which is designed solely to put over one safety point after another in as blunt a way as possible. Show realistic situations, in a realistic manner.

Prestige and promotion

One of the oldest established uses of industrial film is for promoting company prestige. Prestige films aim to present, and promote a company image. Many sponsors make prestige films and some are more successful than others. How can this kind of film succeed and what pitfalls can turn prestige to catastrophe? There are many kinds of prestige films. The most common, and most boring, spend all their screen time telling an audience they are hearing about the best company it is possible to imagine and they have no need to look any further! This approach is often used by companies who insist on their own ideas being followed at every stage of production. It is easy for the management to forget that, though the company they serve is all important to them, to the public at large it is not the last word in anything. If a film goes on trying to prove that it is, it will become boring. Persistence is rarely the key to success. Planning is a much more important ingredient. And there have been some notable prestige film successes.

When making sales promotional or advertising films companies often choose hard-selling techniques. The name of the products or service, and the name of the sponsor, are frequently mentioned. The message of the film is put across as firmly as possible. This approach is sometimes used in prestige films but it can do more harm than good. It is easier to make people believe in a product or service than it is in a company image, and is usually a company image that a prestige film is trying to promote. If the Muggins Trading Company produces a film, and every second line of commentary tries to convince the audience that the Muggins Trading Company is the best at everything it ever tries to undertake, the approach will quickly grow tedious. On the other hand, if the Muggins Company *show* what they do and why it works, audiences will be more readily convinced. It's an old, old cliché that actions speak louder than words, but in industrial film, the truth of the statement is hard to overestimate.

Shell Mex and BP are experienced prestige film sponsors. They set out first of all to interest an audience. They promote a company image in the process. Their films are planned first of all as film subjects. The company interest in these subjects is usually made clear but never emphasised and the name of the sponsor is not usually mentioned in a soundtrack but it appears on the titles. This is a splendid and successful approach to prestige film making. The Swiss engineering group of Sulzer sponsored another kind of prestige film. They sent a film unit round the world to photograph major contracts completed by the company. It was a fascinating film, and a hard-selling one in which the company's name was frequently mentioned. Yet it too succeeded, principally because the film was well made and put together in an interesting manner. If you make a prestige film, consider your audience first, and present your case in an interesting manner. And do not forget that it is the audience you are trying to interest, not the sponsor!

Some prestige films have to present several different points of view. This is often the case when one film is sponsored by a group of companies. A German chemical group, with companies making a variety of products, wanted a film for general group prestige. The film had to show the range of activities carried out by companies within the group and the resources available to any potential customer. The work of five different companies was featured, and the film proved a great success. It succeeded by making each situation interesting, and the variety of work shown added strength to the message of the film. The companies were all large and well equipped and the sponsors had obviously won some big contracts. This kind of group prestige film, showing the activities of a number of companies forming part of one group, can achieve several aims. It can present the activities of the group as a whole, and can also highlight the activities of a number of individual companies. If the film is properly planned, it can sometimes be divided into several self-contained sequences, each dealing with a separate factory or product. While the main composite film is distributed as a prestige production, parts of it can be used by individual companies for more direct sales promotion purposes. Sequences may need re-editing and a different soundtrack may have to be prepared. Such alterations are not difficult to arrange if they are envisaged from the scripting and planning stage. A well-made prestige film can earn its keep. The great danger is in being too pompous or self congratulatory. If a film seems too self assured it will achieve little. Prestige films do not have to use hard selling techniques.

So, if you plan your film well and produce it carefully it can achieve a great deal. But will it be a good investment? Production costs vary enormously and depend on the type of film to be produced. Subject matter, film size and the number of locations all have a bearing on total production cost. One film may cost ten times as much as another, depending on the subject and the necessary treatment. Now, knowing something of what can be done with a completed production, we can explore its real value.

Investment and result

The success of any film depends on its ability to do what it is designed for. It may be designed to increase sales of a product. Increased sales figures will then prove its success. It may be designed to promote company prestige: large audience figures may justify its cost. It may be designed to train or recruit. Again the results are already visible and will prove the success or failure of the investment. Aims and achievements in relation to costs prove the value of investment. A sponsored film is usually a long-term investment, though this is not always the case. There are exceptions. A few films are produced for one special showing.

A company making aircraft sponsored an expensive twenty-minute film about their activities. The film was produced for showing to a dozen senior airline executives at a conference in New York. Its aim was to convince the heads of several major airlines that the company had the equipment and experience to supply and maintain aircraft in all parts of the world. The film was shot at a number of large airports and some very small ones off the main air routes. It was an expensive film to produce and it was designed for only one showing— at the airline conference. The film was planned as a short-term investment, for if one of the airlines placed an order at the conference, the cost of the film would easily be recovered.

Film can be a good short-term investment but comparatively few productions are planned for such limited use. Most industrial films have a long life of between three and five years and the initial production cost must be considered in the light of what can be achieved in that time. Sponsored films are not seen by millions of people overnight. Television commercials already take care of the demand for an instant mass audience. Industrial films take longer to reach a smaller audience. In 30 seconds a television commercial can be seen by millions of people. It may take an industrial film two years to reach ten thousand. The figures are not impressive, and if the aim of a film is to reach a large number of people quickly, sponsored films are not the answer. But the aim is not usually to reach a mass audience, but more often to reach the right sort of audience. It is in this kind of controlled use that the sponsored industrial film excels.

Television commercials are excellent for national products. Repeated showings are usually needed if demand for a product is to be sustained. And screen time is expensive. Sponsored films are usually presented to audiences attending rather more of an occasion than watching interminable television. A weekly film show at a club or a show in school or at college is more likely to be remembered by an audience than a short flash on television. Moreover the sponsor does not have to present his case in 30 seconds. Time is on his side, unless he is greedy and uses too much of it and bores his audience. The time scale is one reason why industrial films are often remembered by those who watch them.

A film can be given a general distribution or a selective one. General showings cover most types of audience. Selective ones can be chosen by the sponsor and he can ensure that his film is seen only by people he considers worthwhile. A specialist film will reach a specialist audience and it will have several years in which to earn its keep.

Of course, a film can prove to be a waste of money. A company operating cruises sponsored a film and bought five copies. Three of them were held by the company head office. The other two were held in company ships. For two years the film was only shown when travel agents wrote and asked for it! It was never advertised so few agents knew it existed. In the first two years of its life, it was seen by only a few hundred people. When the film company who produced the film wrote to see if the sponsors were interested in making another, they were amazed to be told that the first one had proved to be a waste of money. They quickly investigated the situation and arranged for ten copies of the film to be put in a film library. Fifteen hundred people saw the film in the first month of library use.

If a film is to prove worthwhile, distribution must be arranged. The success and value of the film depends on its planned approach to its subject and on skilful production. The way the film is used also influences its success.

The initial production cost should be considered in the light of the life the finished film should have. Other costs, too, must be taken into account, for other charges will have to be met. The production contract may include the cost of one copy of the film. Others will have to be bought. They must be allowed for and replacements anticipated. Prints do not last for ever. Schools have a fine reputation for eating 16-mm films! A student projectionist let loose on new copies can produce remarkable results! Distribution costs must always be anticipated though they are not usually excessive. The main costs a sponsor has to consider are:

Initial production cost:	What will the film cost to make from script to screen?
Subsequent print costs:	How many copies of the film will be needed and what will they cost?
Distribution costs:	How will the film be used and what will its use cost be? Film library charges, postage and booking costs should be considered.

Replacement print costs: Always allow for the replacement of the occasional damaged print.

Insurance: Copies of the film should be insured against loss or damage in transit.

Promotion: Advertising costs and leaflets should be considered and allowed for if they are to be used.

Against these costs, the following points should be considered:

Film life: The average life of an industrial film is between three and five years.

Distribution outlets: The film production company should be able to arrange for the film to be seen by the people the sponsor wants to see it. If the film is of general interest, library distribution may prove profitable. Most libraries require about a dozen prints and the larger libraries want more. Each copy is seen by an audience approximately every 10 days. Audiences usually consist of at least 50 people. Specialised audiences can also be contacted.

Presentation: On film, much can be said in a short time. Presentation of a subject can be detailed and persuasive. The finished film can be dubbed in any language and can be shown almost anywhere.

You will by now have noted that I am rather biased in favour of industrial film! The bias is the result of experience of film used in many different situations, by a variety of sponsors trying to achieve totally different aims. I have, of course, met dissatisfied sponsors. Detailed accounts of the way disasters occured have been passed on to me from time to time. While some sponsors move from success to success, others seem doomed to rest with failure. Why do some sponsors lose money and decide to abandon film altogether?

Sponsors' success and failure

"We made a film once, but we'll certainly never make the same mistake again." Cheering words from a thoroughly dissatisfied film sponsor! Having decided to make a film the company concerned set out to do it as cheaply as possible. They hired a camera and gave it to their publicity manager. The results might have been of interest to an amateur film makers' convention, but for commercial use they were disastrous. By saving a few pounds, the firm had missed the boat. The publicity manager shot far more material than any professional and almost everything he photographed had to be shot twice. The film was produced without prior planning and, when the different takes were put together, the lack of forethought showed. A professional soundtrack did little to make the film attractive and consequently very few people booked it. When I met the publicity manager, two months after production, it had been publicly shown twice.

Films which fail to do the job they are planned for usually fail for one of four reasons. The reasons are concerned with cost, treatment, distribution and quality. Many industrial films are abysmally badly made. Sponsors may sit and purr with satisfaction at seeing their own company or products on the screen. Outside audiences will be more demanding. They do not share a sponsor's view of the product and if the sponsor's message is to be made clear it must be done in a professional and interesting manner. Bad films are released every day. Occasionally, they succeed. Usually they do not, for audiences remember a bad film for the wong reasons and the sponsor seldom benefits. Inadequate use is another cause of failure. As I have mentioned, it is useless making a film if you cannot be sure it will be used. Distribution must be planned in advance. There are still a few sponsors who make a film and wait for the world to write in and ask for it. They are usually the first people to say that their films have not proved a great success.

Unrealistic costing can also lead to failure. "We want a new film to be shot in our main European factories. It should be the sort of thing we can show on the continent and in America. It mustn't cost more than . . ." and then quoted a very low figure. This sort of statement is heard from time to time. There are sponsors who want the moon and do not expect to pay for it. Film making is not a cheap occupation and, if a low-cost film is wanted the subject matter and treatment must be planned with a low budget in mind, by using few locations and simple techniques. Film costs must be realistically assessed.

The treatment must be planned carefully. It is no good setting out to make "a 20-minute film". A film should be as long as the subject will stand—every subject dictates its own length. Audiences should be entertained and not held to ransom. It is also easy to try to accomplish too much in one film. Say too much and your audience will not listen. Try to speak to several different kinds of audience at once and you may run into trouble. Take one subject and one kind of audience and you will be on the road to success.

2

Preliminary Planning

THERE ARE PEOPLE who think that if you go out with a camera you come back with a film ready for use! Unfortunately, they are wrong. Every film must be planned. There are seven main stages in the making of an industrial film and the first important stage is the preparation of a brief by the film sponsor. The brief must clearly state what the film is meant to do and what kind of audience it is to be made for. When these two points have been settled, other work can proceed.

The next stage is to prepare an outline script, or treatment, as it is often called. This treatment can then be discussed with the sponsor and alterations made where they are needed. This is the time to make alterations; once the final shooting script has been agreed, changes can be difficult.

When the treatment has been finalised a shooting script must be produced. It must be written in terms of film. On the right-hand side of the page the sound is listed and on the left-hand side details of the camera position and movements and also the action. A script is a plan. It tells the production team exactly what has to be produced and it tells the sponsor what form the finished film will take. When the final shooting script has been agreed it must be broken down into different locations and individual days shooting, and then a shooting schedule must be prepared. A set number of scenes must be photographed each day. Each shot must be set, lit and photographed individually. The action must be "taken" over and over again until the director is entirely satisfied. When he is happy, the next scene can be prepared and shot.

So, there is rather more to making a film than going out with camera and coming back with a reel ready for the screen! There is plenty of hard work, even in the early stages before shooting begins. Location shooting will bring its own problems. Let us imagine a small film unit on location and see what kind of problems can arise.

Unit at work

The film unit visited the factory some days previously to make a "reccy": reconnoitre the location. They went, without their equipment, to find out exactly what they would need to shoot the film. They now know what the lighting conditions are like and how much room there is to work in. The factory is dark, and as the film is in colour, lights have to be used. It is not a very large factory. There are half a dozen lathes set out in banks of three on opposite sides of the floor. The roof is high, and there are several fluorescent lights, mostly situated above the lathes giving pools of light where the men are working. On film, these lights are a problem. They are not strong enough to give a reasonable exposure for colour film. And there are not enough of them to give even lighting. On film, the room might well look dark and dingy, so additional film lights have to be used. The factory electricity supply is not enough to power all the film lights needed, so a generator must be brought along too. And all the lights have to be rigged, or set up on stands, in places where they will not be seen by the camera. It takes time to light a set. And it is a skilled job. The scene must look realistic, and shadows must be very carefully controlled. So lighting the factory takes several hours, during which time the camera is also moved into position.

The first general view is being shot without synchronised sound. When the lighting cameraman is happy with what he sees through the viewfinder, he tells the director that he is ready to proceed. The director sorts out the action. He briefs the people who appear in the scene and makes sure they look right and know what to do. And he ensures that they look smart and efficient and do not appear in dirty overalls, or with untidy hair—small points which, on film, can assume unjustified importance. Anyone familiar with factories will know that postcards are often pinned near work benches and official notices are to be found peeling from walls. These must be removed or tidied up before a scene is filmed. When everything is set and ready to proceed, the action will be rehearsed.

It is not always possible to rehearse. Some production lines cannot be interrupted. When this happens, the director has to ask for the camera to be run at what he judges to be the most suitable moment. If he is wrong he will have to try again. He may well have to try again anyway. Very few scenes are perfect first time. Several takes are usually needed before cameraman, recordist and director are all entirely satisfied. When they are, they can go on to the next shot.

Filming has now been going on in the factory for half a day. And several hours have been spent beforehand making preparations. In the finished film, probably 10 seconds of what has been photographed will be used. Now the unit is preparing the second shot. It shows a lathe and the camera has to be set up at the end of the lathe, shooting along its length. It is a much closer shot than the last one, so there is a smaller area to light. First the camera is moved. This time the scene is to be photographed with synchronised sound, so the recordist and his assistant also have to set up their equipment, and all the lights have to be moved. It takes half an hour to reassemble the lights and set up the camera. While this is going on, the recordist chooses the microphone he wants to use and fixes it on to a microphone boom, suspended above the lathe. It looks as if everything is ready for action. The lights are turned on and the cameraman checks the view through the camera view-finder. There is trouble. The overhead microphone is casting a shadow across the end of the lathe. The boom will have to be moved, or the lights repositioned. A compromise is reached, and the viewfinder is checked again. This time the cameraman looks at the edges of his picture. On the right of the lathe is a small patch of dark floor. It needs light. One of the overhead lights will have to be moved. It is adjusted, and all seems ready to go. The action is rehearsed and the recordist listens carefully to ascertain the correct sound recording level. The director briefs the man who works the lathe. He tells him not to look at the camera and asks if the lights are dazzling him or if he can see satisfactorily. He says he can, so the camera and recorder run up to speed and the action is photographed. All seems to go well for the first few seconds, then, as the lathe operator moves forward, the cameraman notices a small piece of lighting cable on the floor behind where the operator was standing. It will appear on the film so it is moved, and the action retaken. This time the operator makes a mess of it and, as the lathe cuts too deeply, adds his own explosive comments to the soundtrack! Take three goes perfectly, until someone in the background drops a spanner and the crash ruins the sound. On the fourth attempt all goes well. Another 7 seconds of screen time have been completed. Eventually work is completed and the exposed film is sent off for processing.

Internal units

Making an industrial film requires expertise and experience. If you are asked to make an industrial film is it best to attempt all the work yourself or to work with a team of freelance technicians employed for the time needed to produce the picture? Or should you advise the sponsor to start his own internal company film unit? Let us consider the last possibility first. When is an internal film unit a worthwhile proposition?

Internal film units (often called "in plant film units" by those wishing to be deadly technical) do a very fine job. There are some internal film units with very high standards who regularly turn out excellent films. British Transport Films are a classic example of a film unit usually working for one major sponsor and regularly turning out first class material. In Italy, Fiat also produce films of a very high standard. And there are other leading sponsors with their own production units. Some are very good and produce films which are, in every sense, professional. They are made with care and skill, and the people concerned have all the equipment and resources needed to do a job properly. Unfortunately, this is not always the case. Lack of money, lack of equipment and lack of the right sort of staff often hamper internal film units. Often, films officers are grossly underpaid and are expected to work miracles with nothing at all to help them. Here is how one recent job advertisement read:

> *Films Officer Required by leading National Company. Experience and interest in all aspects of photography, knowledge of editing and sound recording essential. Successful applicant will be required to undertake film production for the company and supervise the running of the company film library.*

For that they offered a salary of less than a junior office worker. I wish I was joking, but, alas, I am not.

This is not just an isolated advertisement picked out of a British newspaper and saved for this book. It is a regular occurrence, and not only in the UK. It is another result of the general lack of knowledge about industrial film. The advertisement has probably been placed by a company run by people who know very little about making and using film. They think one man, on a ridiculous salary, can go out and make a film. And, of course, they are right. But I would not want to be shown the film. And I would not expect it to do the sponsoring company any good. Cut price film making is commercial suicide. A bad film does more harm than good and only satisfies a stupid sponsor. When is an internal film unit a sane proposition, and what equipment and staff are needed to run it satisfactorily?

An internal film unit is not cheap to equip or to run. It is something only a large company can usually afford. There are, of course, exceptions and a number of small companies do run very successful film units though they do not compare in any way with professional film units. This is an important point, for although most internal film units have to work without the equipment or staff of an outside company, the results they produce will often be seen in competition with, or in the same programme as, other films professionally produced. I said *professionally* produced. There are, I know, some thoroughly professional film makers running and working in internal units. But, alas, they are a minority. The average in plant film unit consists of two or three people, a clockwork camera, a pair of rewind arms, an animated viewer and a projector. Total cost excluding the salaries of the people concerned amounts to about the same as the junior office worker mentioned before. This is ideal for making amateur movies or films with limited scope. But most sponsored films need more. They need the work of a number of people, each a specialist in a different field. A scriptwriter who was trained to write scripts will usually produce a better treatment than a man who has got the job because he happened to know how to use a camera. A cameraman may be brilliant at getting first class pictures, but his knowledge of editing may leave much to be desired. A good cameraman may produce good raw materials and ruin them by trying to edit the results on a hand rewind and a viewer. Editing, too, is a job for experts. It needs a specialist, and expensive equipment. And, like all key film making jobs, it needs experience. A film unit needs trained people and it needs good equipment. A one man band, or a team working on a shoestring with inadequate equipment, cannot be expected to produce results which will have any lasting value. A basic crew might include the following:

> Director
> Cameraman (and assistant)
> Editor (and assistant)
> Production secretary
> Recordist (and assistant)
> General assistant (electrician/handyman)

These nine people mean a large salary bill for any internal film unit. Yet there is an alternative. It is quite possible for a company wanting to establish its own film unit to just appoint a films officer. But he cannot be expected to produce a film on his own. He should operate with outside contractors capable of doing the technical work, preside at all production meetings and liaise between the film unit and the sponsoring company. This kind of appointment ensures that a company's interests are always safeguarded. And the sponsor does not have to buy his own equipment. It is an economical way of making films properly, and it can work well, if the company concerned makes several films in the course of a year. Much will depend on the ability of the individual films officer. He must know film making thoroughly and be able to check a script and spot any discrepancies in a production budget. It is a job for a man with professional film experience.

It is only worth a company setting up an internal film unit if they intend to make a number of films. One film does not justify the cost. In fact, regular productions will be needed to justify buying or hiring the necessary equipment and keeping a reliable full-time staff. There are several ways in which a unit can be established. A full-time director can be taken on, and freelance camera crews and other technicians hired when needed. If this is done, the director concerned must have a first-class knowledge of all film-making procedures. An alternative is to keep a full permanent staff. I have already listed the people needed to complete a film unit. A very small internal unit, making low budget films, could possibly exist with the following staff:

Director
Cameraman
Editor
Recordist or electrician/handyman
Secretary

Five people: the absolute minimum. The moment you start doubling up on different jobs, you have to settle for less than perfection. It is impossible for a cameraman to shoot and record simultaneously. Very few cameramen know anything about editing, and I do not know a recordist who can shoot film under all conditions. Directing is a full-time job and a secretary is also essential. So an internal film unit should pay five basic salaries. And good salaries will be needed to attract competent staff.

Equipment for internal units

When you have the staff you have to find the equipment. I would consider the following items essential:

1. Camera with lenses and zoom lens.
2. A portable lighting kit.
3. Portable tape recorder, with microphone and wind gags.
4. Motorised editing machine capable of running sound and picture on different pieces of film.
5. Synchroniser
6. Projector capable of running film with separate magnetic sound.

These are basic essentials. If you are going to make several films they could be bought. The cheapest camera worth buying will cost about a tenth of the price of a really good outfit. A good tape recorder outfit will probably cost a little less than this cheap camera. It is impossible to do any creative editing with an animated viewer. A motorised editing machine is also essential. They cost anything from the price of the cheapest camera upwards and most models cost far more. A projector for picture and separate magnetic film will also prove expensive. Yet with these few items it is just possible to make a film. But must they all be bought?

Most film equipment can be hired, on a daily or weekly basis. Many film units, professional and otherwise, hire all their equipment. There are advantageous tax reasons and hiring also gives you a chance to choose from a range of equipment you could never afford to buy. For each film you can hire the gear best suited to the job. This is not a bad policy. Lights, too, can be hired and if generators are needed they can be supplied as well. Editing machines can be hired, but the more normal procedure is to hire a fully equipped cutting room, again on a weekly basis. A projector is worth buying, if only to show the finished film. Other equipment can be hired. And film crews, too, can be taken on individually for short periods. But someone must be in control from the start.

Decision making for the sponsor

When making an industrial film, decisions must be taken at many stages of production. The first obvious decision is to make the film at all. Other decisions must be made before production begins. The film gauge must be determined and the aim of the film must be clear from the start. Decisions must be made about shooting dates and procedures. And editing will require decisions too. There are decisions of every kind, most of which need to be made quickly. Someone has to do the deciding and a chain of command must be established before film making begins. The sponsoring company should have one man who can put the sponsor's point of view. This is essential. Every company has its managing director used to taking decisions, but he is not always involved in all the stages of film production. Sometimes he is only brought in at the very beginning and given the briefest possible facts. He is told how much the department concerned wants to spend and what they hope the finished film will achieve. Once the go ahead is given, many managing directors lose touch. This is all very well, but there are occasions when a director, seeing the finished job, does not like what he sees. This is often because the sponsoring department has not outlined its intentions before production begins. Occasionally, a film may have to be remade. Money is wasted and frustration caused. A managing director should always be given the facts. Make him agree the script and keep him informed. But even then, he may not be the right man to take all the decisions.

Committee decisions are all very well, and the preparation of a script will usually call for a lot of committee work. Time spent discussing a script is not usually wasted. Many good ideas come from committee discussions. But a time limit must always be set and someone, again with executive powers, must be able to look at committee comments and make a firm decision. This is vital when a script is being pre pared. Every department wants to climb in on the act and most people have their own ideas and views. Let them express their views in committee, then, when the views have been explored, let someone decide what is to be included in the treatment and what is to be left out. The following chain of command can work well:

On behalf of the sponsors

Managing director: He must be kept informed of all stages of production.

Executive contact man: When a film is made with an outside company, an executive contact man must be appointed by the sponsors. He must be a man who is able to deal at both high and low levels in the sponsoring firm. A man able to take quick decisions without consulting a lot of other people is usually best for the job. He should be entrusted with, and made responsible for, the film project. The sponsoring company can then rely on him to see that their views are made clear and respected at all production stages. The film company will know that he is the man they can approach for quick and reliable decisions. They know, too, that he has the backing of his company and will be a reliable person to work with and listen to.

Production committee: When the script is first being prepared, ideas can often be aired in committee by all the interested departments. This makes them all feel they are contributing to the finished job—even if they are not! And it makes sure that no ideas or views are left unexplored. When the final script has been prepared, copies should be sent to all executives concerned. Make sure they agree the script in writing. Then, when they see the finished film, if they find something omitted, they have only themselves to blame. Committees can sometimes be invited to see a "fine cut" edited version before a film is finally completed. The fine cut edited stage is the last point at which alterations can be made easily and cheaply.

On behalf of the film production company

Project director: One man should be appointed by the company to deal with liaison for the production. He should contact the sponsor at a very early stage. The more he is taken into their confidence, the better. In a small company (often the best to work with), the film director may supervise all stages of the work himself. This is the ideal situation. In a larger company, script researchers may start the probing work, and the director may meet the sponsors on site when reconnoitring before filming begins. Whatever the size of the company, one person must be named and known as a permanent point of contact.

When an internal film unit is engaged in making a film, a similar chain of command must apply. It should be easier for decisions to be made when one department is dealing with another department of the same company. Unfortunately, this is not always the case. It can even prove harder, for some internal film units are very low on the list of management priorities. Again, someone must decide what the film is to achieve. When the film is being made with internal company resources, there may not be a need for a permanent contact man. There is, however, often a need for a technical adviser to be present. I do not mean a man to advise on film techniques, or on how each scene should be handled. The film director and his team will look after that. The technical adviser I envisage is there to advise on technical aspects of the subject being filmed. If the film is about paint, he must make sure that the right painting techniques are used. If it is about engineering, he will keep an eye on the technical side. When advertising agencies are involved in making films, they love to send a sea of advisers, most of whom have nothing to do except claim expenses at the end of the day. A good technical adviser can sometimes be a great help.

Decisions in an internal unit will often be made by the unit director. He should be in complete control, answerable only to the board or one of its members. If he has to answer to the head of another department, who himself has to re-submit all matters for higher approval, work may be delayed.

Premises for an internal unit

I have already outlined the minimum number of staff I consider necessary for running a fully equipped internal film unit. If such a unit is to be established, it will need its own premises. What, exactly, will be needed? It is impossible for a film unit to work satisfactorily in one room which happened to be empty when the decision to start a unit was taken! Again, in finding office space, film units will often find they are not given a very high priority. Let us discuss the ideal layout first, and then give some thought to ways of achieving a compromise.

The unit director and his secretary should each have a separate office. Accommodation department managers, eager to put both in one room, should try reading or writing a script with telephone calls and a typewriter clanking away in the background. A separate office for the sole use of the director is essential. The other rooms in the unit premises can each be planned to cope with one part of the film-making programme. The main rooms needed will be:

Office for the unit director
Reception/office for director's secretary
Camera room and unexposed film store
Cutting room
Film vault

Preview theatre and projection area
Studio
Production office.

Many industrial units have to make do without these individual rooms. A few have even more space. Let us consider the minimum essentials. Apart from the two offices already mentioned, I have listed a camera room and film store. These can be the same room, and daylight, though pleasant, is not vital. The room should have enough storage space for the camera equipment to be kept under lock and key. Film stock, too, will need its own storage compartment away from heat, damp and sunshine. One small unit I visited recently had all their film stock in a large metal cupboard. It was locked up and the film was kept on three shelves inside. They only kept about 20,000 ft of film, but it was neatly stored and could easily be seen and quickly identified. An index system provided a check on the amount of stock used on every job.

A film-cutting room is also essential. You cannot edit film in a room used for any other purpose. And you cannot do any other job satisfactorily in a room where there is a motorised editing machine. The cutting room should contain the main editing machine and synchroniser bench. Wall racks will also be needed for filing film trims. And do allow plenty of rack space for storing cans. The floor of a cutting room should not be carpeted. Lino is quite sufficient, and easier to keep clean and dust free.

A preview theatre sounds the ultimate in luxury to anyone starting a new unit. It is really an essential. In the course of production it will be used many times. It gives the unit a chance to see the daily rushes on a decent size screen. It gives the editor a chance to see the edited version on a screen larger than his editing machine and the mood and pace of the film can be more easily judged. And it is always available for showing the completed film to clients. Few company cinemas are a waste of time. Properly equipped, they can be very useful. Again, no daylight is needed, though adequate ventilation is essential. A theatre should be well away from noise and walls may have to be insulated with wire wool, polystyrene or other materials. There is no need for a large number of seats. Most company cinemas seat less than 25. A large screen and stereophonic sound are not needed either. Make sure the sound is good and clear and project a picture which is steady, properly lit and always in focus. And do make sure the screen is high enough. Internal cinemas do not usually run to the luxury of a sloping floor. The screen should be at least two foot higher than the top of the head of someone sitting in the row in front of any member of an audience. Sit down and look, before placing the screen. And do not put it too high, or your neck will ache after the first reel! Light dimmers and curtains do much to make a cinema look professional. Curtains, drapes and carpets also improve the quality of sound by cutting down echoes and absorbing some of the sound. Do not curtain the whole room—it will make it sound dead. At least one wall and the ceiling should be given a different treatment. Acoustic tiles can be used quite satis- factorily. Projectors should always be in a separate soundproofed room and the seating should be chosen for comfort.

Now let's consider the film vaults and the production office. Film vaults again do not need daylight. A strong floor and plenty of rack space will suffice. The room must be ventilated and a constant air flow maintained. Dampness and heat must both be avoided. Film vaults are essential, for in the course of making even one film, a large amount of material and many cans will be used. Not all the material will be kept, but it is normal procedure for the final edited version of the film and the trims of master material to be kept for future use and reference. All this takes up space, and plenty of extra space should be allowed for future use.

It may also be useful to have a production office. It is a handy room for unit personnel to meet when filming is not going on. It is also a good place for production meetings to be held. If space is at a pre- mium, the director's office may perhaps suffice. It is sometimes possible for a production office to be combined with a secretary's office and reception area. A production office is not a technical area and indi- vidual film units will be able to do what suits them best.

Many internal unit directors, reading my recommendations for a company film studio, will be having a good laugh! It is a luxury few companies can afford. Although it is not often possible to establish a fully equipped studio, it is a good idea if an area where basic photo- graphy can take place can be set aside. If the area can be soundproofed, so much the better. Even a small space can be most useful—for filming title cards and pack shots and for close-up work, which can be time consuming and difficult when shooting on location. And it can serve for filmed interviews.

A studio is undoubtedly a luxury, but if a room is going spare, it could perhaps be adapted for use. The cheapest equipped studio I have ever seen was also extremely efficient. It was built by a religious order, and five monks had done all the work themselves. I went down to see it before work began, and when it was completed. The monks started with a bedroom measuring only 20 × 15 ft. They fixed scaffold poles to the ceiling and vertically up two of the walls. Simple lights were mounted on the poles in a way that enabled them to be removed quite easily. The floor was rather uneven, so they nailed hardboard over the top and painted it a dark non-reflective colour. The floor was then smooth enough for a camera to move across on wheels. If you had stood in the room at this stage and clapped your hands, you would have heard a very noticeable echo, far too much for the studio to be used for any kind of sound recording. Proper soundproofing was too expensive to contemplate so the monks decided to experiment. They bought two thousand egg packing boxes and nailed the shaped part designed to hold the eggs to walls and ceiling. The effect was quite astonishing. The room was acoustically very much improved. A coat of paint applied to the egg boxes disguised their real purpose and the studio was brought into use. The whole room, including the lights but excluding the camera equipment, cost half the price of the cheapest good camera!

Inter-departmental liaison

When a new internal film unit is established, one of the first problems to be encountered is that of dealing with other departments in the same organisation. When a film is being made, every department wants to climb in on the act, and most departments seem to feel that the film unit is there to work for them and them alone. The head of training is not interested in the problems of sales, and the sales director does not lose much sleep over training. When both want a film at the same time, problems arise that need tact and planning to overcome. The day-to-day running of an internal unit is full of problems. Timing and information are at the root of many of them.

When a film is planned and the script finally agreed, a definite production timetable must be arranged. All the major stages of production must be given firm starting and completion dates. Dates must be fixed for locations to be visited and for filming to take place. A detailed schedule should be prepared for this. Dates must be fixed for editing and dubbing and a final completion date must be decided upon. Fixing these dates presents one set of problems. Making sure they are met presents others, and the unit director will have to sort them out. Two wet days alone can cause chaos and mean rearranging a complete shooting programme. Time must be planned, and used profitably, and information on the progress of work in hand must be passed on to interested parties.

A company press office or public relations officer will often want to know when films are being made. A judicially released still of a new film in production can often get good press coverage and do a lot of good. In some companies, the public relations officer is himself directly responsible for the film unit. He then has an excellent opportunity to see that information is only used when it is up to date. The unit director must also see that information is fed to other departments at the right time. If, for example, filming is to take place in a factory on a particular date, the date must be agreed with all interested parties, well ahead of the actual filming day. Everyone even remotely concerned must be consulted. In a large factory this can mean consulting the departmental manager and his foreman, union representative, security officers and firemen, as well as the electricians and others who want to know about the filming, and who could cause trouble if they are not consulted. Inter-departmental liaison is a vital part of the work of running any internal film unit.

Equipment will need periodical attention too. If the basic equipment I have recommended is purchased, it will have to be written down in value each year in the company books and, when it has ceased to be of practical value, replaced. How long should equipment last, and when is it best replaced? Obviously much depends on how the equipment is used. Camera equipment will not wear out very quickly, unless it is misused or used under very bad working conditions. It may not, however, be a good move to keep it for longer than two or three years. The cost of buying the equipment in the first place may by then have been written off in the company books, and, of more interest to the cameraman concerned, more up-to-date equipment may have been produced. If a camera is to be bought (and there is always the alternative of hiring) the possibility of selling and replacing it should be considered every twelve months.

Editing equipment often has very hard use. If it is regularly maintained, good equipment will last for a long time, even if it is working constantly. Although economy may be the first consideration, it still pays to buy a good machine. Such a machine will last much longer, though its initial purchase price may be higher than one needing replacement because of breaking down at an earlier date. I used a machine costing as much as a good camera for five years without any major problems. I used another costing one-third of this for six months and it broke down completely. Another make of machine at the same price worked satisfactorily for five years, though it did need a lot of servicing and several expensive replacement parts. Costs must always be carefully assessed. An expensive machine may be worth keeping for longer than three years. A cheaper machine should only be bought if it is known to be reliable. Even then, its purchase price must be considered in the light of the likely maintenance and repair bills which will follow if the machine is required for heavy use. It pays to review each machine at the end of every year, and consider its state of repair, its cost and its possible future use.

It is important to only buy equipment which is known to be reliable and thoroughly tested and made for professional use. If you want to save money, hire good equipment rather than buy inferior machines When you have enough money, and enough demand to justify the cost invest in good machines of your own. But it is better to hire good equipment when you want it than to buy poor machines which break down when needed. Good technicians simply will not put up with bad machines and the morale of a unit and the quality of its films will suffer.

Staffing an internal unit

If you are starting an internal unit, how do you find the right staff and what is involved in interviewing staff for technical positions?

Everyone and his wife wants to get into films! They are all mad, of course, thinking it is a fantastically romantic and exciting industry! A few nights on a cold location or in a film cutting room would cure them. But the view that film making is fun persists. Interviewing applicants for film unit jobs can thus sometimes have its lighter side. One company I know advertised a trainee's job in a national daily newspaper. They did their best to make it sound thoroughly unattractive, emphasising low salary, hard work and long hours. The day the advertisement appeared was quiet and peaceful. It had been placed under a box number. When the company directors got to their office the following morning, they were amazed to find over 200 letters applying for the job. I was involved in interviewing the candidates and read many of the letters. I found some of them among the most amusing I have ever seen. I also interviewed the applicants. From experience of appointments boards and staff interviews, I have managed to pick up a few points which may interest others facing applicants for technical posts.

We did not interview the man who wrote to say he had just written "a great new biblical epic", or the chap who thought "film was a wonderful expressive vision of flowers, music and the realities of life"! We stuck to those who from their applications showed they had an experience of, and an interest in, film. Interest is the first quality to look for. If the applicant is interested, he will have taken practical steps to follow up his interest. The steps are worth retracing. Many applicants can produce visual evidence of their past experience.

Interviewing people for responsible positions in an industrial film unit is not really difficult. It is like finding top people for any other job, with one important difference. They must be technically minded, yet able to communicate these things in a non-technical way, to people without any such knowledge. One of the problems an industrial film maker faces is the complete lack of technical knowledge which many of the people in control of film-making projects have. Sponsor committees often consist of people with no film experience at all and a firm conviction that films grow in cameras! The ability to explain what has to be done at all relevant stages is important. In selecting personnel for an industrial film unit, this problem must be remembered. But this is not the main problem. Professionalism is the word most easily forgotten in industrial film making, and it is a word which should be written on the top of every staff application form.

Getting into films is, as I have mentioned, many people's ambition. The main professional film-making areas are already overstaffed and rigidly controlled by unions. There are thousands of professional film makers in the USA and the UK who are unemployed following the near-demise of the entertainment feature film. They can be traced by getting in touch with any of the major film unions. Union representatives will always put an industrial unit in touch with their members looking for work. It is one way of finding experienced staff, and it can offer a satisfactory solution, but this is not always the case. People used to working in the main parts of the professional film world may not be suitable for a small industrial unit. If they are used to large scale productions and elaborate equipment, they may find the industrial scene rather limited, though good technicians interested in quality work will usually prove worthwhile. People who opt out of television companies can also prove suitable. They are used to working on 16-mm film and are normally quite experienced, though here again checks must be made. Before taking anyone on, find out all you can and establish the limits of their experience. An application form will provide the basic facts and an interview will fill in the details.

Application forms can be very misleading. For an office job, a staff application form may well list the most relevant facts. Education is often given great emphasis. The BBC, like a number of large organisations, lays great stress on education, and a person applying for a job as a holiday relief projectionist will find his application form asks for details of all his schools and colleges, and leaves spaces for details of degrees obtained! This situation is really rather absurd. Though I certainly agree that a good general education is essential, film makers can often offer experience which is much more useful than a degree. Some graduates are a complete waste of time. They may be very good in other fields, but for film-making purposes, practical experience and evidence of interest are often more important.

Many industrial units take on young people with very little experience. This is not a bad idea, provided they are employed as trainees and are thoroughly trained, and not expected to do a job for which they are not qualified or experienced. I have already stressed the importance of using professionals for all key posts. Asking a young man who has made two 8-mm home movies to shoot a complete company film, or edit one, is inviting trouble. Employ him by all means, but let him work with someone who has the relevant professional experience. Let him see how a professional cameraman or a professional editor uses professional equipment, and let him learn the techniques. He will, in time, become reliable himself. How do you find suitable trainees for an industrial unit?

The film unit first mentioned, who advertised and received 200 replies eventually found a first class trainee. They found him by reading all the applications and by shortlisting ten candidates. You will remember that the advertised job was made to sound as unattractive as possible. Low salary, long hours and hard work were all promised, yet many people still applied. A shortlist was compiled by choosing only people who had either professional film experience or extensive experience of amateur film making. The letters written by applicants helped to weed out the time wasters. Some did not mention an interest in film at all. Many wanted to become film directors! Ten people managed to convey their interest in film, and in the post advertised. Each of these was sent an application form, asking for the names of three referees and details of education, career and experience. From these completed forms, seven were finally invited for interview. One arrived drunk. Two more appeared to be more interested in the prospect of being able to tell other people they were "in film" than they were in the prospect of being able to make films professionally. One candidate had seven years of first class professional experience. He did not get the job because the committee conducting the interviews gained the impression that he thought he knew everything and was not prepared to learn, or try new ideas or techniques. The job went to a young man who had worked as a display artist and made two films, at his own expense, in his own free time. He was a first class artist and his interest in film, and in the company, was clear and genuine. He still holds the job today, though he now has a more responsible post.

So, to summarise, when finding staff for internal film units, it pays to shop around. Unions may be able to provide people who are out of work. They will have film experience but, like applicants for any advertised post, should be interviewed and checked. Trainees should be tested for an interest in film and in the company. Only experienced people should be given key posts.

Many potentially good industrial films are ruined because internal film units try to take on more than they are equipped to cope with. Most units can produce a camera team and make a good job of shooting a film, though stills cameramen should not be asked to shoot cine film without a training on the equipment and camera movement techniques. The trouble usually starts in the later stages of production, for although the camera team may produce material of a high technical standard, the shots may be wasted in the course of editing. One solution is to subcontract part of the production work.

Sub-contracting

If you are running an internal unit you will have to decide what work to sub-contract and when to do it. If a film is to be photographed by contracted crews, contracts must be drawn up showing exactly what is required. Camera crews often provide their own equipment and film stock. When a contract for shooting is prepared, the number of shooting days should be specified, together with full details of the locations and materials required. Make sure the crew is told in advance what film stock you want it to use—whether it is 35 mm or 16 mm, colour or black and white. And tell them, too, what they have to shoot, so that they will know what kind of equipment is required. Crews engaged on a day-to-day basis are only responsible for shooting. Their responsibility starts when they start to shoot, and ends with the processing of the raw materials. They are not expected to find or negotiate the use of locations; all that preparatory work has to be done beforehand. So if you take on freelance crews on a daily shooting basis, do not expect them to make all the pre-shooting preparations.

Shooting a film always needs plenty of preparation. When an internal film unit commissions outside crews on a daily shooting basis, the unit will have to do all its own preparatory work. Locations must be chosen and reconnoitred. Wherever possible the cameraman responsible for shooting a film should always visit each location before shooting is due to take place. This may involve engaging a cameraman for a few extra days but the time will not be wasted. When filming is due to start he will know what equipment has to be provided. Actors and extras will have to be auditioned. Many industrial films do not involve actors but there are other items which have to be prepared: clean overalls for production line staff in a factory sequence; extra power to cope with film lights: catering arrangements for the crew, and so on.

When a freelance camera crew is employed, the internal unit commissioning the work will have to provide its own film director. It is possible to take on a freelance director and indeed many of the best documentary film directors only undertake freelance work. It is useless commissioning a director for the period when shooting is in progress. Most directors worth employing like to be called in well before shooting takes place. They want to study and get the feel of the script and work out every detail of the action before a scene is shot. They may well be used to working with a particular crew and if a freelance crew is needed, may be able to produce people known to be good. Some directors work on a shooting basis only but most prefer to see the film through the cutting rooms to completion.

What other stages of production can be sub-contracted? Writing a film script is a specialised job. Writing dialogue scenes and commentaries requires a great deal of skill if audiences are not to be bored and if the point of the film is to be explained in a way which satisfies both the sponsor and an audience. The work of producing a script can be sub-contracted. It is no good simply commissioning *a* script. More detailed instructions are required.

What sort of script is wanted? You will probably want a detailed shooting script, but the script writer must first prepare a treatment for discussion. A treatment explains what the film is to be concerned with and outlines the main points to be explored. A shooting script develops the theme and shows how the points are to be handled in terms of camera movement, angles, action and dialogue. When a treatment has been agreed, work can continue on the preparation of the final blue-print—the shooting script. If a freelance scriptwriter is commissioned, he must be given all the research facilities he needs. He must also be provided with a very detailed brief and the contract of employment must state exactly what is to be done, and what is to be paid. Writing a script normally includes three main tasks:

1. Carrying out research and visiting locations.
2. Preparing a draft treatment.
3. Developing the draft treatment and producing a detailed shooting script.

Before this work can be done, the script writer must be given all the basic facts. He must meet the key personnel concerned and be given all the facilities and access needed to carry out his research. He must know what the film aims to achieve and the audience it is intended for. He must know how much money is to be spent on the film, so that he does not write scenes which are too expensive to produce. And he must know exactly what the sponsors do, and do not, want to show. Then, he can produce a script.

Sub-contracting post-production work

Editing work too, can be sub-contracted. Editing means cutting the pictures to length and for effect. Each sequence must be edited so the film has its own pace and is interesting to watch. Several sound-tracks must then be prepared. Some will consist of music, others of sound effects and more still of commentary. We will examine the methods in detail later.

A film can be put together by using a pair of rewind arms and an animated viewer, but it cannot really be said to be edited in the pro-fessional sense. Editing is a highly skilled job calling for first class equipment and considerable experience. A small unit may perhaps decide to edit the picture and then go along to a sound dubbing theatre and add a bit of music and record a commentary. It is a shoddy, cheap way of making a film, and many good films are ruined by taking short cuts. Just as there is more to photographing a film than pointing a camera in the right direction and pressing a button, there is more to editing than cutting out the bad scenes and joining the rest together. Advanced editing is beyond the scope of many internal industrial film units. They do not have the equipment or the staff, and the work is often best sub-contracted. It should not cost too much and it will ensure a good film, if the raw materials are there to work with.

When film editing work is sub-contracted, contracts can be drawn up on a weekly or monthly basis, or a rate can be agreed for editing a film from rushes to completion. The normal procedure is to contract work from rushes stage. When filming is completed at the end of each day, the camera crew sends the original film for processing. Laboratories process the original and make a copy for editing purposes. This copy is often produced overnight and is thus made in a hurry, hence its name "rush print". In the USA, rushes are more often known as "dailies". Internal units sub-contracting edited work should commission an editor from rushes stage. It is a fatal mistake to try and make the first assembly, and then employ an editor to finish the job. Let him work from the rushes stage, so that he can then be held responsible for the results.

Many industrial films are edited by freelance editors. It is a pity more are not handled in this way for many films are ruined by bad editing and countless opportunities are lost. It is easy to sub-contract editing work. It only involves two people: an editor and an assistant, and the work to be done can be specified quite easily. These are the main tasks an editor should be asked to undertake:

1. Check the rushes and make a first assembly.
2. Fine cut the assembly.
3. Produce a full and detailed soundtrack.
4. Dub. (Mix several soundtracks together.)
5. Neg. cut. (Match the camera original to the edited cutting copy.)
6. Supervise the preparation of the first show print.

Again, when sub-contracting editing, let the sub-contractor get on with the job. The film director will, of course, need to be on hand. Sometimes even he does not hang around. Directors often choose editors because they are used to working with them and they know that once they have outlined what they want to achieve, the editor will get on without close supervision. It is the ideal working situation and there is a safety check built in. If the editor is left to get on with the work until his fine cut version is ready for inspection, work will proceed at speed. And, if anything is wrong with the fine cut, alterations can still be made. An editing contract should always specify exactly what has to be delivered when work is complete. When the work of shooting a film is sub-contracted, the exposed film has to be delivered for processing. When editing is sub-contracted, the master material of the final edited film and one first show print should be supplied. One graded combined sound print of the final edited version of the film, ready for showing, should be included in the contract. This can only be produced when the last stages of editing have been satisfactorily completed. In addition, the final mix master magnetic soundtrack should also be supplied, together with the cut picture and sound negatives used to produce the first "show" print. If foreign versions are to be made at a later date, it may also be worth specifying the need to supply an international soundtrack, in master magnetic form. An international soundtrack is the penultimate soundtrack produced in the course of dubbing. It has all the sounds and music contained on the finished film, except commentary. It is thus free of dialogue, and foreign language versions can easily be added later without conflicting with the original language version. Known as an M & E track (standing for music and effects), this kind of track may also be worth including in the delivery requirements of an editing contract.

Is an internal unit worthwhile?

Films cannot be made on the cheap or as a sideline, and a film department is not just another office. Good cameramen and directors and worthwhile creative ideas cannot be drawn from a pool of surplus staff. It is a full-time job, as some companies who have tried to make their own films, with disastrous results, have found out. Often it is not worth a company even considering an internal unit.

In my opinion, it is only worth establishing an internal unit if two questions can be answered with a definite "yes". The first concerns output. Is there a real need for an internal film unit and will it have enough work to do? It is not worth establishing a unit for one film. Regular output must be guaranteed and there must be enough subjects worth filming to keep a unit profitably employed. This tends to suggest a large company with plenty of interests. Today, when takeovers and mergers are everyday events, there's much to be said for a group internal unit. Such a unit can be attached to a group publicity department and make itself available for filming the activities of a number of companies forming part of one group. Apart from the obvious possibility of a group prestige public relations film, the unit should be able to justify its keep by producing separate sales, training or publicity films for individual companies in the group. The group should have funds to pay for equipment and professional staff. This kind of unit can be a first class investment. For individual companies, not forming part of a group, the same cannot always be said.

The second question which should be asked before any internal unit is established is concerned with costs. Can the necessary equipment and operational costs be met and can the output of the department justify the sums involved? When these two questions have been thoroughly explored, the final decision can be taken. It may well prove more satisfactory to put all film production work in the hands of outside film production companies. It is always far better to take this step than to try to cope with inadequate resources. Making films on the cheap is commercial suicide.

The European passenger manager of a shipping line came to see me a year ago. He had read an article I had written in a travel trade magazine and was keen to produce a cruise promotional film. His company had never produced a film before, and the board were not keen to spend any money or explore the medium properly. I strongly advised him not to make a film—and that's an unusual event in itself! I explained the costs involved and the need to do the job properly, if it is to be done at all. Two weeks after his first visit he returned to tell me that he had succeeded in persuading his board to put up some money —an absurdly low figure. They had, however, pointed out that the sales director was "used to making films" and would be pleased to shoot the film himself without incurring additional costs for the company. The passenger manager who first approached me had returned to ask if I could arrange for the film to be edited and for some sound to be added. His visit was typical of so many visits made by inexperienced sponsors of industrial films. His company had agreed to provide a small amount of money, from which they expected to get a full-scale cruise film. They were, as I explained, heading for disaster. The facts were clear to see. The company has agreed to put up too little money to do the job properly. And they had tried to cut costs by putting the vital shooting stage in the hands of a man used to making 8-mm home movies—their own sales director. And they had no idea whatever about the shape or form the finished film should take. They had made only one plan: to produce a film on their Greek Island cruise. The other details hadn't been given a thought. This kind of stupidity occurs quite often in the world of industrial film.

I did not agree to edit the cruise film, though I did do all I could to talk the firm out of the idea of using the sales director to shoot it. My comments had no effect at all and six weeks later the company telephoned me to ask if I would like to see the film, which had just been returned by the processing laboratory. Out of interest, I accepted the invitation. The event was exactly as I had anticipated. I have been to many similar showings. I arrived to find the whole board gathered round a 16-mm projector and a number of rolls of film. The film was the original film exposed in the camera: no copy had been produced. The projector was not in good repair and would clearly damage the original film. I sat and watched while the sales director laced up the machine and projected two hours of indescribable film. The shots were all fairly well exposed, but the camera movements were unbelievable and the shots were all far too short. Used to shooting at silent speed on an 8-mm camera, the sales director had not realised that he needed to keep the camera running for much longer. And, most noticeable of all, the shots had no overall plan. They were simply moving snapshots, without any plan whatever. No one had ever thought of the form the finished film would take. And they had already succeeded in badly scratching the original film. Today, the film has still not been finished. The money has been written off, a lot of useless material produced and valuable time wasted. All through lack of planning and a determination to economise.

I would like to report that few companies are as stupid as the shipping line I have mentioned, but alas, I cannot. The events I have outlined have been repeated again and again, though I am glad to say I have not been involved myself. The end is not always quite as disastrous. Sometimes the raw materials are put together, and occasionally a professional editor does do what he can to redeem the rubbish he has to work with. A film may eventually be released, and, quite often, the company concerned will like it very much. They see their own product, and hear their own company name. But their enthusiasm isn't shared by audiences, and when the film is shown with other professionally produced films, it does its sponsors untold harm. Making films on the cheap is not a good investment.

The ideal situation would of course be for one man to make the whole film. Unfortunately, it is not a practical proposition from any point of view. Just as one man cannot run a company as managing director and do all the individual jobs himself, no one man can undertake all the individual parts of film making on his own. Film making calls for a variety of expertise. It is a strange combination of artistic feeling for what looks and sounds right, and a methodicial scientific approach to technicalities. And, as in so many other fields, experience pays off. If you can find a man with three heads, twenty arms and four pairs of legs, with a science degree and an appreciation of music, he may be able to make a one-man film! If you do not know anyone who meets the specifications, try the normal way of using a film production team. Let us consider why one, mere normal man cannot be expected to turn out first class results on his own.

Film making needs expertise. Expertise in writing and in

photography. Expertise in editing and in recording good quality sound. It is unlikely anyone will achieve a high standard in all these fields. Any-one can become competent in them, but expertise is more than com-petence, and it is worth looking for. Even if someone does succeed in mastering all the different major stages of production, there are practical points which make one-man filming impossible. You need at least two people to shoot film and record sound simultaneously and you should use four. One will have to operate the camera. And an assistant will be needed to zoom, or pull focus, to load and unload film magazines and to adjust lights. A recordist will have to watch his recording levels and look after the recording apparatus. His assistant may have to hold a microphone boom. So, one man would be rather overworked! Even silent filming is usually beyond the scope of one man. One man may be able to do the work, but two can do it better, and more quickly. The finished films will only show the results achieved. Setting up will take longer and there is a definite limit to the amount of camera equip-ment one man can operate and carry. The same problems apply right through production. You may have a brilliant cameraman. If he does not know much about editing, he will ruin his own raw materials, if he has to put them together.

"We did it to save money," the cruise director said when I asked him why the film he had decided to shelve had not been shot by pro-fessionals. And how much did he save? He lost the money invested and countless opportunities. He is not alone. Many films never reach an audience. A number of very costly professional feature films are con-sidered too bad for presentation and are permanently shelved. In the sponsored film world, where standards are lamentably low, films are often released when they should be thrown away. Low budget, and occasionally high budget films, so badly made they can do nothing but harm for their sponsors, are regularly released .And the reputation of industrial films in general suffers. Standards must be raised. Film making is a job for professionals.

3

Pre-production Stage

EVERY DETAIL OF a film must be planned if anything worthwhile is to be produced. It is useless going out with a camera and shooting an unplanned number of different scenes. Even if it does prove possible to put them together satisfactorily later on, they will probably fail to do the required job satisfactorily. More often, scenes shot without any prior planning will prove impossible to put together in any coherent form. When edited, they continue to look like a lot of unplanned scenes put together. They constitute an assembly and not, in any sense, a film. An assembly is an intermediate stage in film making. It is not the ultimate end product. Film—the correct end-product—must flow smoothly to achieve its purpose and the flow and sequence of events must be carefully planned.

The brief

Before a script is commissioned the sponsors should set an overall price limit. Then, with the sum in mind, a script can be produced. The limit must be realistic—or to express the same point another way, the brief must be realistic. They must not expect the earth for a minimal outlay. They will get what they pay for. If the amount of money available is small, limit the number of locations and opt for a simple film. It can be just as effective. Money does not breed success. Ideas are much more important than scale. A well-made film, with a simple treatment and interesting script, will usually prove worthwhile whereas large-scale productions can easily misfire.

A sponsor's brief should set out at least three basic guidelines.

1. *Aim of the film:*   To show what, how and why?
2. *Audience:*   Who is the film intended for?
3. *Limit to costs:*   How much money, in general terms, is available?

Before despatching the brief to the producers, sponsors should read their answers to point 3 and then the first point to see that the answers are realistic when the two are related.

With the brief as a guide, work can now start. Every production company has its own way of dealing with a brief and of planning and producing a film. I shall outline the way I personally use, and have used over many years to make sponsored films. To explain the processes, I shall explore some examples. Let's begin by tracing the history of two different films, one for a general audience and one for specialised showings, both concerned with the subject of paint.

General audience

The sponsors were makers of a very well-known brand of non-drip paint. So all production stages can be explained without embarrassing any of the personalities involved, we shall use the fictitious brand name of "Painton" in this text. Here is the brief provided by the sponsors. It was drawn up on the 18th July.

Painton Non-drip Paint: Brief

Aim: To increase the sales of Painton non-drip paint, by demonstrating its ease of application, quality finish and range of colours.

Audience: Primarily intended for use at evening presentations made by our dealers to clubs and societies. These presentations are arranged by company reps who agree to show a film to any organised group looking for entertainment. Women's clubs, YMCA and school audiences are most common, and the company's representatives are always available to introduce the films. They are also available to answer questions asked by the audience. Sometimes the showing is accompanied by a practical demonstration of paint application techniques.

Cost: Our last film was made for . . . [the price of a basic camera]. We look for something comparable.

Note: The film must be completed for showing at our annual sales conference on the 29th September. It should be 25 minutes long, in colour, with sound.

This brief arrived on my desk on the 20th July—10 weeks from the completion date specified. There is nothing very unusual about the short space of time. Sponsors often seem to think late and expect results early. Fortunately, I was working with an organisation large enough to meet close delivery dates with reputable material. Used to turning out two complete television programmes a week as well as a large number of sponsored industrial films, production teams could usually be made available at short notice. So we started to sift through the brief.

The last paragraph gave me a particularly good laugh! The madly

echnical reference to sound and colour often appears in briefs prepared
)y inexperienced sponsors. Armed with some facts, I went to see the
ponsors. The brief had been prepared by the company public relations
)fficer, on behalf of the brand manager of Painton. He said he thought
₁ new film was needed. The old one had been made four years before
₁nd some of the colours shown were no longer available. Pack changes
₁ad also been made and the paint was being supplied in a different type
)f tin. The existing film was out of date.

The budget

My first meeting with the PRO was enjoyable and useful. The
)udget was, of course, the first point for discussion and the unrealistic
igure had to be reconsidered. I was also concerned about the stipula-
ion of film duration, "The film must be 25 minutes . . ." as stated in
he brief. Stipulations of this kind can do no good at all. My philo-
ophy has always been that a film should be as long as the subject
equires. It should be long enough to make all the necessary points
learly, without undue repetition and without boring an audience.
These views, when explained, usually meet with approval. The
'ainton PRO certainly approved, and we agreed to say what had to be
aid, and let the film dictate its own length. Next, costs had to be dis-
:ussed, and before discussing the figures I wanted to know exactly what
₁ad to be shown in the new film. I also wanted to see the old one.

The original film had, I was assured, done a very good job. I was
₁gain reminded how little it cost. It certainly looked it. It ran for 25
₁inutes and felt like two hours. Every point was made over and over
₁gain.

The film had been produced four years ago and the work had been
ntrusted to a one-man band film unit. Like so many solo operators, he
:laimed to have worked for some time with the BBC. He had—I
hecked. If the sponsors had checked before, they would have dis-
:overed that the man's BBC experience consisted of 6 months as a
₁oliday relief assistant, in the gramophone library! The Painton film
vas made on a shoestring. It was adequately shot and edited in a
:ompletely uncreative way in keeping with the script which read rather
ike a sales catalogue. The soundtrack consisted only of a commentary.
There was no music and no sound effects. The film completely lacked
ife and, by cutting costs at every corner, the producer had churned out
he film for a ridiculously low sum. No doubt the economies had been
₁oticed by countless audiences.

This kind of film is not worth making. It does very little good for
he sponsors. If it is shown at a gathering attended by company
epresentatives they may be able to get over some of its drawbacks.

There is, however, a much larger audience. There is a definite limit to the number of showings company representatives can attend. There is no limit at all to the number of copies a film library can distribute. Copies of a well-made film, in the hands of a library, can do a very good job for the sponsors. The film must be good—it must stand on its own. And that means professionalism at all production stages. The figure offered for the job was not very enticing.

At the end of my first meeting with the Painton PRO, I suggested two steps be taken. As the company's reps were to use the completed production and had already used the earlier film, I felt we ought to have their comments and suggestions. Each rep should be asked what he thought a new film should include and what successes and failures the last production had encountered. I also suggested that the same questions be put to all interested parties at the company's head office. The answers to these questions would provide valuable raw material for a script.

Preliminary research must always be carried out before a firm quotation is given. The Painton PRO understood this point and agreed to take the matter up with the company management.

I could not produce a firm quotation after our first meeting because I did not have enough information to work with. I knew the subject and the audience and the aim of the film, but did not yet know how many locations or how much studio time would be needed. I knew the film subject, but a way of handling it had still to be decided. So, I could provide only a general idea of costs, based on the probability of the film being shot on 16 mm and running for what I estimated to be an adequate time for exploring the subject: 15 minutes. A figure of more than three times their quoted price was submitted with a letter explaining what could, and could not, be expected for the price. A firm price would be provided when detailed plans for the film were finalised and a contract drawn up.

Painton had expected a new film for the price of the old. They were now being told that any film worth making would cost more than three times as much. This may seem odd, but it happens quite often. Sponsors often believe they can get good films for next to nothing. A few are stupid enough to set a low and very firm price and demand a film for it—they get one, and often it sits on a shelf. A sensible sponsor takes advice and Painton did not make any further contact with me for two weeks.

During those two weeks they put the same brief in front of three other film producers. One of them agreed to make a film for the old price. One refused to quote for anything under double the figure suggested by myself and insisted on shooting on 35 mm. Another submitted an estimated price of slightly less than I had quoted. Painton then took negotiations a stage further and arranged to see examples of films produced by the companies expressing an interest. I was later told that the standards of the films seen were generally high, though some were far too long.

I had already made my point on that score, and it was remembered when the films were presented. The man quoting the old price produced other films made for that amount, and he lost the job.

Two producers were commissioned to produce a script. I was one of them.

Commission for a script

I had already suggested that the Painton representatives who were to use the finished film should be asked what they thought it should contain. A letter was sent to each representative asking him for suggestions about the film content, and for his comments on the successes and shortcomings of the existing film. Facts and figures were also asked for on the number of showings carried out in a year. Simultaneously, the Painton brand manager was asked for his ideas, and the marketing manager provided notes on how he wanted the subject to be handled. A full set of current promotional literature was provided. I also visited the factory and called on several retail decorating shops, without identifying my interests, to find out what retailers felt about the product.

These explorations took a week. At the end of the week I had all the facts and figures I needed. I was also beginning to discover what the finished film had to consist of.

Painton is a non-drip paint and the first job the film had to do was to show the advantages of non-drip paint. The brand manager wanted to emphasise the range of colours available and the marketing manager pointed out that the colours are all available in three different types of finish: gloss, emulsion and vinyl. The managing director felt it was important to emphasise that the Painton organisation is one of the world's largest producers of paint and thus has all the experience and resources needed to make a worthwhile product. The representatives, too, came up with some useful information. The first point they made was that 80% of their audiences consisted of women. Paint is often chosen and bought by the woman of the house. The representatives, in direct touch with the customer, had the benefit of first-hand experience in the use of the product. They recommended the paint, and if anything went wrong they were the first people to hear about it. They were anxious that the film should explain what could go wrong, so that potential customers could avoid making mistakes. There is nothing wrong with the product, the reps were quick to point out. But the way

Painton products are used often leaves much to be desired. Pain
cannot be applied to an unprepared surface if satisfactory result
are to be obtained. Good paint needs a carefully prepared surface anc
a good brush. The representatives wanted these points explained i▮
the film.

So we had five main points to make.
1. A non-drip paint has many advantages.
2. Painton is available in many colours.
3. There are three different types of finish to choose from.
4. Before painting you must first prepare the surface.
5. Painton is made by a vast organisation.

These five points were all made by Painton staff. In my explora▮
tions I unearthed a few other views which guided me when planning th
film.

My visit to the Painton factory impressed me very much. It wa▮
very modern, and paint was being produced at great speed and i
amazing quantities. It was clearly a busy place and there was obviousl
a demand for the paint. "Who uses it?" I asked the works foremar
"It's not all for home use," he explained. "We're making sever▮
different kinds of paint here. Some of it is for marine use. Some goes o▮
cars, and there's a lot of it used in industry." Three interesting fact▮
which I noted and later used in my script, to illustrate the experienc
of Painton as a company. My visit to the retailers also proved wort▮
while.

One of the retailers I visited had been selling paint for yea▮
and summed the situation up very neatly. "Most people don't care
damn what paint they buy. If they think it's easy to use, or they've see▮
it on the telly, they'll buy it." There was nothing I could do about th▮
"seen on the telly" bit. The new film was for non-theatrical use. B▮
the ". . . if it's easy to use . . ." comment gave me a very good hin▮
and eventually suggested a title—*Decorating Made Easy*.

Outline script

After the visits I have described, I had four days in which to pr▮
duce an outline script for discussion at a further meeting with th▮
company. Although I knew that another producer was also workin▮
on a script, that did not really concern me. My main aim was to writ▮
a script which would do the job the sponsoring company wanted. The▮
wanted a hard-selling film, demonstrating the advantages of the
product.

My job was to get exactly what they wanted, and put in on film ▮
a satisfactory manner.

Few people really want to watch the beginning of a film. When the lights go out, people are usually talking and few are really paying close attention to the screen. This is particularly true in the presentation of industrial films.

Shows often take place in less than ideal conditions, and a projectionist may sometimes have to start the film and then race to the back of the hall to turn off the lights! I am not recommending this—but it does happen, and film makers should bear it in mind when planning the start of their films.

My aim at the beginning of a film is to say two things. First, I want to say to my audience, "Here is a film which is worth watching. You'll enjoy it." Then, I want them to feel involved and to identify themselves with the message of the picture or with the characters portrayed. They will then regard the message with less scepticism and more belief.

Films are very often presented in programmes. Films distributed by a film library are often run one after another in a club film evening, or some other gathering. Possibly, four or five films will be presented in one programme. If they are all industrially sponsored they will all be promoting something. The soft-sell film immediately has an advantage, but so too does the film which says in its opening sequence, "This film is worth watching."

There are many ways of interesting an audience and of attracting attention. In the Painton film I decided it was important for the people in the audience to identify themselves with the difficulties of decorating. Once they had been understood, the advantages of Painton could be presented as a direct and very obvious contrast. I decided to start the film with a series of deliberate jokes. My aim was to make fun of the amateur decorator—the really inefficient do-it-yourself man. And I hoped that an audience seeing the mistake would immediately say, "That's me. I've done that!" Once they had identified themselves with the problem, the Painton solution would be more readily received.

By remembering my own tragic attempts at home decorating (I am the professional's best friend—he always has to come in and put it all right when I have finished) I developed a short and simple sequence. I decided the first scenes of the film should be:

Painton: Sequence

1. An amateur preparing to paint an outside window and putting a ladder through the window by mistake.
2. Another amateur painting a door and letting paint drip over the door handle.
3. Someone painting a ceiling and succeeding in painting almost everything else at the same time.

Scenes from the Painton film. The firs
scene (top) shows a professional decorato
at work. This is to reinforce the openin
remarks made in the commentary. The
follows a humorous sequence showing a
amateur, who is hardly able to handle th
the ladder (centre) and ends up by pushin
it through the window (bottom).

I had these three basic ideas and started to work them out o
paper. I realised that the shots would be funnier still if prefaced b
showing the correct professional methods. So I added an extra shot fo
the first scene of the film. It showed a professional decorator, in whit
protective clothes, holding a professional paint can and carefull
applying paint to the outside of a house. The scene was covered b
an introductory line of commentary. It was short and to the point
"A few years ago home decorating was a job only done by experts
Then the do-it-yourself craze began."

It seemed to me to be wrong for the amusing shots which followe

Further scenes from the Painton film.
Another amateur decorator paints a door
(top) with dribbling paint which spreads
over the handle (centre). A man paints the
ceiling, and his whole face is spattered with
paint.

to have any commentary. Funny scenes should look funny—a voice
explaining that "here the man is using too much paint and it's dripping
on the handle", would kill the comedy and add absolutely nothing. So
I decided to use music: preferably funny music, with the intention of
later editing the pictures to match the beat of the tune. This method
later worked out very well.

After the first shot, attention had to be focused on the amateur
at work.

I decided to start with a view of a very small amateur, stagger-
ing towards the camera with a very long ladder. I wanted to make it

obvious that the ladder was out of control, so I scripted a shot of the top of the ladder waving madly about against the clear sky. For the third shot, I thought we should show the amateur and the ladder at a point where he missed his footing, and let the ladder fall with a crash through the window of a house.

From these three brief shots we could turn, without comment, to our second amateur decorator. This time we would show a girl. She should be a long haired girl so the hair could be made to look completely disorganised and she could look harassed. She should be painting a door, without having previously taken off or masked the door handle in the correct manner. And the paint should be rather too liquid.

We might as well make liquid paint look quite difficult to use, even at this early stage! I decided to start with a close-up of an unidentifiable paint tin, with drips galore running down the side and covering the girl's hand. At the start of the shot a paint brush would come into view, enter the tin and slop out again leaving more drips in its trail.

We would then cut to a second shot, showing the part of the door nearest to the handle. The paint-laden brush would slurp into shot and drips would run down the door, on to the handle. The girl would try to stop the drips running down the handle by wiping them off with her paint sodden fingers. She wouldn't succeed. After five seconds of that shot, we would turn and look at the girl. She loses patience and decides to paint over the handle and forget all about it!

In the finished film this scene always gets a long laugh and I often hear people saying "That's me", which is exactly what was intended in putting it in.

To end this short sequence I decided to cut to a big close-up of a nose and a pair of spectacles seen in profile. The camera would quickly move back to show a more general view. The glasses and the whole face would be spattered with large amounts of paint. We would see a man painting a ceiling . . . and everything else as well. At the end of the camera movements the man would turn from the ceiling to recharge his brush and we would see the front of his face and his glasses—all covered in paint.

Over this scene the second line of commentary would be introduced. "There are still a few people who can paint ceiling, walls and carpet in one operation. But there are many who are rather more expert."

The opening sequence I have outlined consisted of only seven shots. Six of them were designed to get a laugh and make an audience interested enough to pay close attention to the rest of the film. The success of a sequence like this depends entirely on the way in which is handled.

It is absolutely fatal to be seen trying to be funny. An audience will immediately suspect what follows and the attempt will misfire. Comedy must be very carefully handled. If it is to succeed in an industrial film it needs good acting, observant direction and skilful editing.

In my experience, sponsors usually regard the introduction of comedy with grave suspicion. Carefully used, it can be successful.

With the opening sequence planned, I turned my attention to the rest of the film. Having shown the amateur way, and had a good laugh in the process, it seemed to me that the correct professional techniques should be shown next. But Painton is made for an amateur market. The publicity material made that quite clear. "The number one paint for the amateur home decorator," the posters proclaimed. So I had to think again.

I wanted to show professionals, but couldn't, so I would show professionalism—professional techniques being used by experienced do-it-yourself decorators.

From the shot of the man slopping paint, we would turn to someone using the correct techniques. And we might as well start at the beginning, and show him preparing the surface before applying paint. The commentary was written first. After the previous sentence about those who paint ceilings, walls and carpet in one operation, it read, "But there are many who are rather more expert. They know how to prepare a surface before painting." This was illustrated by a shot of a man sandpapering a door before applying paint. Five seconds of film, and one more valuable point. The commentary went on, "And they know how to choose the right kind of paint—Painton." At this point, the action would then change to show a revolving paint tin somewhere in a sea of whiteness. The camera would track in as the tin revolved.

The label on the tin would appear at the same time as the word "Painton" on the soundtrack. The film titles would then follow.

It can take a long time to plan and write an industrial film. You have seen how much work goes into planning just nine simple shots. And the sponsor's message has so far only been introduced. The main sales points have to be explored in the rest of the film. The Painton film is typical of many hard-selling industrial films. The sponsor's ideas had to be planned so they occurred in a logical way throughout the film.

The brief outlined the sponsor's requirements. Ideas and some research followed. Then a way of linking the ideas and sales points had to be found.

And last of all, a shooting script had to be produced. Let's see how some of the sales promotional points were covered.

Covering sales points

It seemed to me that, after the titles, we might as well start where we wanted the audience to finish up: in a paint shop! So, after the title sequence, I proposed showing a general view of a modern shopping area.

This is how the remainder of the film developed:

The camera concentrated on two young people walking into a paint shop. The scene changed and we saw a shop assistant rearranging countless tins on the shop counter. The couple approached him and started to talk. Over these shots the commentary asked the audience a question. "With hundreds of paints on the market, how do you choose the right one?" A closer view of shelves of paint tins followed. There were many different types and a variety of colours though no brand names could be seen. Not even God's gift—Painton! The commentary continued—"A colour card will help you, but it's important to remember that some paints mean harder work than others." The scene again changed to show the girl who entered the shop pointing to a pile of tins on the counter. A card near the tins announced, "Reduced Special offer!"

The commentary then went on—"This conventional paint is cheap and in this large tin there seems to be plenty of it. But if you buy it, you'll soon discover it's thin and very liquid. It needs a great deal of stirring and very careful application. You'll have to apply several coats, and buy reams of newspaper." The scene changed during that commentary to show cut price paint in use. In one shot we saw a brush emerge from the paint, dripping and full. In the next shot we saw the paint being applied to a wall. It failed to cover the existing colour and was obviously thin. Before the paint could be applied, we saw it had to be stirred thoroughly. It was clearly a messy and unsatisfactory paint to use.

From the shot of paint dripping down the wall and so on down the decorator's arms too, we cut to a shot of a new tin of Painton. It stood on a plain laminated surface and looked clean and tidy. A girl's hand came into shot and opened the tin. The tin looked easy to open (we are permitted some poetic licence?) and a brush was produced and dipped in the paint. It emerged again, coated in non-drip Painton. The girl applied it to a section of dark coloured wall. It covered the existing paint satisfactorily. She used long smooth strokes of the brush unlike the man who applied liquid paint in a number of short energetic bursts.

Painton thus looked easy to apply. The commentator made further sales points. "Painton is different. It looks different for a start. It's a gel and not a liquid and needs no stirring. You still use a brush or a

oller but you can take a much bigger load from the can to the wall.
t never drips and won't run down your arm and paint your wrist-
vatch. It doesn't leave brushmarks and its much easier to apply than
onventional paint."

At this point there was a further commentary gap. It is very im-
ortant to avoid the considerable danger of talking all the way through
a film.

Audiences are easily bored and if they are offered continuous talk
nd advice, they will quickly grow restive and cease to heed the points.
A pause, however slight, serves to maintain interest. So we paused,
rought music in again and watched our demonstrator apply the paint.
Ve allowed two commentary free shots. One medium shot showed her
pplying the paint. She wore a blue dress and painted the wall dark
ellow, a contrast and another way of emphasising colour without
pelling it out in commentary. The next shot was a big close-up of the
rush at work on the wall. The paint flowed on and the brush marks
uickly disappeared. From these shots, the camera panned round to
how another girl painting another nearby wall with conventional
aint.

The commentator pointed out the facts: "While the first girl is
dding a second and a third coat, *she* will be enjoying herself. One coat,
asily applied, and her work is complete. The whole job is much
impler."

Having seen the ease of application, and compared the advan-
ages of Painton with the disadvantages of conventional drip paints,
ve could start to explore decorating techniques more fully. In the next
equence we examined ways of preparing a surface before painting. The
ommentary led the way. "Of course before you start painting you
aust first prepare the surface. Old paintwork must be removed with
aint stripper or it must be sanded down. If the existing paintwork is in
ood repair a thorough wash with warm water and detergent may be
ufficient. But don't forget to wash off the detergent before repainting."
The action illustrated the points. We saw a man sanding down a door
nd using a paint stripper on a wood-panelled door. A girl washing a
hird, painted door was then featured. Again, maximum use was made
f colour.

The proposed script suggested sanding down a blue door, stripping
red one with panels and washing a brilliant white one of hardboard.
he commentary went on with further practical hints. "Holes should
e filled up . . . the right way not the lazy one." One sentence to cover
wo shots. One showed a hand applying filler to holes in a plaster wall.
t was followed by a small boy putting a picture over a hole in a wall
nd looking over his shoulder to see if this lazy method had been wit-
essed! The third shot showed someone sanding down the outside of a

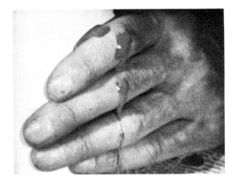

Painton film sequence. Two young people
in a shop are shown the numerous brands
of liquid paint available (top). Problems in
using conventional paint; stirring (centre)
and the thinness of the result (bottom).

window frame, and the commentator ended the sequence by re
minding the audience that "time spent preparing a surface is never
wasted".

At this stage in the film a number of important points had already
been made. The advantages of Painton over conventional points had
been made clear, visually. The need to prepare a surface before paint
ing had been made known, so the Painton representatives would be
happy. The next sequence was difficult to write, for the choice of a
colour scheme is very much a matter for personal taste. This fact was

ainton paint sequence. The virtues of
on-drip paint are shown. An easily
pened tin, and the background suggest
ean working (top). The brush is dipped
entre) and the paint is applied easily
ad effectively over the existing colour
pottom).

ater acknowledged by adding an extra line of commentary—a line
ot in my original draft. I relied on the advice of the Painton colour
onsultant, who had many original ideas for room colour schemes
ad the imagination to try them out; I decided to show examples
f as many different colour schemes as the budget could afford. The
xamples included furniture and were aimed at as large an audience as
ossible by showing antique and modern furniture and an old and a
ew house, with rooms expensively redecorated as well as some re-
ainted at very low cost. To show the versatility of the paint, and its

ability to make every kind of room look attractive, was the aim ⊂
the sequence and it was scripted with this aim in mind. The previou▮
sequence ended with the words, "Time spent preparing a surface ▮
never wasted."

The film then contined with a further reference to time in th
commentary as well as a visual link. "You can also spend time choosin▮
your colours. And with Painton you'll find there are plenty of colou▮
to choose from." The action changed from the shot of a man preparin▮
a window for painting to a close-up of the face of a clock.

From this close-up the camera moved out to show that the cloc▮
was situated on the wall of a living room. Sitting nearby were the youn▮
couple seen earlier in the shop. They were surrounded by colour card
and were looking at a Painton colour card. An establishing long sho
was followed by a closer view of the colour card, showing the wid▮
range of colours available. The sequence then went on to show some ⊂
the colours used in different room settings. Music and commentar▮
were both used.

The music provided a suitable break from monotony and gave th▮
audience a chance to refocus its attention on the general theme. Th▮
commentary did not describe the scenes but identified the colours b▮
name.

The sequence showed that small and large rooms look good ▮
Painton colours and cupboards too can be painted to advantag▮
Emphasis was placed on the wide range of available colours.

The colour sequence lasted three minutes and the film then wer▮
on to explore the company background. It had already explained tha▮
Painton paints are easy to apply and look good when they dry. It ha▮
shown that they do not leave brush marks and dry to a good finish. An▮
the range of colour had been explored. "Who makes Painton, and wh▮
is it so good?" seemed a logical question to ask next. To answer i▮
we turned to science.

"Scientific" sequence

Now many industrial films have laboratory sequences emphasin▮
research and showing all the usual shots of chemists in white coa▮
doing the sort of visually interesting things they only do when fil▮
cameras are around. I decided that any science sequence should be ke▮
very short and made as visually interesting as possible. I limited it ▮
six shots. At the end of the colour sequence we had introduced th▮
science sequence by saying, "The makers of Painton know a lot abo▮
colour.

They also know what the home decorator needs." This w▮

Painton film. Two shots showing how the paint is tested in the company laboratories. Close ups are most effective. One machine tests the thickness (top), and the other the weathering ability of the paint (bottom).

ollowed by "Research and development go on all the time. Many experienced people working to produce a paint which is really hard wearing and easy to apply. And Painton is tested in all conditions." We reminded the audience of two sales points and introduced a visually attractive short sequence. The first shot showed a complete paint laboratory. I had visited the company laboratories while doing research and knew exactly what I wanted to show. General laboratory scenes are often dull and I decided to play the scene in close-ups. I proposed starting with a general view of the whole laboratory just to show the scale of the company resources, and then to cut to a big close-up of a curious little machine testing the thickness of paint. It made a cheerful noise and looked interesting and that was enough. On the reference to being "tested under all conditions", I proposed cutting to a shot of what paint manufacturers call a weatherometer. It is really a large tank where specimen panels of paints are lit by ultra violet light and sprayed with a fine rain spray for hours on end. Three more shots were planned, all with authentic location sound effects. One showed the whole machine with the paint panels in position being sprayed. The

Painton film. Factory sequence showing the moving row of tins (top) and the process of filling them with the various colours (bottom).

second shot showed a meter registering the number of hours during which the panels had been sprayed. A third shot showed a smaller number of panels immersed in water with what looked like a small ship's propeller turning to keep the water moving. Over this shot commentary was reintroduced. "When tests are complete, the paint goes into production."

The next sequence in the Painton film spoke for itself. It was based on my visit to the factory. It was edited to music, using a lighthearted jig, and the tins of paint appeared to move in time with the music. The early proposed draft script listed was later to be one of the most successful parts of the film as a "production sequence". It was to show paint being stirred in vats and machines filling tins with various colours. The sequence was designed to provide a break from commentary and to remind people of the range of colours available. It lasted for two minutes.

"Production" sequence

The production sequence came near the end of the film. Most of the points which the sponsor wanted the film to make clear had already been explored. To finish the film the main issues had to be summarised

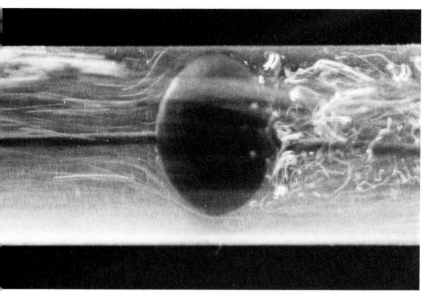

Close ups, slow motion and animated diagrams can often be used effectively in an industrial film. In the Unilever film *Fluid Flow* the pattern of flow round an obstacle is very clearly illustrated. Picture: Unilever Films.

The last shot in the production sequence showed cans rolling off the production lines, ready for use. I wanted to remind the audience that the paint had a number of different applications, so I used a commentary link to lead into a final summary sequence. "When paint comes off these production lines, it's ready for use." The scene changed from the factory to a shot of a young man painting an inside wall with a bright coloured emulsion paint. The paint was yellow and it was being applied to a dark blue wall.

The picture clearly showed that it really covered in one coat, with very little effort. From this interior shot the film moved outside to show someone else painting the front of a house. So the paint could be used inside and outside.

The next point to establish in the film was the experience behind all Painton paints. Here my discussion with the factory foreman came in useful and a line of commentary was based on his comments. 'Painton is the result of years of experience. Its makers supply paints for every possible use. For cars, of every size; for domestic appliances and for shipping." The action at this point provided an opportunity to show something more interesting than people applying paint. To cover the words "for cars of every size", a model car was lined up on a wall and photographed in a way that made it look full sized and realistic. Then the camera moved back, on the words "of every size", to show

Left: In *Simplicity Westaform* the lightness and flexibility of Westaform flue lining materials was emphasised. The film was designed for showing to audiences of builders merchants. Shot at two locations in one day it cost very little and proved a valuable sales aid for several years. Picture: SimplicityWestaform.

that the car was a model on a wall alongside a main road where real cars drove past. Shots of industrial applications were also easy to obtain.

A large vacuum cleaner company used Painton products and shots of cleaners being sprayed provided an interesting five seconds. And shipping too was easy to illustrate. Painton materials had been used on a liner about to make her maiden voyage. Shots of the liner provided additional interest and led into the last sequence of the film. The commentator summarised the points already made: "No wonder Painton is the world's most widely used paint. And, to benefit from this experience, all you have to do is choose the right tin." The action moved from the shipyard to the shop where the first sequence started. The couple standing by the shop counter pointed to the Painton tins and the shop assistant took a tin from the racks and placed it on the counter.

The camera moved in to a close-up of the tin and a final sequence edited to music and free of commentary, ended the film.

The Painton film was thoroughly conventional and rather unambitious but it proved a great success. It cost the sponsors a little over three times more than they originally intended to spend. And nearly half as much again was eventually spent in making copies and preparing foreign language versions. The film was distributed by

On film, it is possible to show the whole of a factory or a complete industrial process more effectively than by actual inspection. Portable cassette projectors enable the results to be shown almost anywhere without fuss. The complexities of glass making and the modern equipment at Pilkingtons factories have been covered in several Pilkington films. Picture: Pilkington Bros.

the Painton company and by several film libraries. It was withdrawn after four years of use because the company changed the shape and appearance of its paint tins, thus making the film out of date. The company has since produced four further films.

The Painton film used hard-selling techniques. I am not at all convinced that these techniques were right. I prefer to show *why* a product or service is good with minimal help from a commentary. Unfortunately, few sponsors are brave enough to opt for a soft-sell treatment. Writing scripts for industrial films is not like writing *Gone With The Wind*. You can't write what you want to write or what appeals to you personally. A film-maker's job is to do everything he can to understand the product and the market. Sponsors know what they want to say.

Film makers should be experts in making films and should thus know how a sponsor's ideas can best be presented on film. If the two can work together, and there is no reason why they should not, success should follow.

Producer–sponsor relationship

In producing any industrial film a working relationship which really does work must be established between producer and sponsor. The producer must understand the sponsor's point of view. The sponsor knows his subject. And his subject is the product, not film. If he is wise, he will acknowledge that the producer knows film and not, initially, the product. This philosophy is important and often misunderstood. My ideas on the subject are easily summed up. Let the sponsor say what he wants, and let the producer suggest ways of saying it, on film. A sponsor may not want to learn about film techniques and he does not really need to. But a producer must learn everything he can about the subject of the film. And this is where so many producers miss the boat. They become so wrapped up in filmic ideas that they lose the subject. And quite often they do not carry out enough research, or bother to even try and understand the sponsor's wishes and point of view.

I have produced many technical and general interest films. I have often been asked "Have you ever made a film on a subject like this before?" This question is often followed by "It's important you should understand what we're trying to get at." You do not need to be an expert to learn all about any subject. All you need to be is an expert on film. The sponsor is the other expert needed. He can provide the facts and information and the producer will suggest ways of putting those facts on film. By asking the right and sometimes wrong questions, he will soon find the necessary facts.

Specialised subjects

The question of expertise is most often raised by sponsors about to embark on making a technical film or one designed for a specialised audience. I firmly believe that research is more important than expertise. A producer should be able to learn the necessary facts. Look now at a further example of interpreting a sponsor's brief—this time with specialised subject matter. I have deliberately chosen another paint film for it provides an interesting contrast with the film for general showing which we have already explored. We are concerned with another type of paint—the type used for vehicle refinishing. So that the subject and negotiations can be fully explored, I have again used a fictitious brand name. Lifton paint does not exist. The film does, and the following notes show how the same production team who handled the general interest Painton film handled a technical subject for a specialised audience. Here is the sponsor's brief:

The Lifton Weight-Mixing System: Brief

Aim: To sell more Lifton weight-mixing systems to trade users. To project confidence in the accuracy, speed and simplicity of the system, and to highlight the customer benefits.

Audience: The vehicle refinishing trade. Particularly garage owners, foreman painters and fleet vehicle operators.

The brief was attached to a letter I received asking for a quotation. The letter was signed by the vehicle refinishing manager of Lifton who had seen the Painton film and had got in touch with the sponsors. I arranged to meet him and explore the subject in detail. We met two weeks later and he explained the reasons for the film. Again, it was wanted for use at dealer evenings, when audiences of refinishers are gathered together and introduced to new products and generally boozed up by the sales hungry trade! The film would also be used on Videotronic projectors. These machines are entirely self-contained and have their own built-in screen and sound system. A sales representative using a Videotronic can slot a film cassette into position, plug the projector into the mains power supply and show his film. Lifton intended to equip their representatives with the film and with Videotronics. A few copies would also be made available to film libraries for circulation to specialised audiences. So much for the audiences, but what about the film, and the subject?

When I first went to Lifton, I knew nothing at all about weight-mixing, Lifton or the vehicle refinishing trade. I was not in any sense an expert and, needless to say, had not made any weight-mixing films before! So, research had to start at basics and I asked to see the system in use. I was shown thirty paint tins, a pair of scales and a book of figures, all being used by one man mixing paint. That, and that alone, was to provide the subject for a 15-minute film. It was a very dull subject, from a film-making point of view. But the film had to be made, and it had to satisfy the needs of the sponsors. And, to satisfy me, it had to be interesting too, so we set to work.

I watched a demonstration of the operation of the system while the sales manager explained what was taking place. In simple terms, the method of mixing paint by weight is extremely accurate and enables colours to be matched without variation of colour or tone. The final script shows how accurate it is and lists the many other advantages that it has. When I first saw the system I could only notice that the operator took one tin from a shelf, stirred the contents by turning a handle on top of the tin and poured a set amount of paint into an empty tin placed on a pair of scales. When the weight of paint in the previously empty tin reached a point determined by the weight shown on the scales, the operator ceased to pour colour one and added another colour to a new predetermined weight. Several other colours followed, all to weights dictated by figures contained in the book of formulas. Then, the mixed colours were stirred and put in a spray gun.

When sprayed alongside a new car of the same colour, the colour match of the original paint and the newly mixed batch was perfect. A perfect match, it transpired, was the success of the system, or one of the successes anyway. There were plenty of others, as my researches soon revealed. After the demonstration I talked to the operator and discovered some more important facts. From the thirty tins in front of him he could mix any colour except black. The book of formulas contained figures for making over 2000 different colours and four different pack sizes. The scales were obviously easy to operate and the whole system looked simple. I tried it, and it *was* simple. I also noticed that the tins were well designed and easy to pour without drips. A special pourer had been inserted in an airtight lid so that paint could not dry out after use, and a stirring handle had been incorporated in the lid. The whole system was compact, took up little space and seemed to work well.

The sales manager provided some more facts and figures. He pointed out that one supplier could provide all the tins needed and that meant a reduction in time spent ordering and in paperwork. Also, as only thirty tins were necessary, there was a tremendous saving in stock investment costs. The colours were repeatable—each of the thirty tins contained paint meeting computer dictated specifications. In down to earth terms that meant that anyone running out of one tin one day could find another tin of the same colour on another day, and know it would be identical in every way. This is unusual, for paint is made in batches and one batch often differs slightly from another so that colours are not repeatable. In the Lifton system, I was assured, repeatability is guaranteed.

After visiting the Lifton factory I went to see a garage. I did not tell Lifton I was going, and I did not mention Lifton during my visit. I just asked the foreman painter how he resprayed his vehicles and what system he thought best. He did not use a weight-mixing system. He used a rival method of mixing by volume and he showed me how it worked and some of its advantages and drawbacks. And he showed me his collection of hundreds of tins of paint.

In drafting my first script I was guided by both of the visits I had made and by the audiences who were to see the finished film. I realised that most of them would have seen enough crash repairs and paint respraying to last a lifetime. They would not want to see more on a cinema screen. And they would not wish to be told how to do a job most of them had been doing for years. So I decided to try and get them on our side from the beginning—to make them laugh at the expense of the people who gave them most work and most trouble: the motorists.

So, I found my first line of commentary. "There's nothing new about a crashed car." The continuation of this introduction was suggested by my visit to the garage. When I arrived, the owner of a car being resprayed was telling the garage owner the details of his accident. Clearly the man had heard it all before and wasn't really interested. So I completed my first script sentence. "There's nothing new about a crashed car, though to listen to some of the owners you'd think there was." To accompany this I decided to show on the screen a damaged car being crushed by a car reclamation machine. At the end of the opening sentence I decided to cut a series of shots of different damaged cars. Over each shot we would hear the voice of the owner giving his account of the accident. Each voice would be different, and we would never see the owners—just their cars. I arrived at the dialogue by looking at various insurance claim forms, and by adding a little here and there. The sequence went as follows:

Lifton Script Extract

1st car. An average family saloon	*1st Driver:* "I was just driving along when this pedestrian came out and hit me. I always thought there were only four lamp-posts on that road but I discovered a fifth." *Cut*
2nd car. A small family saloon. An ideal "second car"	*2nd Driver* (a rather carefully spoken lady): "I wasn't going very fast. I just didn't see him. When I knocked him down he admitted it was his fault. He said he'd been knocked down before." *Cut*
3rd car. Executive limousine	*3rd Driver* (the executive in a hurry): "It wasn't my fault. I mean I collided with a stationary car when it was coming the other way. What could I do about that?"

The fourth and final driver was a working man. We only heard the first sentence. "You see there was this other chap coming the other way so he was obviously going to run into me." His voice was then faded low and a new, formal commentator's voice was heard over the top. It introduced the first facts of the film. "While they bore everyone to death with accounts of their accidents, someone has to repair the damage. Bodywork first, then paint, of the right colour. And accurate colour matching can be a problem. One solution is to mix the paint." The action moved from the car scrapyard to the interior of a garage. A paint foreman was inspecting a damaged car making a note of what had to be done. On the words "colour matching can be a problem" he walked over to the Lifton weight-mixing system. He reached it as "one solution is to mix the paint" was heard on the soundtrack. Then the opening titles followed, with some music.

The introductory sequence was immediately accepted by the sponsors who, with a good knowledge of the vehicle refinishing trade, felt it would be appreciated by motor trade audiences. It later proved a tremendous success. In fact the scenes got so much laughter that one silent pause between dialogue had to be extended so that important information was not lost under the roars of mirth. It took the audience off the defensive, and made them interested in the scenes that followed.

I decided to explore two avenues. I wanted to show how the weight-mixing system worked and illustrate its advantages. To make the advantages obvious and memorable I decided to contrast them with the volume-mixing method. I would feature two different garages, one using the weight-mixing system and one not yet enlightened! The latter had to be realistic enough to make valid points. I also wanted to make the same place look extremely inefficient, so I decided to portray it as a small back-street garage run by a man simply identified as Fred. After the main titles we had our first view of Fred's back-street garage. Cans littered racks stretching from wall to wall. It was dark, and the only wall not cluttered with cans contained a few nude picture calendars, tyre pressure gauges and other decorations often found in the garage trade. Fred, in dirty overalls, was seen to be pouring two different tins of paint into one and stirring frantically. He knelt beside a small Fiat car with a scratch a few inches long on the side of the bodywork. The commentator introduced the scene:

Lifton: Commentary (Extract)

"Fred uses a volume mixing method, and its not very reliable. He goes on trying until he gets the colour he needs. He collects more and more tins from many suppliers and still doesn't get the colour he wants. However, if he keeps on trying he may eventually get there. But at what cost?"

This short scene consisted of three shots. One showed Fred, messily blending the paint, dipping a stick in the mixture and holding it against the body of the car. It showed an entirely different shade. The second shot highlighted the racks of untidy cans. A sea of drip-covered tins, some open, most half empty, all badly stored and dust covered. Scene three showed Fred's office. Files galore, mostly half open, and papers everywhere. No visible desk or clear working surface. Only a cat, asleep on the latest batch of invoices. Fred did not appear to be the sort of man to make a profit.

To introduce Fred and the volume-mixing system took 20 seconds. Next, I wanted to draw a very clear contrast to the efficiency of the weight-mixing system. So I decided to dissolve to the second garage, starting with a general view showing a lot of empty wall and floor space. The shot was designed to look neat and tidy and well organised. Space, sadly lacking in Fred's emporium, must be seen to be abundant. Again, I relied on commentary to make the point really clear.

> "The garage opposite is rather more organised. They have a limited amount of storage space and don't want to clutter it up with hundreds of tins and unnecessary paperwork. Their paint comes from one supplier. There's only one invoice and so it's easy to check. And they only stock thirty tins. Yet from these colours they can make any colour they're ever likely to need. They use the Lifton weight-mixing system. Mixing by weight. Why have they chosen this system? Let's go back to Fred and see why his volume-mixing method can't succeed."

The scene, again short, was kept simple. We saw a general shot of the whole working area, neat and uncluttered by surplus rows of cans. We saw paint being delivered, by a van labelled "Lifton", and we saw one man sign one delivery note and receive five cans. And we returned to take a closer view of the system, noting the thirty cans and the pair of scales. At the end of the sequence, the camera tracked into the scales and the action dissolved from the neatness of organised efficiency, to the chaos of Fred's empire. Fred was still trying to match the colour of his Fiat. And he still could not find the right colour. The commentary continued:

> "A few years ago this garage was rather like Fred's. If they hadn't got the right colour they had to send out for it. And with more than 2000 different car colours on the market, they frequently found they didn't have the colour they needed. Sometimes the first stockist was able to supply it, but often they had to try more than one. All this took time. And it cost money for wages, for telephone calls and for tins of a colour they might only use once. Anything left when the job was completed went into store. Ten tins became twenty; twenty, fifty; and fifty, two hundred. And they found they were keeping hundreds of tins they were unlikely ever to need again. All of them paid for, tying up valuable capital and using valuable storage space, as well as adding to paperwork. The weight-mixing system changes this situation at once."

From scenes of Fred sorting through endless tins, and a montage of his assistant visiting warehouses unable to supply, we returned to the Lifton garage. Having highlighted several of the disadvantages of conventional vehicle refinishing paint systems, we could now explore in more detail some of the advantages of Lifton.

> "You only need thirty cans, and they can all be supplied from one source so it's easy to check and you use very much less storage space. And you're not tying up capital on stock you may never use twice. So you save time. You save space. You save money. And you can make any colour."

In the Lifton film two rival garages were used to highlight the advantages of the Lifton system and the drawbacks of traditional methods. Fred's rundown garage was specially constructed for the film.

Having pointed out the advantages of the system over the direct disadvantages we had seen in Fred's workshop, I now decided to add some further advantageous points. Accuracy was the number one sale point.

> "But the important thing about this system is that it's really accurate. It uses controlled strength mixing enamels—reliable raw materials, the same from batch to batch. And the scales are thoroughly accurate, guaranteed to one ten thousandth of an ounce. Both the results of years of research and testing."

After a short sequence in which we explained some of the tests and research carried out were explored, we returned to the garage for a demonstration of how the system worked. Over shots showing the different processes, I decided to explain the system and reiterate the main sales points.

> "The paint combinations are contained in a book of formulas. All you have to do is look up the colour reference number in the book and alongside the entry you'll find the colours you need. The book lists the quantities you have to use and the figures are worked out accumulatively."

By contrast with Fred's establishment, the Lifton garage was uncluttered, clean and efficient.

"So, zero the scales and add the first colour until you reach the figure indicated in the book of formulas. Then add the second colour. It's easy to pour from the cans. The colour of the enamels is always consistent. And the stirrer makes it easy. The result: a perfect match to the motor manufacturers' official colour standard."

The film went on to explain that as the system was easy to use, anyone could use it without hours of training. "If someone goes sick, someone else can take over," summed up the issue. And the sales points were made clear once more for, as the sponsors pointed out at our first meeting, not all vehicle refinishers are Masters of Arts. A film has to be down to earth and very clear if it is to be remembered. We showed what the system consisted of and how it should be used. We highlighted advantages in cost, ease of operation and economy. And we showed the shortcomings of an alternative system. And we showed the system in international use. The last scene of the film seemed to me to call for light relief. So I returned to the beginning sequence and one of the crashed cars, suitably repaired and resprayed, being collected. The driver got in and thanked the operator of the weight-mixing system. He reversed into the main road and the camera moved across the garage to concentrate on the vehicle refinisher's face as he watched his customer

reverse out of the garage. We heard a screeching of tyres and a tremendous crash and the accident was reflected in the refinisher's face. He
seemed to be thinking "Bloody idiot", but as he turned and retraced his
steps to the weight-mixing scales his words were audible. "That'll be
another pint of canary yellow."

End titles followed.

The script approved

The Lifton film script I have outlined was presented to the sponsors
for approval. A few slight alterations were made but the film generally
met with approval. It was produced and shown to an audience of
refinishers to test their reactions. It was an unqualified success and, with
the exception of extending the shot mentioned before so that laughter
did not obliterate an important sales point, no alterations were made
to it.

Six months after the film was produced, representatives were asked
to stop using it until further notice. It had proved so successful that the
company had run out of weight-mixing systems and twelve months
supply had been sold in twenty-four weeks!

Producer-initiated films

We have so far discussed the planning of two industrial films, both
designed to increase sales of particular products. As I have already
mentioned, sponsored films can do a number of different jobs. The aim
is not always to increase sales. Let us now consider a further production,
a fire safety film which has proved an international success—*Fire At
Work*.

Fire At Work set out to make everyone more fire safety conscious

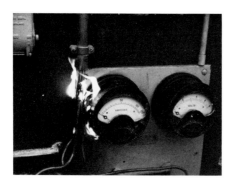

A graphic illustration of danger from the
film *Fire at Work*. The results of an electrical
short circuit were simulated by using wires
soaked in oil which burst into flame when
overheated. Picture: Sorel Films.

and the way the film was sponsored and produced was rather unusual. On this occasion the idea for the film came from a producer and not from a sponsor. Sorel Films wanted to make an up-to-date fire safety film.

They explored the subject and made sure that there was a real need for such a film, put some ideas on paper, then set out to find a sponsor. Several organisations were approached and asked to put up part of the production cost. In return a full screen credit was offered, pointing out that the film was produced in the interests of safety and with the help of the organisation concerned. The organisations approached were all chosen because they were known to have a commercial interest in fire protection. They were told that efforts would be made to demonstrate the capabilities of their products in the film. It was however made clear that products would not be named and the film would not be a hard-selling vehicle. Its main aim was to sell safety and to make everyone more fire safety conscious. Potential sponsors were told copies would be made available world-wide for sale and for hire and a London preview would be arranged. The sponsors, faced with the proposals and a request for cash, considered all the possibilities. Three go-ahead organisations agreed to take part and, as the subsequent success of the film has proved, made a very wise decision.

With three sponsors, the film obviously had to be impartially controlled. The producers made clear that all rights on the finished film would be held by themselves and they would retain editorial control. By retaining the rights of the film the producers were able to keep control of its production and of its use. They were able to ensure that the film was planned without any hard-selling product messages. They wanted to do this so that they could try to obtain a television sale of the finished job—an aim achieved shortly after the film was released. There was very close co-operation between sponsors and producers at all stages of production. To ensure complete technical accuracy, and to guarantee impartiality, a technical adviser from the London Fire Brigade was appointed and the final script was referred to the Fire Protection Association. The film took three months to make. Within five weeks of its completion it was in use in thirteen countries with sixty copies in the United Kingdom alone. It also attracted wide press coverage and a UK television showing in the first weeks of its release.

Joint sponsorship

Joint sponsorship is one answer to continually rising production costs. If the interests of sponsors do not conflict there is no reason why joint ventures should not succeed. Of course a lot of hard work has to be done in preparing a script which is unbiased and which doesn't

The scene is dramatic but the commentary and the next scene had the impact: "All this damage could have been avoided by taking one simple precaution." The next shot showed a hand unplugging an electric fire from a power point. If the fire had been unplugged and not left on at night, the blaze might not have started. *Fire at Work* contains some spectacular scenes and some advice no one can afford to ignore. Picture: Sorel Films.

appear to favour any one sponsor. The first aim of the *Fire At Work* script was to get the urgency of the fire prevention problem over to audiences of every kind. It also had to show how the sponsors' products could help in an emergency. One sponsor, Minimax, make fire-fighting equipment, so sequences showing how fires could be extinguished and controlled were planned within the framework of the script. Another sponsor, The Asbestos Information Committee, represents the main asbestos manufacturing companies, so sequences showing how non-combustible materials can prevent fires from spreading were introduced. Colt International Limited, the other sponsor, make fire ventilators which are extremely effective in clearing smoke from a burning building so firemen can get to a blaze quickly and put it out. Sequences dealing with the problems of smoke were incorporated in the script. All this took time and a great deal of research. It was a difficult film to plan and to produce. It had to appeal to a wide audience.

The sponsors wanted to remind management audiences of the

In Sorel Films *Fire at Work* the results of leaving doors open when fire breaks out were clearly shown. If the door had been closed the fire might not have spread. Picture: Sorel Films.

dangers of fire and to explain how their products could make the dangers less. It was agreed that this had to be done in a way which didn't "plug" any product or mention it by name. Though management audiences had to be the primary target, the producers felt it should be possible to make a film which was interesting enough to appeal to everyone from a managing director to an office cleaner. Then it could really do some good. It could show how fires are caused, how they can be extinguished and how they can be prevented. With this aim in mind and the instructions of the three sponsors, I set out to produce a script.

The Fire Script

I sat through every existing fire prevention film I could find and read numerous books and leaflets dealing with every aspect of industrial fire prevention. I went and talked to fire brigades and government departments. I studied fire reports and gradually began to learn what fires really do mean to the companies involved in them. I learned that 45% of companies having a fire go out of business. I met firemen who had rescued dying people from offices and slowly began to realise the seriousness of the problems the film had to deal with. It was a London fireman who first made me realise the really major problem. "When you point out a fire hazard and suggest they take precautions they don't want to know. They think it'll never happen to them. Fires just happen to other people. They don't concern them." The fire officer who told me this had been called the night before to a fire in a house. He had had to fight a half crazed woman trying to get back into the burning building where five minutes before she had left two young children with an oil heater, while she went out to buy some cigarettes. Fires mean much more when you see what they involve. The film had to put this across.

We decided to base the script on fire case histories. By reading hundreds of fire reports I found three good examples of what happens quite often. I wanted to use them near the start of the film, but not right at the beginning. They weren't visually strong enough, so I went on trying to find a powerful start. I went to a telephone exchange handling emergency calls. Listening to the voices calling for help I again appreciated the urgency of the film's message. How could the urgency be put across on film? The answer came out of another conversation with a senior fire officer. Over lunch he told me about some major fires that he had been concerned with. "Have you ever heard the Manchester tape?" he asked in the course of our chat. I said I hadn't and asked him what it was. He explained. It was a recording of an emergency call, made by a man who failed to tell the telephone operator where he was speaking from. He dialled the emergency number, shouted "Fire!" and left the phone. Because he didn't say where he was speaking from, the telephone operator had to call in engineers to trace the source of the call. It took three minutes to trace, and in those three minutes the man, his wife and child died. I heard the tape recording of those three minutes —one of the most unpleasant tapes I have ever heard. While the operator tried to trace the call, the screams and sounds of fire can be clearly heard in the background. Screams and the words "Alistair, there's a fire . . ." The last words the man's wife ever spoke.

The tape recording made the seriousness of the fire problem abundantly clear. I wanted to use it for the start of the film. Two major problems had to be overcome first. I had to get permission to use the material and to make sure that its use wouldn't offend anyone actually concerned with the fire. And, as the tape was only a sound recording, I had to think of a way of using it visually on film. The fire authorities were very helpful and I eventually got permission to use the tape provided the address and telephone number at the end were not used, so the actual victims' relatives could not be traced. I sat down and worked out a sequence of pictures showing shots of a telephone exchange and switch room and a fire brigade control centre. The tape was edited down to one minute the shots planned round the edited tape. The shots were planned so that it would appear that the people seen on the screen were trying to trace the call heard on the soundtrack. When the film was produced, it started with the shot of a hand lifting a telephone receiver and dialling the emergency services. This was followed by a shot of the central telephone exchange, where the call was answered by an operator who said: "Emergency. Which service do you require? Hold on, I'll put you through." The next shot was filmed in the fire brigade control room. The main titles went over this shot. At the end of it the camera moved into a close-up of one of the fire brigade telephone operators. Then, we began to hear the taped incoming call. As the tape ran through, we saw a montage of shots of the exchange and shots of various pieces of telephone equipment. At the end, after the screams, we returned to the fire brigade control room as the operator finally succeeded in tracing the call. At this point, so the correct address was not revealed, the film's commentator started to talk. He explained what the audience had heard. "The voices you heard were not actors. The telephone operator was trying to trace the source of an emergency call, made by a man who didn't give an address or a telephone number. It took three minutes to trace the call and these three minutes were recorded. You heard part of them just now. In those three minutes, the man whose voice you heard, his wife and child, died." The opening sequence ended with a still photograph taken by the fire brigade at the scene of the fire. It showed the man who made the call. In the fire he had collapsed behind a chair. His two clasped hands could be seen amid the rubble.

Dramatic starts like this do have their place in the world of industrial film. *Fire At Work* dealt with a serious problem and if the message at the main part of the film was to be properly understood the seriousness of the problem had to be made abundantly clear at the beginning. By using dramatic techniques the urgency of the situation was made plain. After the opening the film went on to make clear that fire prevention concerns everyone—especially those who think its no concern of theirs. We took three more case histories and Patrick Allen, who read the English commentary, continued. "Fires at work cost lives, jobs and millions of pounds each year. No one is immune. Fires can and do break out in factories, shops, offices and stores of every kind and size. And if you think it'll never happen to you, remember some of the other people who felt the same way. The shop assistant who dropped a cigarette on waste materials and burnt a supermarket to the ground. The storeman who dropped a cigarette between two cardboard cartons and thought it would go out. The fire he started cost £373,000. The company director who thought fire protection was an expensive nuisance. Last July he went out of business . . ." All hard hitting material. And all real case histories taken straight out of official fire brigade reports.

Making an industrial film of this kind presents major problems. We had, as always, to produce a script. And we had to make sure that the script was completely accurate and that the case histories referred to were as relevant overseas as in the UK. As we had decided to base the film on facts, we wanted authentic fire shots. We viewed miles of library film and checked shots against official fire reports. We sat in the London Fire Brigade control room and waited for suitable fires to break out. Gradually, we got the right shots for the job. Shots of an office on fire with staff desperately trying to rescue what they could while flames swept towards them. The ruins of a hotel, where faulty electric wiring started a blaze which completely destroyed a man's life work. A fire in a department store, started by an office cleaner misusing an electric plug. The film gradually took shape. Of course, some of the shots had to be staged. We showed fire exits blocked up and clear. We spend half a day trying to make a cigar fall off an ashtray the right way at the right point. But the efforts were worthwhile. The film was completed and released. It is now being used by fire prevention authorities, company staff training departments and governments all over the world, demonstrating the sponsors' products and making audiences more fire safety conscious. It has proved very successful and two of the sponsors have already commissioned other films.

Film budgets

When a script has been produced, a detailed film costing can be prepared. Preparing film budgets requires skill. Every company has its own method of tackling what can be an expensive task. I do not intend to provide figures. They vary too much from country to country and from film to film. It is however sometimes useful to have an idea of the general areas to be considered when reviewing the various film production costs. Some of the technical production costs of industrial film making can be considered under the following headings:

Staff: Research and script
                         Director
                         Camera crew
                         Sound crew
                         Editor and assistant editor
                         Production secretary
                         Commentator
Technical costs: Film stock and processing
                         Equipment hire
                         Magnetic tape and magnetic film stock
                         Sound recording and transfers
                         Hire of film-cutting room

                        Dubbing
                        Commentary recording
                        Optical effects
                        Titles
                        Negative cutting
Sundry expenses: Insurance
                        Travel and living costs
                        Facilities fees
                        Royalty payments

Technical costs

Let us first consider some of the technical costs—Film stock first. New stock must be bought. It can be either 35 mm or 16 mm, colour or black and white. We will discuss the choice later. When the stock has been exposed, it must be developed. That is a further expense. Developing costs about three-quarters the price of the film stock and a black and white print for editing may cost the same again. Colour films are often edited in black and white—one way of cutting production costs. When films are cut in black and white, a sum should be allowed for printing up test sections in colour. It is a good idea to test print some of every roll and any difficult or doubtful scenes should always be printed in colour. Again, allowance must be made in the budget. Magnetic recording tapes can be bought outright for a small sum. Lights are often best hired. If they are hired, the rental company will be able to provide a daily or weekly rate which can be taken into account when preparing the filming schedule. If the film unit possesses its own lights, as is often the case in an internal company unit, each production should include an allowance for depreciation costs on the light fittings and an allowance for bulbs and carbons used in production.

Camera equipment too must be carefully costed. Cameras can also be hired on a daily or weekly basis. Most hired cameras are supplied with a set of basic lenses. On some cameras, zoom lenses are permanently fixed. On others they are extra. Motorised zooms are always extras and their cost must be taken into account. Tripods are normally included when camera outfits are hired. If, however, a geared head is needed, the cost will be an additional charge. Internal units with their own equipment may well find their basic equipment needs augmenting by hiring special items. A sum allowing for the depreciation of their own equipment should always be included.

When a film has been shot, it has to be edited. Apart from the processing charges, there are other costs such as the hire of a fully equipped cutting room, perhaps manned by an editor and an assistant editor. The cost of magnetic film stock needed for preparing the different soundtracks also has to be taken into account. And the cost of matching the edited cutting copy to the master has to be assessed. This is often calculated on a footage basis, the charge being made according to the length of the final edited roll. The cost of making the first showprint must be included, and any optical effects, like fades and dissolves, must also be anticipated. Also transport, living expenses and insurance must not be overlooked.

Insurance

Insurance should be taken very seriously indeed. Not only must the equipment and staff involved in making the film be covered, the subject being filmed should also be insured before work starts. This may sound an unneccessary extra, but I can assure you it is not. Accidents happen and on a film location they happen very easily. Even a small accident can prove very expensive. It only needs one person to trip on a cable and knock over a light. If the light falls on a highly skilled person, or indeed, anyone who is injured, substantial claims may have to be met. A comprehensive accidents policy must be taken out in advance.

It is also worth insuring the exposed film against damage during processing. The cost of film stock and processing is very small compared with the cost of reshooting. Shooting scenes again, because the master has been damaged in a laboratory, can prove expensive. It is possible to insure against this kind of damage and cover should include provision for meeting reshooting expenses up to a set sum agreed in the light of the premium payable. Accidents do happen, even in laboratories. It is better to allow for a safety measure, and include a realistic sum for this in the production budget.

Artistes and technicians

One of the highest costs to be met will be the cost of artistes and technicians. Actors are not always necessary in industrial films. Every one has views on this subject. Mine are simple. If acting skills are required, or if a dialogue scene is included, I recommend using actors. If not, ordinary people may suffice. It is sometimes better to show people who are used to doing a job than to import actors who have never done it before, and try and teach them how to do it.

The films I outlined earlier were made without professional actors. They were, however, completed by a small army of professional technicians. A professional film team is essential, and it may represent the highest part of any production budget. The script writer and researcher may be paid an agreed sum for producing the script. This sum should be agreed before work is started and should cover all stages up to the delivery of the final shooting script. The film director too may be taken on for a film at an agreed sum. Cameramen and their assistants can be paid on a daily basis. Film unions lay down basic daily rates in all countries and many companies pay considerably more than the lowest daily rate. Good technicians tend to be expensive.

A good editor is essential and his work can be costed on a weekly basis, depending on the number of weeks it is anticipated the picture will take to cut. Three weeks is enough for many industrial films, though some of the more complicated ones run on for far longer. These are basic costs. They must all be allowed for in the production budget. The various factors involved in costing can be summarised in a checklist as follows:

Film stock:	There is a choice between 35-mm or 16-mm colour or black and white. Negative or reversal.
Processing the original:	Laboratory cost for development of the original.
A cutting copy:	The laboratory cost of making a copy of the original for editing purposes. Colour films are often printed in black and white for editing. Like film stock and development costs, this cost is calculated on a film footage basis.
Colour tests:	If a colour film is being edited in black and white, a sum should be allowed for test colour printing some rolls.
Recording tape ($\frac{1}{4}$ in):	Allow for reels of sound tapes to be purchased for use in recording.
Lights:	Allow for the hire of fittings and replacement lamps. Generators, filters and other extras may be needed. A visit to every location will determine the amount of lighting needed. Internal units with their own lights should allow for depreciation.
Cameras:	There is a daily or weekly hire charge for most cameras supplied by rental companies. Include the cost of zoom lenses or other extras like geared heads if these are needed. Internal units may need to hire extra gear and should also allow for depreciation of their own equipment.

Studio hire: If a studio is to be used the cost must be
                      worked out in detail. How long is the
                      studio needed for and what is the daily
                      cost. Does it allow time for building and
                      striking sets and have their costs been
                      included? Is electrical power an ad-
                      ditional charge? Does the studio have its
                      own resident crew or equipment?

Sound transfers: Sound recorded on $\frac{1}{4}$-in tape must be re-
                      recorded on perforated magnetic film
                      for editing purposes. This is costed on a
                      time basis. Allow for transferring all
                      sound needed in the course of building
                      up music and sound effects tracks as well
                      as dialogue and commentary.

Editing: The cost of a fully equipped cutting
                      room, and the services of an editor and
                      assistant can be assessed on a weekly
                      basis. Do not forget to allow for raw
                      materials like film spacing.

Dubbing: Dubbing theatres can be hired on an
                      hourly basis. It is no use booking half an
                      hour for a half-hour film. Allow more
                      time than you expect to use. A simple
                      half-hour film usually takes around 2–3
                      hours to complete.

Magnetic film stock: The final master soundtrack and an
                      international soundtrack free of dialogue
                      should be kept at the end of the dubbing
                      session. The cost of the stock should be
                      allowed for.

Commentator: A professional commentator will make a
                      set charge for reading a film com-
                      mentary. Charges are based on the
                      number of reels. Foreign version com-
                      mentators often prefer to translate their
                      own scripts.

Negative cutting: The process of matching the edited
                      version to the film originally exposed in
                      the camera. Again, costs are assessed on
                      a reel basis.

Showprint: The final edited version of the film can
                      be printed and the first copy off, known
                      as an "answer print", must be allowed

	for in the budget—assessed on a film footage basis.
Royalties:	If music is used in a film, copyright payments may have to be made. These sums are assessed on the amount of music used and the type of film. Films intended for non-theatrical showing to non-paying audiences are not as expensive as films intended for advertising use on television. In the UK the Performing Rights Society lays down a list of standard charges and similar organisations exist throughout the world.
Insurance:	Cover staff, actors, subject matter and the film in every way possible. And do not forget the equipment.
Travel and living:	The cost of moving from one location to another has to be allowed for and overnight stops must be included in the budget. Entertainment costs should also be included.
Theatre hire:	Is a theatre needed for viewing rushes or for showing the edited versions at any stage? Theatres can be hired on an hourly basis.

Film stock

Before the budget can be completed there must be a firm decision on the gauge to be used. What are the differences between the three film gauges and which is most suitable for industrial film use?

The 35-mm size in the professional film used in cinemas and, in some countries, on television. Fifteen years ago it was *the* professional gauge, and 16 mm was dismissed as a toy for amateurs. And 8 mm was still comparatively unheard of. Today, 35 mm is still a professional gauge and it is still used in almost every cinema. But 16 mm is now also a professional gauge. Television has brought about tremendous technical development and now makes 16-mm film its staple diet. Videotape and 16-mm film are more commonly employed in television studios than 35 mm and, indeed, some of the new small cinemas are also being equipped with 16-mm projection equipment. So, the future of 16 mm is bright, or as bright as it is for any existing photographic process. Standard 8-mm film is now being replaced by super 8 mm. Although the manufacturers remind us that it has a large picture area and improved technical-performance, and these points are perfectly true, in my opinion, super 8 mm is still unsuitable for wide professional use such as industrial film making, as there are too many limitations. Films made on either 35 mm or 16 mm can of course be copied on to super 8 mm, for projectors used in display work, etc. I would never shoot on super 8 mm, unless cast adrift on a desert island with nothing else.

The 35-mm gauge has much to recommend it. Its main drawback is its cost. A thousand feet of 35-mm film runs for the same time as 400 ft of 16-mm film and stock and laboratory costs are thus considerably increased. But it is a pleasure to work with and to look at. Results can be as technically perfect as it is possible to achieve with film. But the high cost of 35-mm production limits its use for industrial filmmaking purposes, and 16 mm has been far more widely adopted.

Now, 16-mm film, too, can be technically excellent. Within certain limitations, it can be very good indeed. The picture area is, obviously, smaller than 35 mm and it is not ideal for large screen presentation. I never like to see 16 mm on anything larger than a screen 12 ft wide and prefer a small well-lit picture to a large one which looks as if the glow worms in the projector have given up the ghost. Modern technical developments have done much to improve the quality of 16-mm film stocks. Cameras too have kept pace, largely due to the demands of television. And costs are lower than on 35 mm. The equipment is more versatile and more manoeuvrable. For sponsored industrial films, 16 mm has much to offer. Indeed, if the film is not intended for large screen showing, it may be the best gauge to use.

For flexibility, 35 mm has most to offer. A film shot on 35 mm can be presented on 35 mm in cinemas. Copies can be made on 16 mm for general showing and super 8-mm copies can also be made for use on cassette machines. And the film can be recorded on videotape. Film shot on 16 mm can be presented in an enormous number of places in 16-mm form, and copies can also be made on super 8 mm. It, too, can be copied on videotape, but it cannot be satisfactorily blown-up to 35 mm. If a 16-mm original is of superb quality it is occasionally possible to make 35-mm prints, but the feasibility of this depends on the quality of the 16-mm original and the nature of the film stock used. Generally speaking, 16 mm is best on 16 mm, or reduced. Super 8 mm should stay on super 8 mm or videotape. It is not good enough to enlarge to 16 mm as the results always look like a blizzard.

Detailed shooting script

Once the film size has been decided upon, the production budget can be finalised and a detailed shooting script can be prepared. You will have noticed that I have emphasised the need to attract and maintain the attention and interest of an audience. This can be done in a number of ways and the final shooting scripts should outline them

Quite apart from the choice of attractive subject material, the method of presenting every subject and every scene must be made as interesting as possible. Film is a visual medium, and scenes must be made visually appealing. This is the basic difference between a draft treatment and a detailed shooting script.

In a draft treatment, the dialogue to be spoken and the actions to be shown are listed side by side. The dialogue may be the actual dialogue to be used, but the action is unlikely to be written in the precise technical terms used when preparing a final shooting script. The last script must be written in terms of camera. It is a plan for the production team to follow. It must list dialogue and action. It must state who speaks the dialogue and describe what happens in the action, and it must say what the camera sees. The directions must be listed in terms of camera movements and positions.

Indicating camera movements

There are seven basic camera positions from which each scene can be observed. Each is listed in a script by an accepted abbreviation: DS (sometimes listed as VLS) stands for Distant Shot or Very Long Shot—a general view of a very wide area (now rarely used), LS a long shot—showing a wide area but not quite as wide as a Distant Shot. The remaining shots narrow the field of view down more and more. MLS Medium Long Shot: MS Medium Shot; CMS Close Medium Shot; CU Close Up and BCU Big Close Up. In addition to these static camera positions, film cameras can move by panning up or down, or round, and by tracking in or out. Zooms in and out are also often used. When a shooting script is prepared, these movements and positions must be worked out and listed. The needs of the subject and the requirements of the editor should be the two main considerations.

The human eye tires quickly and needs constant change of scene if interest is to be maintained. If you sit down and look at someone sitting in a chair talking into a camera, you may find the scene interesting for the first 15 seconds. After a minute you may start to get bored. Ten seconds is about the average screen time for one shot to remain on the screen. With this in mind, a script writer can plan his sequences. He can plan to move from a general view to a closer one and so focus the audience's interest on a particular part of the scene. He can go to a close-up, to give added emphasis or to study detail. He can pan round from one point to another, to reveal the whole scope of a scene. Or he can start with a general statement and zoom into a detailed point.

Film grammar

Every operation can be observed from a number of different camera positions. In the weight-mixing film, the operator standing by his rack of tins and operating the scales could be seen from the opposite side of the garage or from close up. The camera could go wide and show that the garage was not cluttered up with tins, and it could go close to show how accurate the scales were. The choice was there, and the script was planned to make maximum use of the choice and concentrate interest on the point where it could be used to best advantage. Every sponsored film should be planned with this in mind. Start with long shots and cut, frequently, to maintain the pace of the film. Do not sit on one shot and expect the audience to remain fascinated. Constant scene changes are needed and they must all be allowed for in the shooting script. The following example will serve as an illustration.

All Systems Go was produced for the Ford Tractor Operations Europe. It was designed to train audiences of farmers in the basic points of tractor maintenance. Look at one sequence, first in dialogue form only, and then again in a shooting script. The dialogue read:

All Systems Go: Dialogue (Extract)

"When a new tractor is delivered, the local Ford dealer will make arrangements for two free services to be carried out after 50 and 300 hours. After that, responsibility for maintenance rests with the owner. There are recommended daily and weekly maintenance points which must not be neglected. Proper care ensures that the tractor is always ready for the job in hand. It cuts down repair time and saves money. Let's look at some of the points which are often forgotten. For a start, the engine. The oil is changed regularly, tappets are adjusted and injectors cleaned. But elementary areas like the induction system are often forgotten. How does the induction system work? Air reaches the engine through an air cleaner unit. It passes through a pre-cleaner which is specially shaped so the air is forced to swirl around. This creates a centrifugal force and any bits of dirt are ejected through two vents at the top. The air continues down the centre of the cleaner until it reaches the lower end where it is forced to double back on itself. It then passes through steel mesh packing . . ."

I am sure you are not riveted to the page! Let us see now how this material was interpreted in the film script.

All Systems Go: Script (Extract)

Ext. Day. LS. Farmyard. A large lorry arrived with a Ford tractor on it. It stops in the farmyard near a small van labelled "Ford Service". Beside the van a Ford Agent is talking to the Farmer who has bought the tractor. He holds an instruction manual and points from it to the tractor. The farmer looks interested.

Commentator: When a new tractor has been delivered the local Ford agent will make arrangements for 2 free services to be carried out after 50 and 300 hours.

Cut

Ext. Day. MS. Farmer and dealer standing by service van. The agent puts away the instruction book and suggests the farmer and he walk over to the tractor (out of shot) and they start to walk away L to R in the direction of the tractor.

After that, responsibility for maintenance rests with the owner. There are recommended daily and weekly maintenance points which must not be neglected.

Cut

Ext. Day. MS. The tractor about to be driven off the back of the trailer. Farmer and agent walk into shot *Camera left* and stand on left of frame watching the operation.

Proper care ensures that the tractor is always ready for the job in hand. It cuts down repair time and saves money.

Cut

Ext. Day. CMS. The tractor starts to move off the trailer on to the ramp down which it will drive into the farmyard. *Camera concentrates* on the engine.

Let's look at some of the points which are often forgotten. For a start the engine. The oil is changed regularly, tappets are adjusted and injectors cleaned. But elementary areas like the induction system are often forgotten.

Dissolve

CU. Diagram. The induction system. We see the whole system in this general view.

How does the induction system work? Air reaches the engine through an air-cleaner unit. It passes through a special precleaner . . .

Dissolve

BCU. Diagram of pre-cleaner showing air circulation path.

. . . which is specially shaped so the air is forced to swirl around. This creates a centrifugal force and any large bits of dirt are ejected through the holes at the top.

Dissolve

Ext. Day. BCU. The pre-cleaner on the new tractor. *Camera is taking an identical viewpoint to the section seen in the diagram. Camera pans down length of cleaner unit and stops on* steel mesh packing.

The air continues down the centre of the cleaner until it reaches the lower end where it is forced to double back on itself. It then passes through steel mesh packing.

Dissolve

And so the film continues. Every film must be planned. Ideas must be turned into treatments. Treatments must be discussed and approved. Scripts must be produced and camera angles chosen. Budgets must be prepared and all the ideas and plans must be brought together in a shooting script. The script dictates the form of the end product.

Shooting schedule

When a shooting script has finally been agreed by the sponsors the production team can start to plan a shooting schedule.

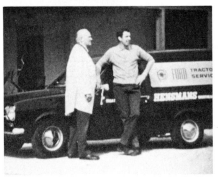

A sequence from the Ford Tractor Operations Europe film *All Systems Go*. A straightforward film produced in seven languages by Sorel International, and designed to encourage new tractor owners to carry out simple maintenance procedures. The sequence discussed in the text deals with the arrival of a trailer and the unloading could have been shown in one shot, but it would have taken two minutes and would have been very boring so a sequence of shots was planned to maintain audience interest. 1. In the first shot the trailer and tractor drive up and stop. We then cut to: 2. The

ord dealer and new tractor owner watch-
ng (a cutaway shot). 3. The trailer driver
ets out of the cab and walks out of shot.
. The Ford man suggests that he and the
ustomer go and take a closer look at the
ractor. 5. At the start of this shot only the
ractor is in shot. Dealer and customer
ralk in and stop left of frame to watch the
ractor being driven off the trailer. 6. At
he start of this shot the tractor is out of
iew. It drives into frame and stops. The
amera then tracks into a close up of the
ir filter and the scene dissolves to the first
iagram. 7.

Film, unlike many television recordings, is always shot discon-
inuously and often out of script order. The first scenes in the film are not
ecessarily shot first, and it is extremely unlikely that the scenes will be
hot in the order in which they appear in the final edited version. The
rder depends on the availability of actors and locations. All the scenes
o be shot at one location will normally be taken together, regardless
f where they occur in the final film. The shooting schedule must be
lanned to keep costs to a minimum, and time spent travelling between
ocations must be minimised. The script must be rearranged in shooting
rder and every detail of each day must be planned.

The location

Before any film is shot, the cameraman and director should visit all the locations and work out exactly what equipment is needed and how each scene is to be handled. Reconnaissance is important, for it ensures that the film unit arrives with the right equipment and starts work straight away without wasting time. Electricity supplies must be checked to ensure that enough power is available and the amount of cable required can be estimated. The available light can be assessed and a note made of any filters needed.

It is not always easy to find locations and getting permission to use them is sometimes even harder. Industrial films often call for quite a number of outside locations. Sometimes they are under the direct control of the film sponsor, but not always. Often scenes at other locations have to be included. So extra locations must be found, and permission to film obtained. This can take time and it can also cost money. There are a few saints who will let a film unit move in and shoot without charge, but not many. A facilities fee normally has to be negotiated for the use of a location. The fee can sometimes include the provision of

Scenic shots alone, however beautifully photographed, are not enough to hold audienc interest. The Institute of Civil Engineers Film *Build Yourself a New World H.S.* relied on fascinating script written by Dick Need who also directed. Picture: Stewart Films.

A sleepy world of waterways was featured in British Transport Films *World of the Waterways*. Travel and holiday promotional films must always be planned in advance. It is hopeless shooting randomly and then trying to make a film out of the results. A script, or at least an overall plan must be prepared beforehand. Picture: British Transport Films.

power. I used to think that people who did not welcome film units with open arms were mean and cautious. Then I used my own house to shoot a television commercial. Never again. Facilities fees are a necessary expense!

Industrial film makers often have to shoot film in factories or offices belonging to the film sponsor. It is easy to think that because the premises belong to the same organisation, detailed preparations need not be made. This is not the case. The same reconnaissance must be carried out, well ahead of the date set for filming. And permission must be obtained, in writing, in advance. And, do make sure everyone likely to be interested is consulted. If one person who should be contacted is left out, chaos can follow. The head of the department concerned should be contacted first. Then the foreman of the area to be filmed should be met and anyone else in charge of any section where the film is to be photographed should be briefed. Always consult the union representatives. A few words beforehand can save any misunderstanding and time-wasting trouble. In a large factory, security officers should also be warned that filming is to take place. I remember one occasion when a film unit arrived at a factory to spend the day shooting a scene. The unit was stopped on the way out of the factory gates and the security officers refused to let the crew leave until every box containing equipment had been checked! A few words beforehand would have saved a lot of lost tempers, valuable time and unnecessary trouble.

When filming in an industrial location, I always ask for an electrician to be made available to work with my production team. This is a worthwhile move for the local man always knows where every connecting point is and, as filming is often a new experience, is usually quite helpful in showing the film electricians where to connect supplies and where control points are to be found. A contact man, able to take decisions and liaise, is absolutely essential. It is useless having someone who has to go and ask someone else whenever a problem arises. An executive contact man, with a thorough knowledge of the location and the people who work there is essential if filming is to go ahead without trouble.

Call Sheets

Shooting industrial films can be very satisfying. Many pieces of machinery are pictorially interesting, and people in factories and offices are usually helpful. But if everything is to run smoothly when filming is in progress, it must be planned in advance. Arrangements must be made for the use of every location. And agreement must be put in writing by both parties. Detailed lists of times and dates for filming must be prepared and entered on call sheets for the use of all concerned with production. Lists of equipment needed must be prepared and arrangements must be made for the day's exposed film to be processed. Here is a specimen call sheet for one day's shooting on an industrial location:

All Systems Go: Call Sheet: Day of shoot: 16th June.

Production.	*All Systems Go.*
Client.	Ford Tractor Operations Europe.
Client Contact.	Mr. Robin Walters (Telephone ....)
Director.	Fred Bloggs.
Camera Crew.	Unit 3.
Location.	Hill Farm, Boreham, Chelmsford, Essex.
Telephone.	....
Call Time.	08.30.
Rendezvous.	The Crown Inn, Turners Hill, Boreham, or for *coach* leaving production office at 06.50.
Artistes.	Charlie Brown. London Casting. Tel. .... Bill Campbell. Tel. ....
Wardrobe.	Charlie Brown. Old, tatty looking jacket. Wellington boots and baggy trousers. Open neck, faded shirt. Cloth cap.

	Bill Campbell. Smart, creased brown slacks and open sports shirt, clean brown shoes. Overalls hired by production company in three sizes.
Props.	Old petrol cans and oil drum (On location)
	Packet Woodbine cigarettes (Office)
	Spare tractor oil filters (2) (Fords)
	Grease gun (1) (Forge Garage, Boreham)
Product.	Ford 2000, 3000 and 4000 tractors (new) supplied by client direct to location.
	Ford 2000 tractor pre-1965, in dirty condition collected from Forge Garage by production office. P.M. June 15th.
Equipment.	1 Arriflex BL camera with 9–95-mm zoom.
	Unit Box.
	From Cine Europe Ltd. Tel. ....
Lighting.	Colortran half kit and 4 Bashers.
	2 sun guns. Honda generator. From Mole Richardson. Tel. ....
Stock.	2000-ft 16-mm Eastmancolour 7254 from Production Office. (Mrs. Jones.) Tel. ....
Travel arrangements.	All personnel not able to travel to location rendezvous direct should meet coach departing production office. The coach will leave at exactly 06.50 am.

Any further information, contact Valerie Jones at production office. Tel. ....

This kind of call sheet is designed to prevent the possibility of arriving on location with the wrong film or the wrong equipment. It is also designed to ensure that everyone arrives at the same location on the same date and that is not always as simple as it sounds. The example I have quoted was prepared by a film company producing a film for a film sponsor. Similar sheets should however be prepared by internal units for internal use. Check lists help to avoid errors and save time when it is most needed. Filming can then start on time.

Stock shots

If you cannot obtain a scene by shooting it, you may sometimes be able to use library film. Library footage can be useful when scenes are too expensive or difficult to obtain first hand. Stock shot libraries exist all over the world. If you need a scene which is too difficult or too expensive to obtain, it is worth asking a library if they can supply the necessary material. If the scene is of general interest, they may well be able to help. Establishing shots of well-known places and archive film material are library specialities. Yet most libraries contain a lot of unfamiliar material too. Shots of industrial sites and machinery are often available.

A telephone call to any film library will ascertain whether the required shots are likely to be available or not. Tell the librarian the subject you want to find and give as much detail as possible. It is useless ringing up and saying you want general interest shots of an industrial scene. The librarian, who has thousands of feet of industrial material, will want to have a more precise brief. He will want to know if you are interested in heavy industry or light industry or in any particular kind of production techniques. He will want to know what country you are concerned with, because most libraries contain a considerable amount of foreign footage. Be as precise as you can and you will find librarians helpful.

If the library has material likely to be of interest, the librarian will select footage for you to view. Prints, usually of atrocious quality and sometimes deliberately scratched so that they cannot be copied on the cheap, will be made available for viewing, for a nominal search fee. If you find a suitable shot, tell the library which scene you want to use. They will then obtain a good quality copy which you can include in your edited film. All this is charged for. A search fee is normally charged for finding material to view. It does not cost a fortune, but a small charge is always made. If you find a suitable shot you will be charged a further sum, based on the quantity of film you use, and the type of film the scenes are used in. Charges are calculated on the basis of a fixed sum per 35-mm foot of film. The charge made differs from one audience to another. If a film is being made for advertising on television, the charge will be quite high. If it is a sponsored industrial film for non-theatrical showing to non-paying audiences in the country of origin, the charge will not be as high. Here is a guide to the way in which charges are assessed. The figures are a guide to *relative* library costs and are therefore quoted in units.

Type of film	Black and white Charge per 35-mm foot used	Colour Charge per 35-mm foot used
Feature films (over 3000 ft in length).	2. (Minimum 20.)	6. (Minimum 60.)
Documentary films under 3000 ft incl. industrial films.	1. (Minimum 10.)	3. (Minimum 30.)
Sponsored TV commercials.	4. (Minimum 40.)	6. (Minimum 60.)
Direct TV. (One country of origin only.)	1. (Minimum 10.)	1.50. (Minimum 30.)
Direct TV. Worldwide use.	2. (Minimum 20.)	6. (Minimum 60.)

Search fees. Per hour: 8

Processing charges are in addition to the licence fees outlined above.

Stock shots, as library footage is usually referred to, can save time and money, but they should not be used if a scene can be photographed first hand. Sometimes for reasons of cost or accessibility it is not practical to film a scene. Library footage may then come to the rescue. Library shots are never as good as original material. The quality of the image is not the same. Original film should always be perfect but a library will never part with original material, only a copy. So the original is kept and copies are made from it. When library film is used the source should be noted in the script.

Planning saves time

It can take months to make a cinema entertainment film. Some directors make one film every two years. Weeks are spent perfecting a script and making technical preparations. Industrial film makers do not have the same problems or the same time because their films often have to be produced in a hurry. Sponsors have a terrible habit of sitting on a brief till the very last moment. Then they pounce and want the film tomorrow. Film making must take time, though it does not have to take months; some films are more complicated than others but the average industrial film can be produced in around twelve weeks, from script to screen. Three or four weeks are adequate for shooting. It takes about a month to perfect an edited version and prepare the final sound-track. The remaining time is spent preparing to shoot and supervising the laboratory processes needed to make final prints. The time spent in making any film can be considerably reduced if the whole operation is planned, as far in advance as possible.

4

Film Stock and Equipment

I HAVE ALREADY DISCUSSED how important it is to give a full briefing to all those concerned before a day of filming begins. Other preparations too must be made before any film is photographed and some decisions have to be taken a long time before the film unit even assembles. One of the questions to be resolved is the choice of raw film stock—not the gauge, which was discussed in an earlier chapter, but whether the film is to be in colour or black and white and whether negative or reversal stock be used.

Colour or black and white?

The choice between colour and black and white is really quite obvious, but the difference between negative and reversal, though just as simple, is not quite as clear to see. In industrial filming, the choice between colour and monochrome will sometimes be dictated by cost. Colour film is a firm favourite with most industrial sponsors. Black and white is often dismissed without even being considered. This is a pity, because some subjects can benefit from black and white treatment and considerable savings can be made with this material. Colour film is expensive. For a full-scale professional film, film stock and processing are probably not the most expensive items. Salaries will be higher. For a small industrial unit, or for a film company making a short sponsored film on limited resources, the situation is not always the same. Film stock costs and processing charges can prove expensive. And colour film is always far more expensive than black and white.

When a film is being shot most scenes are photographed more than once. I have myself often shot scenes more than ten times and still been dissatisfied with the results. So, in film making a considerable quantity of film stock is used. The final edited version of a film may run for around 800 ft, but in making it very much more film passes through the camera.

For every scene that is used, three are thrown away, and that is with considerable shooting success. Professionals often shoot to a ratio of 5 : 1, one take is used for every five thrown away. And this figure is frequently surpassed. Industrial film makers are not quite as bad as television producers. They often shoot 20,000 ft of film for a programme which will eventually consist of 1000 ft. Budget limitations control the industrial producer.

Stock costs

Here is a general guide to film stock prices and laboratory costs: the figures here are a guide to values in relation to each other and do not correspond in value with units quoted elsewhere in the book.

If a foot of colour 35-mm film costs 6 units, it will cost about 1·5 units to develop. A black and white cutting copy costs about 2 units and an ungraded colour rush print around 8 units. And remember, 1000 ft of 35-mm film only lasts for 10 minutes at normal sound projection speed, so it is quite expensive when you consider the amount of film shot in the course of making an ordinary, straightforward film. Black and white 35 mm is considerably cheaper. If a foot of 35-mm black and white negative costs 2 units, you will have to pay around 1 unit to have it developed. A cutting copy costs about 2 units per foot.

With 16-mm film there is a wider choice of film stocks. You can choose between colour and black and white and between negative and reversal. We will consider the alternatives in a moment. First, compare the costs. If a foot of 16-mm colour reversal film costs 3 units it will cost around 2 units to process the master. In relation to this a black and white reversal cutting copy costs about 3 units per foot to produce, and a colour cutting copy about 6 units. But these charges normally vary from country to country and from one laboratory to another. Colour negative (16-mm) film costs around 2 units per foot. Processing the original costs around 1·5 units and a black and white cutting copy costs about 2 units. Colour rush prints cost around 5 units. Black and white negative film on 16 mm is cheapest of all. It costs around 1 unit per foot and developing the original costs about the same. A cutting copy costs about 2 units per foot. These figures are not, as I have mentioned, intended to be a laboratory price list. They do, however, give an idea of the difference between the alternative types of film stock and the costs which apply. Shooting on 35-mm film is always more expensive than on 16 mm and processing charges too are higher. Do not forget that 400 ft of 16-mm film runs for the same period of time as 1000 ft of 35 mm. So, 16-mm black and white negative is cheapest of all, but is it best?

We live in a colour conscious world. Colour television is now in use in many countries. People expect to see colour and industrial colour films do sometimes have a definite advantage over productions completed in black and white. The general interest film, promoting a company image or a product, can look very drab if filmed in black and white. Colour goes better with the glowing message on the soundtrack! But black and white does still have a useful part to play. Research films and staff training productions can often be just as good in black and white and considerable savings in cost can be made.

Negative and reversal stock

So you can shoot in colour or in black and white on either 35 mm or 16 mm. You can use colour negative 35 mm or 16 mm or colour reversal film 16 mm. You can shoot black and white negative on either 16 mm or 35 mm. What are the differences between the various types of film stock and which is the best type to use?

Negative film, when processed, gives a negative image in which the tones of the original scene are reversed. On processed black and white negative original film, black appears as white. To restore the tones of the original scene, the processed negative must be printed on a reel of positive film stock. When the tones originally reversed on the negative are themselves reversed (when the positive copy is processed) the original values will be restored. In simple language, a negative film produces a negative image where the tones of the original are reversed. To get back to stage one, the processed negative must be printed on positive stock. The tones of the original scene are then restored.

Reversal film, when processed, immediately gives a positive image on which the tones of the original scene are preserved. To make a copy of a reversal original, the reversal master must be printed on another roll of reversal stock. The tones of the original remain unchanged. When working with colour, you can immediately check the colours of a scene by looking at a reversal master. Colour negative is difficult to interpret without expert professional knowledge. You have to make a test print so that the quality of the colours can be determined. Is it best to shoot an industrial film on negative or reversal film?

We will consider colour film first, as it is the most widely used in industrial filming. On 16 mm there is a choice of stocks. On 35 mm, Eastmancolor negative is the most widely adopted. It is designed for exposing under tungsten lighting but with a Wratten 85 filter on the camera, it can be used in daylight quite satisfactorily. It is a versatile film with a speed of 100 ASA (for tungsten). This is reduced to 64 ASA when a filter is used in daylight. Both speeds are fast enough to interest industrial film makers. I have seen good results on Eastmancolor shot in dimly lit factories. Many television films are shot on Eastmancolor and the stock often has to be used under difficult conditions. When conditions are good, results are superb. When they are difficult, the stock can still produce results of a surprisingly high standard. But remember that the negative has to be printed before the colours in a scene can be appreciated. Eastmancolor is widely used in 35-mm (Type 5254) and in 16-mm (Type 7254) forms. The 16-mm version has a different type reference number but for all practical purposes the stock is identical. If you shoot on 16 mm you have several other stocks to choose from, and with 16-mm colour there is a choice between negative and reversal.

The most widely used colour reversal films are also made by Kodak. Ektachrome films have a variety of applications, some of which are of particular interest to industrial film makers. All Ektachrome 16-mm films are reversal, and there are three types of stock to choose from. For normal purposes there is Ektachrome Commercial (Type 7252). Again, this is a film designed for exposure under artificial light or, with a filter, in daylight. It is not a fast film, but has a fine grain and superb results can be obtained with optimum picture definition. In daylight, the film speed is only 16 ASA and in tungsten 25 ASA is the normal speed. In bright light, it gives excellent results.

There are two other Ektachrome films, both with the suffix letters EF—standing for Extra Fast. The films are designed for application where the general level of illumination is very low. There are two types of Ektachrome EF. Type 7241 is designed principally for daylight exposures. It has a film speed of 160 ASA in daylight. It can also be used in artificial light with a filter but the film speed is considerably reduced. For artificial light work, Ektachrome EF Type 7242 is a far better bet. It has a speed of 125 ASA, and it can be used in daylight with a Wratten 85 filter, though the speed in daylight is only 80 ASA. Ektachrome stocks are all well tested and are available world wide.

Low light level work

Industrial films often have to be shot under difficult conditions. It is not always easy to get enough light. I recently produced a film about driving at night. It set out to show some of the special driving techniques needed for driving at a time when roads are always very dark and often full of unexpected hazards. It also had to demonstrate a complete range of reflective products. Reflective number plates, signs and armbands all had to be shown. Ten years ago, the film would have been almost impossible to make. Only by banking up a large number of lights would it have been possible to get anything at all on film. It is impracticable to use film lights on motorways and, as much of the film consisted of action shots taken on location, the production could have presented some very serious problems. Ektachrome EF solved many of the problems and the whole film was shot with hand-held lights and two special high power portable lighting kits for the larger scenes. Ektachrome EF has many industrial applications. A week before shooting the night driving film, the cameraman had been filming in a Lancashire cotton mill. It was a vast place with machinery stretching far into the distance. The sponsors wanted to show the size of their works and a shot of the machine room seemed to them to be the ideal way of putting the message across. From a film point of view, the shot could have presented many expensive problems. The room was light, but not light enough for a normal speed film. The scene was shot, without lights, on Ektachrome EF. To light the entire floor area would have taken at least a day and would have cost a lot of money. On Ektachrome EF Type 7241, the results were perfect.

So, for filming in dim and difficult locations on 16 mm, Ektachrome EF can be very useful. Ektachrome Commercial is ideal for places where light is readily available—for films shot in studios or on well-lit locations or for holiday promotional productions, selling places with plenty of sun, and for films where optimum definition is essential. Ektachrome reversal films can all be intercut, so it is quite possible to shoot one scene on Commercial and another on EF. But, of course, reversal and negative can never be intercut.

When scenes have been photographed, the original film exposed in the camera is processed and a copy made for editing purposes. When the final edited version has been perfected, the original is matched to the edited cutting copy. After this is done, copies of the final film can be produced. At this stage, duplicate master materials are often produced. If, for example, film is shot on 16-mm Eastmancolor negative, a cutting copy will first be made for editing purposes. When editing is complete, the original negative is matched to it. Copies of the edited version can then be produced by printing the cut Eastmancolor negative on a reel of new positive stock. This works well, but there is a limit to the number of prints that can be produced without damaging the original negative.

Master film should always be copied as soon as the first satisfactory final print has been produced. From an Eastmancolor negative you make a duplicate Eastmancolor negative. For reversal films there is a choice. You can either make a duplicate reversal master or you can make a negative. We will explore the technical processes later. At this stage, we will consider the cost. Prints made from reversal originals are more expensive to produce than copies printed from a negative. So it may be worth making a negative from a reversal original if several prints are to be produced. If you are producing more than five copies you should recover the laboratory costs.

As with colour, monochrome film offers a choice of film stocks. In fact there is a much wider choice, for many companies have perfected good monochrome film. It is possible to find very fast stocks, for monochrome films can be rated at considerably higher speeds than colour. There are also some very slow stocks, where definition is excellent. Among the most widely used films are Kodak Double X, which is rated at 250 ASA for daylight and 200 ASA for tungsten. Ilford Mark V film is another excellent and versatile stock. It can be rated at 500 ASA though 250 ASA is recommended. It is a very pleasant stock to use.

Film types

We have discussed several stocks suitable for industrial film making. We can now study each type in rather more detail and consider the manufacturer's recommendations.

Eastmancolor Negative.
Type 5254 (35 mm)   Type 7254 (16 mm)

Characteristics: This is a multilayer colour film consisting of 3 light sensitive emulsions, each sensitised differently, coated to a safety film base. Incorporated in the emulsion are dye couplers which react simultaneously during development, to produce a separate dye image along with the silver image on each layer. The silver images are removed later by bleaching. Two of the dye couplers are themselves coloured and the original colour of these couplers is discharged during development in proportion to the development of the emulsion. The remaining colour couplers serve as automatic colour correction masks to help obtain good colour reproduction when the negative is printed on its companion film product Kodak Eastmancolor Print film Type 5385 (35 mm) and 7385 (16 mm). Black and white prints can also be produced.

Use: Exposure Index: 100 ASA (tungsten). 64 ASA (daylight with W85 filter).

Lighting contrast: The lighting contrast should be considerably lower than that used in black and white photography. The ratio of key light plus fill light, to fill light alone, should be 2 or 3–1 and should only exceed 4–1 where a special effect is desired. The film is balanced for use with tungsten lamps of 3200 K colour temperature. It may also be used with tungsten lamps operating slightly below or above this value as final colour balancing can be done in printing.

Ektachrome Commercial. Type 7252 (16 mm).

Characteristics: This is a reversal colour camera film balanced for exposure in tungsten illumination with a colour temperature of 3200 K. It is a slow, very fine grain film, designed for use where light levels are high. Colour prints can be made by two different methods. The Ektachrome original can be printed on reversal print film or an internegative can be made and it can be printed on Eastmancolour print film.

Direct printing is usually the most satisfactory way of producing a limited number of prints. For larger print orders, it is more economical to use the internegative process.

Exposure index: 25 ASA (tungsten). 16 ASA (daylight—with W8 filter).

Ektachrome EF (*daylight*). Type 5241 (35 mm) Type 7241 (16 mm).

This is a high-speed reversal camera film designed for daylight conditions. It is specially intended for use where the illumination level is very low or for high-speed photography where sufficient exposure cannot be obtained using slower films. It can be exposed at one half to twice the normal exposure indices with very little loss of quality. Colour prints from the processed original can be made on Ektachrome reversal stock or via the internegative process.

Exposure index: Daylight 160 ASA.
Artificial (3200 lamps). 40 ASA (with W80a filter)
Artificial (3400 lamps). 50 ASA (with W80a filter)

Ektachrome EF (tungsten light). Type 5242 (35 mm) Type 7242 (16 mm).

This is a high-speed reversal camera film balanced for exposure in tungsten illumination with a colour temperature of 3200 K. It will give very satisfactory results when underexposed by one stop, with adjustment of the first developing time. It may also be underexposed by two or three stops, again with adjustment of the first development time giving results satisfactory for news coverage.

Exposure index: 25 ASA (tungsten). Daylight (80 ASA with W8 filter).

Colour prints from the processed original can be made Ektachrome reversal films or via the internegative process.

Eastman double x negative film. (*Black and White*)
Type 5222 (35 mm)   Type 7222 (16 mm)

A high speed black and white negative film for general production photography either out of doors or in the studio, it is especially preferred where lighting economy is necessary. It is also useful where greater depth of field is required without an increase in the overall illumination level.

Exposure index: 250 ASA (daylight). 200 ASA (tungsten).

Ilford mark V.

A fine grain high-speed monochrome material with a wide exposure latitude, this film is suitable for producing high quality pictures under

lifficult lighting conditions. Great depth of field is possible without the
need for exceptionally powerful lighting units.

Exposure index: Average 250 ASA   Minimum 500 ASA (daylight)
Average 200 ASA   Minimum 400 ASA (tungsten)

So, we have a choice of six different kinds of film stock. And, in fact,
here are even more. The six I have listed are possibly the most widely
used. An industrial film can be shot with confidence on any of the
stocks mentioned. It is often worth shooting a test before production
gets under way. If a cameraman is using a stock he is not used to, he
will want to shoot a test anyway. If a location presents special problems,
a test may solve the problems in advance. I recently had to shoot scenes
in a car factory near Liverpool. The script listed only one scene, starting
with a wide general view of the car production lines and concentrating
attention on the part of the lines where cars are sprayed with paint. To
light the whole area would have been very expensive and time consuming, and with paint and other inflammable materials around, could
have presented a lot of problems. So a test was shot with available light.
The factory was lit by fluorescent lights and some daylight. The cameraman shot a hundred foot using a number of different filters. The results
were printed in colour and a satisfactory combination of exposure and
filters was agreed. The test, though it cost extra, proved an economy,
for it saved the expense of lighting a very large area. And it proved that
the fluorescent lights did not flicker and gave a colour cast which was
correctable in printing. It was worth shooting the test.

There are other reasons, too, which can make a test worthwhile.
Films stock is made in batches, and cans and boxes of film always
mention a batch number. The numbers should not be ignored. Film,
though technically the same from batch to batch, can in fact differ slightly. It pays to shoot a test on each new batch (i.e. each change of number)
used. Shoot the test, process the original and make a print. You will
then know exactly what to expect when you go out to shoot a film.

We have already considered some of the costs of film and processing.
They vary from country to country and from state to state so there is no
firm way of giving a price list which is both accurate and up to date. The
costs can however be considered in relation to each other. So far we have
only explored cost per foot. Though the costs of 35-mm filming and
16-mm work obviously differ, the difference is more readily seen when
footage is translated to time. If you buy ten minutes of 35-mm colour
film you will have to pay around two and a half times more than if you
buy the corresponding amount of 16-mm stock. Processing and printing
costs will be similarly higher. And the costs remain higher throughout
production. How, then, can money be saved?

You can cut the cost of colour filming by printing the day's colour rushes in black and white for editing purposes. It is, however, important to get a laboratory report on the original film to ensure it is all right. I also pays to test print sections in colour. There are two ways of making black and white prints from colour. A colour original can be printed on an ordinary black and white stock or on one which is "panchromatic" (i.e. it responds to all colours of the spectrum). A panchromatic copy usually costs a little more but it is a good investment. This is particularly true where a film is shot on short daylight-loading rolls. The black and white stocks used to produce an ordinary cutting print are not sensitive to all the colours of the spectrum. Red and orange tend to get lost and other colours too can look deceptive. So, if a film is edge-fogged you may not see it on a cutting copy. Panchromatic film is sensitive to all colours and a black and white print made on pan stock will immediately show any fogging or colour faults.

The choice of stock used should depend on the film subject and cost, and the preference of the lighting cameraman. With 16-mm colour it is worth noting that colour negative is less tough than Ektachrome reversal. This is not a drawback but it does mean that Eastmancolor film is more easily damaged and worn. Do not use an original colour negative for making a large number of release copies. Make a duplicate as soon as you can. The ideal situation is to produce a handful of prints from the original and, when the colour correction and printing exposure have been perfected, to make a duplicate negative for making further copies. When a duplicate wears out, it can be replaced. You just take the original and make another duplicate. If an original is worn out or damaged, nothing can be done to replace it.

Although Ektachrome is physically tougher than colour negative it is still unwise to produce a large number of prints from an original. A dozen is the limit, and the fewer times the master is used the better. Industrial units working on tight budgets sometimes decide it is not worth spending money on a duplicate. They forget that, if the original is lost or damaged, their film is lost for ever. Duplicates are not cheap but they are essential, if only for safety and insurance purposes. They can save money. It is often difficult to estimate the number of copies of a film that are likely to be required, and some spectacular mistakes can be made. A Tourist Board recently sponsored a film shot on 16-mm Ektachrome. When it was completed, three copies were ordered. "No, it's unlikely that more than two or three will be needed," the laboratories were assured. Fifty have now been produced. A negative was produced after 30 had been made. If the duplicate had been made earlier, print costs would have been halved. And the quality of the original master would have been preserved from wear and tear.

We have discussed six different film stocks suitable for industrial use. And we discussed the choice between 35 mm, 16 mm and super 8 mm. As stated earlier, most industrial producers, for reasons of cost or convenience, use 16-mm film. Some of the more expensive productions are shot on 35 mm. Nothing worth mentioning is shot on super 8 mm, though it is widely used for sales demonstration showings of films produced on the two major gauges. Whatever gauge is used, prints of other sizes can be produced. The formats and systems are conveniently interchangeable.

Printing: enlarging and reduction

The sponsor of a 35-mm industrial film can show his film in any conventional cinema but he may not be able to project 35-mm prints in his own company offices because many companies are only equipped to show 16-mm films. So he will have to arrange for 16-mm prints to be made from the 35-mm master. This should not present any problems if the laboratory entrusted with the work takes the necessary care at all technical stages. Here, too, are lessons to be learned and money to be saved.

There are two alternative ways of making 16-mm prints from 35-mm masters and both should be considered. If you need one or two 16-mm copies and do not intend to make a lot of prints on the smaller gauge, ask the laboratory to make a direct reduction print. To do this they will lace up a motion picture film printer with the 35-mm original film on one side and a reel of new 16-mm stock on the other. A film printer is rather like a camera. The two pieces of film run through the machine at the same speed and at one point light is allowed to shine through the original film on to the unexposed reel of new stock. The original is thus rephotographed on a new roll. If 35-mm film is printed on 16-mm positive stock, the resulting 16-mm copy will be ready for projection when processing is complete.

If a number of 16-mm copies are needed, it is cheaper and better to make a 16-mm duplicate negative from which further 16-mm prints can easily be made. To do this, the laboratories may still use a motion picture printer. One part of the machine still contains the 35-mm original. But, on this occasion, the other side will be loaded with 16-mm negative stock and not the positive stock needed to make one 16-mm reduction print. The two pieces of film will run through the machine together. The newly printed 16-mm negative can then be processed and printed on a reel of 16-mm positive stock in the normal way. 16-mm copies can then be made until the duplicate 16-mm negative shows signs of wear.

So there are two ways of making 16-mm copies from 35-mm originals. By direct reduction printing of the 35-mm original on a reel of

16-mm positive. In this manner one copy is made. Or by reduction printing the 35-mm original on a reel of 16-mm negative which, when processed and itself printed on 16-mm stock, can be used to produce 16-mm copies *ad infinitum*. For making a few prints only, the first system may suffice. If more than a handful of 16-mm copies are required, the second method of making duplicate master material in 16-mm form should be used. The reduction printing process can be reversed. 35-mm copies of 16-mm originals can be made. I do not, however, recommend this procedure as it is not technically very satisfactory. 35-mm film can be satisfactorily reduced to 16 mm but when the reverse is attempted, all the imperfections of 16 mm are magnified. When the results are projected, the faults are magnified again. A perfect 16-mm original can be blown up to 35 mm, but it will never look anything like a 35-mm original. The grain size of the 16-mm film will be visibly magnified and the quality of the image and its colour will suffer. If it is essential to blow up a film, a 16-mm Ektachrome commercial original may be the best stock to use for the 16-mm shooting. The stock is fine grain, for a 16-mm colour material, and when enlarged to 35 mm it may not look too bad. It is however best to keep to 16-mm copies of 16-mm films.

Although super 8 mm is not used very much professionally, probably its only serious professional use is an industrial one. It is widely used in cassette projectors designed for salesmen. And it does do a good job, though its quality should not be compared with 35 mm and 16 mm. Super 8-mm prints can be made from originals shot on 16 mm or 35 mm. Again a laboratory process is involved. Never attempt to blow 8 mm up to 16 mm.

Film storage

Whatever its size or nature, film must be looked after before and after it is exposed. In the USA insurance underwriters describe film as "slow burning—hazards in use and storage are small, being somewhat less than would be presented by common newsprint in the same form and quantity". But underwriters are usually more concerned with fire and damage than with results of perfect photographic quality. To ensure optimum results and long life of master material, a few simple precautions should be taken. Do not keep large stocks of unexposed film. Only a major company turning out a considerable daily footage can afford to tie up capital and space storing reels which may not be used for a long time. And even if money and space are no object, unexposed film should not be kept indefinitely. As raw film gets older, age may affect it. It may lose its sensitivity or the fog level may increase or it may lose contrast. With colour film, one of the colour sensitive layers may suffer more than the others in the same piece of film and the colour balance of the material may suffer. If the film is stored in a damp or hot place, this sort of damage is more likely to happen. It is true that raw film is usually supplied in a can which is sealed. That certainly offers some protection. But once the seal is broken, the protection will cease, and if the can is stored in the wrong temperature, the film will probably suffer.

Unexposed film should be stored at a low temperature. When I last visited the Kodak factory I arrived on a warm summer day and the raw stock storeroom felt like the edge of the Arctic Circle. In fact it remains at the same temperature day and night throughout the year. The ideal temperatures for film storage are:

Black and White negative and reversal	13C (55F) Maximum for up to 6 months
Eastmancolor films	10C (50F)
Ektachrome and Kodachrome films	18C (65F)

There is no harm at all in using lower temperatures than those I have outlined. Film must always be allowed to warm up above dew point before a can is unsealed or moisture may spoil the film.

Once a film has been exposed, it should be processed as soon as possible. Do not shoot a film and keep it for weeks. You do not have to print it, if you think it may not be used. Exposed but unprocessed colour film is particularly vulnerable. Each of the separate layers of a colour film is liable to change independently and colour quality can suffer if film is kept for a long time after exposure. And do not leave shot ends in magazines. Processed rolls should again be stored where extremes of temperature and moistness are avoided.

Integral tripack films

I have mentioned the different layers which make up a piece of colour film. If you look at a piece of colour negative or reversal you will not immediately see all the inherent characteristics of the stock so let me explain how the layer film system works.

In the early days of colour filming, there was a special Technicolor camera. Every scene viewed through the lens was analysed by a prism block consisting of two prisms mounted together to form a cube. Light, passing through the lens, entered the prism block and was split up three ways. On one side it was photographed on one strip of film, sensitive to blue. It was simultaneously photographed on a separate piece of film, sensitive to red, and a third exposure, also made at the same time on a separate piece of film, took care of green. So three separate records were obtained simultaneously in the same camera using three separate strips of film, each sensitive to a different primary colour. Any scene can be rendered in a full range of true colour by mixing these three basic colours.

Today, all three pieces of film are incorporated in one. Known as a tri-pack the film is made up of different layers each of which, like the original process, is sensitive to a particular colour. Layers of filter material are also incorporated in the stock, to ensure that only the right colour is recorded on each layer. This method is now standard and you can shoot colour film on any camera. The Technicolor camera has gone for good. Technicolor prints are now made from ordinary colour materials.

The characteristics of colour film stocks are quite interesting to study. Colour film is physically slightly thicker than black and white stock, because the emulsion consists of three separate layers, each of which is sensitive to a primary colour. The top layer is most sensitive to blue light. Light of other colours pass through this layer without altering it. The second layer is sensitive to green and the third to red. A very thin filter of yellow-dyed gelatine is placed between the blue and green sensitive layers. This filters off colours other than red and green and prevents them fogging the surface below.

The film is exposed in the normal way and processed. The first part of the development process is similar to that used for black and white films. All that part of the film which has been exposed to light is turned opaque. Next, in the case of reversal colour processing, the film is exposed to red light, through the cellulose base. The blue and green sensitive layers of the emulsion are unaffected but in the red sensitive layer the parts of the emulsion not already developed in the first developer are made ready for development. The film is then developed again in a "red" developer which does not affect any of the parts of the film already developed. The blue and green layers remain unaffected. The red developer simply converts the parts of the red layer not exposed to light in the camera, to cyan. Next the film is exposed to blue light from the opposite film base to that used for the red light exposure. A "blue" developer acts in similar manner on the unexposed areas of the blue sensitive emulsion and produces a yellow dye. The green sensitive layer is exposed to green light and a "green" developer produces magenta and metallic silver in the areas previously undeveloped. All remaining unexposed silver is then removed in a fixing solution and the remaining silver is bleached away leaving only the tricolour image of yellow, cyan and magenta. Now, when the film is projected with white light, the coloured layers will act as filters allowing only light of the same colour as that in the original image to pass through.

Lengths and windings

Film can be bought in a number of different lengths and windings. The 35-mm gauge is normally sold in lengths of 100 ft, 200 ft, 400 ft and 1000 ft, whereas 16-mm stock is normally available in 100-ft and 400-ft lengths, though 200-ft and 1200-ft lengths are also available in most countries. This film can be supplied on cores or, in the case of 100-ft lengths, on daylight loading spools. It is also made available in differently perforated forms and in several different windings. It can be double perforated, with sprocket holes down both sides. Or it can be either an "A" or a "B" winding which are perforated on one side only. It is very important to order the right type, for if the wrong one is supplied, the sprocket holes may be on the opposite side to the teeth fitted in the camera. There is a simple way of remembering which is "A" winding and which is "B" winding. If you hold a roll of film, wound emulsion in, so that the outside or leader end of the film leaves the roll at the top, pointing to the right, an "A" winding film will have the perforations along the edge of the film which is nearest to you. On "B" winding stock, the holes will be furthest away. When you order your stock, specify the correct winding and as a double check, let your supplier know the type of camera you intend to use. Then you should not have any trouble.

Choice of camera

A film camera can be divided into three parts. A film magazine, the camera body and a lens mounting or turret.

A conventional film magazine usually fits on to the top of a camera. It consists of two compartments which are sometimes separated from each other. One part contains the unexposed film. It must be loaded in a darkroom or changing bag. The film passes out of this compartment though a light trap at the base of the magazine, in the camera. After passing through the camera, it again enters the magazine via a light trap. The end of the film is then would round a takeup core. This conventional type of magazine is often made as one unit, with a single chamber used for both exposed and unexposed film. When this kind of magazine is used, the raw stock must be put in one side, fed through the first light trap, and then taken back into the magazine via the second light trap so it can be wound on the takeup core. All this must be done in darkness. When the work is complete, the side of the magazine can be closed and the lights turned on. The magazine is then safe to handle in daylight and can be attached to the top of the camera in daylight. On some of the more recent magazines there are two separate magazine chambers. The raw stock must still be loaded in darkness, but as the two chambers are entirely self contained, the takeup side can be "laced up" (i.e. threaded up) in daylight. Some of the most modern magazines lace themselves up when the camera motor is started.

A camera body consists of a film gate and mechanism to drive the film through at a constant speed. On some cameras drive sprockets are situated before and after the camera gate. On other cameras the drive is accomplished without these additional aids. Movement through the film gate is controlled by a pull-down movement. This is sometimes known as the "intermittent movement" for it moves the film forward frame by frame and holds each frame stationary in the camera gate for a momentary pause while the image is recorded. In a camera running at normal sound speed, twenty-four pictures are exposed in a second, so twenty-four times every second the film is advanced, pulled down into the camera gate, held still, exposed then moved on. And the movement is very precisely controlled to ensure picture steadiness. Practically all cameras move the film forward by using a claw which engages in the film sprocket holes and advances it frame by frame. Some of the more expensive cameras also employ a register pin for when the film is stationary. The register pin ensures stability and makes certain that each frame is located in exactly the same place. Some register pin systems work by inserting two moving pins in the right perforations. Others use fixed pins on either side of the frame. Cameras fitted with register pins are noted for steadiness and smoothness of movement. Cameras without register pins are quite suitable for most industrial work, but for ultra close-up work and special effects photography, a register pin camera will give optimum results.

There are two ways in which a camera lens can be fitted. It can be screwed into a threaded camera turret or into the camera body direct, or, if it has a bayonet fitting, it can be slotted into place. A lens turret is a panel on the front of the camera, with two or three lenses of different focal lengths fitted into it. By turning the turret one lens can be quickly interchanged with another of a different focal length. Lens turrets are going out of fashion as many new cameras are equipped with zoom lenses which offer a choice of focal length at the touch of a lever—and other advantages. Zoom lenses on 16-mm cameras are always removable though not always with ease. The standard three-lens turret is still used on some Arriflex models and on Bolex cameras. Eclair cameras continue to use the two-lens turret with which they have long been associated.

Today many cameramen prefer to select their viewpoint by using a zoom lens, though for optimum quality single lenses mounted in a turret are still difficult to rival. When positioning three lenses of different focal lengths in one turret care must be taken to ensure that those of longer focal length do not obstruct the view of shorter length lenses mounted nearby. It is easy for a 10-mm lens on a 16-mm camera to

have its view obstructed by a 75-mm lens mounted nearby. The Arriflex overcomes this problem by using a divergent axis turret.

Camera sound systems

There are many cameras to choose from but are they suitable for
industrial use? Let us consider sound cameras first. There are two
different types: single system and double system.

A single-system camera incorporates its own magnetic recording
head and allied equipment. It records sound directly on to a magnetic
stripe on the edge of the film in the camera. A double system camera
records on $\frac{1}{4}$-in tape while the action is photographed on silent film stock
in the camera. The speed of camera and recorder is governed by a
synchronising pulse recorded alongside the actual sound recording on the
tape. When filming is completed, the tape is re-recorded on perforated
magnetic film. The same pulses are used to drive a synchronous
motor at exactly the same speed as that at which the sound was recorded
and at which the camera simultaneously photographed the action. The
re-recorded sound thus continues to match the action.

In a single system camera sound is recorded on a magnetic stripe
always on the edge of the film. On 16-mm film, the sound is recorded
twenty-eight frames ahead of the picture. This sound and picture separa-
tion makes editing very difficult, for if you wish to cut the picture at one
point, you will also have to allow twenty-eight frames for the sound.
Of course, you can get over this problem by re-recording the magnetic
stripe on separate, perforated magnetic film stock. You then have all
the flexibility of the double system, and have the same raw materials to
edit: a mute print and a separate magnetic track. The single system
is not ideal for industrial filming. And it is mainly applied in filming
television news programmes, where time in getting the material processed, edited and flashed on a screen is of paramount importance. A
striped original can be processed and edited quickly. Double system
sound has to be re-recorded on magnetic stock before it can be edited.
But for industrial use, and indeed for most kinds of film making, the
double system is better, and more widely used.

When moving pictures first became possible, the cameras were hand
turned and the pictures jerky and unevenly exposed. Cameras today are
very much precision products, designed to give first class results at all
times. Yet their main function remains the same: to expose a continuous
reel of film. Cameras still consist of a lens and two chambers to hold
film before it has been exposed and after exposure. And the film still
passes through an aperture where the light is allowed to pass through a
lens. But today, cameras are not hand powered, and film no longer
consists of oil soaked paper! The modern motion picture camera is a

piece of precision equipment, and it can be expensive. Cameras suitable for industrial use can cost anything from £200 to £5000. The type of camera used will depend on the work which has to be done and on the amount of money available. Never buy a cheap camera just for the sake of economy. It is better to hire a good one. Before choosing a camera at all it pays to consider the main camera characteristics.

Cameras can be powered by electric motor or by clockwork spring. You can enjoy a much longer running time for any shot with an electrically driven camera and, if necessary, a complete magazine can be exposed in one take. The spring-operated camera is often more portable. Most 16-mm spring-powered cameras are designed to take 100-ft or 200-ft daylight loading spools. Electric cameras usually take magazines and 400 ft is the normal length to use. Most magazine cameras will also take spools if required to do so. A 400-ft magazine has one obvious advantage. You can shoot for longer, without stopping to re-load. There are also some disadvantages, which although slight, should not be overlooked. You cannot load a magazine in daylight. You have to use either a darkroom or a changing bag, because 400-ft reels of stock are supplied on plastic cores and not on spools for loading in daylight. If you use an electric camera with magazines you will find you have to carry more equipment. You need the camera body and lenses, together with a tripod, and pan and tilt head, also spare magazines, boxes of batteries, filters and a changing bag. A spring-operated camera can be carried in one case.

"Viewfinder systems"

There are two main kinds of viewfinder system: reflex and non-reflex. The reflex system allows you to see through the actual camera lens at all times. This can be expecially useful when shooting in close-up or with a telephoto lens or zoom setting as you see exactly what the camera is lined up on. If you use a separate, non-reflex viewfinder, you may not see exactly what the camera sees. The angle of the viewfinder can be adjusted so the angle it points at gives a corresponding view to that passing through the camera lens, but it is easy to forget to make the necessary adjustment and, if alterations are not made, you may find you cut off part of the picture or line it up incorrectly when working with a long focus lens. The difference between the view from a separate viewfinder and that seen through the camera lens is known as parallax distortion. Today, most professional cameras employ a reflex viewing system.

Some cameras using a reflex finder also offer an additional non-reflex finder as well. This can be useful, especially when filming in bright light with the lens stopped right down. With the reflex system.

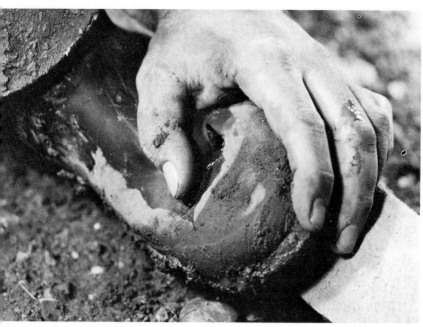

n a safety film visual impact can be used to advantage. In the Drayton Films production *Fifty to One*, the results of not wearing protective footwear were made memorable. Picture: Drayton Film Productions.

you are looking straight through the camera lens, so the amount of light passing through the lens decides how bright your image is in the viewfinder. If you are working at $f2 \cdot 8$ you will probably be able to see the pictures quite clearly. But if you are working on a bright day, with fast film you may have to stop the aperture down to $f16$ or $f22$, as the amount of light passing through is then very small, and it may be difficult to see adequately through the lens. The answer to this problem is, of course, to open up the lens for setting up and rehearsals. Find exactly what you require, focus, then close the lens and make the exposure. If you need an additional guide, you can use the non-reflex finder.

Lens characteristics

Lenses have two main characteristics: focal length and speed. The focal length of a lens is usually measured in either millimeters or inches. A standard lens produces a picture in which the perspective of the original scene is reproduced as near normal vision as possible. For 16-mm cameras, lenses of 25 mm are generally regarded as standard. A wide-angle lens is one of shorter focal length—16 mm or 10 mm when shooting on 16-mm film. The picture it presents is smaller, as it covers a wider field than a standard lens. A telephoto lens is a longer focus lens and it produces a correspondingly larger image than a standard lens. It also covers a correspondingly smaller field of view. A 50-mm lens covers half the area of a 25-mm lens but the image it shoots appears twice the size of that produced by a standard lens shooting from the same point. The other important lens characteristic is its speed.

The speed of a lens is dictated by the maximum aperture to which it can be opened. The "*f*" number on the front of any lens tells you how fast it is. An *f*2 or *f*1·8 lens can be classified as fast. Lenses only opening up to *f*4 are not fast enough for many kinds of industrial work. When you choose a lens you must find one which is fast enough to record the scene you want to shoot. You must also be sure that the focal length of the lens you propose to use is right to show the field you wish to cover. You may find the normal lens is the one you use most. On 16-mm film the 25-mm lens covers a horizontal angle of 23½ degrees and a vertical angle of 17 degrees. It can be used without fear of undue distortion. A wide-angle lens, however, tends to exaggerate the distance between objects. This has some advantages as we shall see when we consider the control of depth of field. But, continuous use of wide-angle lenses can be tedious. Perspective for wide-angle filming depends on maintaining a suitable distance between camera and subject. If you get too close the view will be distorted. A face seen really close up on a wide angle lens shows distorted features. The distortion is far greater than that encountered when shooting the same scene with a lens of normal focal length. This is because the wide angle lens has to be brought much closer to the subject being filmed. If the distance between camera and subject is greater, the perspective will be more normal. A wide angle lens should be part of every industrial film-maker's equipment.

Some lenses can be focused. Others are described as "fixed focus". The fixed-focus lens does not permit the same amount of control, for you cannot dictate the exact area you want to remain in, or out of focus. With a wide-angle lens, where the depth of field is very great anyway, this is not such a disadvantage as with lenses of normal focal length. Lenses with adjustable focus can be set and controlled at will. One of the most important controls is the choice of area on which to focus. The part of any shot which is sharp is known as the zone of sharpness. Each lens has a different and variable zone of sharpness which is known as its depth of field. Let us consider how this works.

If you set up a camera and focus the lens on an object 20 ft away from you, it is safe to assume that anything which is exactly 20 ft away from the camera will be in focus. It is also true to say that, depending on the lens in use, an area of sharpness extends some way in front of, and some way beyond, the 20-ft mark on which your lens is focused. Perhaps this area will range from 15 ft to 25 ft. This area is known as depth of field. The exact extent of the area of sharpness depends on the type of lens and the aperture at which the lens is set. A wide angle lens has a greater depth of field than a normal lens. Any lens, used at a small aperture, such as $f16$ or $f22$, will have a greater depth of field than when the lens is fully opened. Definition is also improved by stopping down. You can, therefore, choose the area you wish to remain in focus by arranging to use a lens of suitable focal length, and by lighting the scene in a manner that will make it possible for you to use a suitable lens aperture. If the scene is flooded with light and a small aperture is needed the depth of field will be greater than if the lighting is dimmed to give a lens aperture of say $f2\cdot8$. When choosing the lens you wish to use, you must therefore decide how you want the scene to appear on the screen, and what area you wish to remain in focus.

We have so far considered the characteristics of individual lenses of different focal length which could be mounted in a lens turret on the front of the camera. The range of a zoom lens for 16-mm work may extend from 12 mm to 120 mm or a 10:1 ratio. By moving a lever a wide angle focal length or a telephoto shot can be obtained. And, of course, if the lever is set between the wide and telephoto position, shots of other, medium, focal lengths can be obtained. Using one zoom lens, it is possible to do the work of a number of different separate lenses. And it is possible to make a tracking shot by moving gradually from one focal length to another while filming the movement known universally as a zoom. This kind of lens has much to recommend it.

When zoom lenses were first introduced, there were a number of drawbacks. The large number of elements which together make up a zoom tended to reduce the amount of light passing through, so the maximum aperture of early lenses was often around $f4$. And the quality of the picture, passing through so much glass, also suffered. Today, many of these problems have been solved. Some zoom lenses are of superb quality. They can be used in extremely difficult lighting conditions and the quality of the pictures produced can be relied on. Zoom lenses are now a worthwhile proposition but, for complete perfection, it still pays to use an individual lens for every scene. Light still has to pass through a lot of elements in a zoom lens and even today definition is not quite as good as on a scene exposed with a standard lens. But there is no doubt at all that the zoom lens is here to stay. Many new cameras are now only supplied with a fixed zoom lens. And the quality of the equipment is extremely good.

Automatic exposure control

When automatic exposure systems were first introduced, a separate exposure meter was usually built into the front of the camera, just below or above the lens. If a standard lens was used to shoot an evenly lit scene, the system could work well provided that the acceptance angle of the meter corresponded. But with a zoom lens the results were not nearly as reliable. While the zoom lens could take a telephoto shot in some darker or lighter areas, the exposure meter continued to provide a general reading of the scene viewed as far as the standard lens, so exposure readings tended to be unreliable. The system was unreliable for other reasons too. One of the chief faults was that the meter usually took an average reading, and bright sky or heavy shadows could easily mislead it. The system worked, but only just. It was never used professionally.

To-day on some cameras, a very small exposure meter is positioned behind the lens, the idea being that the meter only reads for that part of the subject area actually covered by the lens. Readings can be taken with a zoom lens in any position, so at long focal lengths for instance it is posible to obtain quite accurate readings of distant subjects. This kind of integral exposure meter is not used very much in professional filming but I think that in the near future it will come into very much greater favour. One 16-mm professional reflex camera, the Bolex Pro, has three separate servo motors which control exposure, focus and zoom. It is an interesting development, for if the three actions can be closely allied, there is every hope of developing a successful system.

This development is the first step on the way to success. But it is a step which has only recently been taken, and developments are still going on. Probably most development has taken place in the super 8-mm amateur market where such TTL (through the lens) exposure meters are now much in evidence. The high standards required by professional users have required more research. Arnold and Richter have produced an Arriflex camera (the BL) with a built-in exposure control and Bolex have developed the PRO model. For an industrial film maker these are interesting developments. They offer an alternative to the standard method of taking either incident or reflected light readings with a separate meter. At the moment, I do not think they offer any very positive advantages, except possibly simplicity. For industrial use, the present standard system is probably the best, though for shooting scenes where it is often difficult to get a light reading before you shoot, the new system—when thoroughly tested—would seem to have much to recommend it. So, what camera is best for industrial filming?

The Arriflex range of cameras is one of the best known in the whole field of cinematography. There are three models which are ideal for industrial work. The Arriflex 35 Model 2C is a thoroughly reliable camera for 35-mm work. With the Arri blimp 120S the camera can also be used for shooting with sound. It takes standard 35-mm film. For 16 mm use, the Arriflex 16 m and the Arriflex 16BL have much to recommend them.

The 35-mm Model C is a well proven camera. For a 35-mm camera it is portable and can be used for studio or location work. It is a reflex model with a 3-lens turret into which Arriflex lenses can be slotted quite quickly. A zoom lens can also be fitted. The camera has a variable speed motor built into the base, rather like a pistol grip. By turning the base in either a clockwise or an anti-clockwise direction the speed of the motor can be increased or reduced. A tachometer fitted into the back of the camera records the exact camera speed. Other advantages are that the ground glass screen in the viewfinder can be changed. 35-mm film can be shot in a number of different formats—normal ratio, wide screen or cinemascope formats can be used, and for each of these frame sizes, a different glass screen can be fitted. The eyepiece of the viewfinder can be supplied with a spring shutter which closes across the viewfinder whenever the eye is taken away from it. This prevents stray light reflecting into the reflex system and thereby reaching the film.

Film is contained in 400-ft magazines. The magazines for the Model C are well designed and it is possible to get 500 ft of black and white film into a 400-ft magazine in an emergency. The magazines are easily attached to the top of the camera and, as a take-up motor is built into the side of each magazine, once the film has been laced up, shooting can begin. A film footage indicator is built into the magazine. The lens turret is easy to rotate and the lenses themselves just slide in. Arriflex lenses are not screwed into position, they slot into a bayonet mount. The front of the camera consists of a matte box and filters and special effects masks can be slotted into this. It also prevents stray light shining into the camera lens. The weight of the Arriflex Model C camera body with matte box and magazine is around 14 pounds without film. That is not heavy for a 35-mm camera and the design is so good that the body is easy to grip. It is ideal for location work and for all 35-mm mute shooting. By encasing the camera in the 120S blimp it can also be used for synchronised sound work.

The blimp 120S is heavy, for the camera mechanism is encased in a metal casing which reduces the camera noise to a very acceptable level. I have used a 120S blimp to shoot interviews with the camera six feet away from the recording microphone and no hint of camera noise has been recorded. The makers claim that the sound level is reduced to 24 db one metre in front of the camera. This is quite an achievement when you consider the amount of equipment and the motors churning away inside the blimp casing. Again, the 120S permits the use of a standard 400-ft magazine. 1000-ft magazines can be used with an Arri 300 blimp, but for most industrial purposes, 400 ft will suffice.

One of the problems of using blimped cameras is gaining access to the parts which have to be controlled in the course of a take. To deaden the sound of camera motors and mechanism a blimp must be very solid. On some earlier cameras, this meant that controls were often inaccessible when the camera was in use. With the Arri 120S, this is not the case. All the lenses can be controlled from outside the case and switches, controls and indicators are visible and accessible all the time. The main controls are set into the back of the camera casing. Separate push button controls for on and off are mounted above a window showing a film footage indicator. Alongside, there is a spirit level which can be very useful when setting up. A circular wheel, looking like a telephone dial, enables the mirror reflex shutter to be turned by hand so the view through the viewfinder can be cleared when the camera is not running. Other external controls govern focusing. There are two handles, one for focusing normal lenses and the other for use when an Angineux zoom lens is in position. Zoom lenses can be focused and the focal length can be altered by using the two levers provided. Arriflex 35-mm equipment has been produced since 1937. It is robust, well made and thoroughly reliable.

There are two 16-mm Arriflex cameras of particular interest to industrial users. The 16M and the BL. The Arriflex 16M is basically a camera for silent shooting. It is relatively noisy. If sound is to be recorded the 16M can be housed in a blimp, but the blimp is very heavy and not really very practicable for industrial purposes or indeed for use anywhere outside a studio. The Arri BL is a perfect camera for sound shooting. But let us consider the 16M first.

The Arriflex 16M is a reflex camera with a three-lens turret and electric motor drive. A variable speed motor, similar to the motor on the 35C, can also be fitted. The motors on M cameras are easily replaced by slackening one screw and sliding one motor out and another one in. The 16M normally operates with 400-ft magazines though 100-ft spools can be used and 1000-ft magazines are also available for long runs, if required. The camera is very easy to operate and can be hand-held for short periods. With three lenses fitted in the rotating lens turret, rapid change from one lens to another is easily achieved by swinging the turret around. The shortest focal length lens produced for use with this camera is now 5·7 cm and that is more than wide enough for most industrial applications. A zoom lens can also be fitted into one of the turret positions.

The 16M Arri uses the mirror reflex shutter system invented by the two people responsible for the Arriflex range (Arnold and Richter (AR-RI)) in 1937. In the Arri 16M the light passing through the camera lens is allowed to pass unhindered to the film. When the film is running the light is deflected by means of a rotating mirror shutter, arranged at an angle of 45 degrees to the optical axis of the lens. The rotating mirror shutter turns at half the speed of the film movement—once every two frames, so light entering the lens is available alternatively for viewing and

lming. The camera shutter is divided into two segments made in one
art and carefully balanced. The surfaces of the blade are provided with
mirrors of flat optical glass. The balancing shutter ensures smooth
ibration-free running and the precision of the shutter ensures com-
lete steadiness and sharpness of the viewfinder image. The whole
amera mechanism is made with true German precision.

The Arri 16M is a successor to the 16ST used by industrial film
nakers for many years. It is a well proven camera, similar to the 35-mm
Model C. The film magazines are slightly different, for whereas 35-mm
magazines have take-up motors built in, 16-mm magazines do not. A
eparate detachable panel has to be attached when a magazine is
itted. At the end of one magazine, the panel must be detached and
itted to the next magazine to be used. It only takes a matter of seconds.
The controls are basically the same as the 35-mm camera. There is a
achometer to check film speed, film footage and frame counters built
nto the camera body and a footage indicator on the back of the maga-
ines. The viewfinder magnifies each scene ten times and the whole
hape of the camera body has been designed for ease of handling. It can
e hand held, though a shoulder pod will give extra steadiness and
upport. For runs longer than a minute, a shoulder pod is highly recom-
nended. The camera can be used with a synchronous motor on mains
ower. The more normal method of operation is by using portable
echargeable batteries.

There are a number of accessories made for use with the Arri 16M
vhich may interest specialist industrial film makers. There is a very
vide range of different lenses and for really close-up work, a microscope
an be used in conjunction with the camera. Any microscope with a
ertical eyepiece can be used but the lens must never be allowed to
nake contact with the eyepiece. With the mirror reflex viewfinder
ystem, it is quite possible to view the action through the microscope in
he normal way. Time lapse and animation equipment has also been
roduced for use with this camera. A single frame mechanism and an
uxiliary shutter to prevent fogging during long intervals between
xposures form part of the equipment. An intervalometer giving
utomatic control of the camera, and adjustable to intervals between
seconds and 3 hours, is also available. The camera can also be used for
ome kinds of X-ray work. The Arri 16M is a versatile camera. It can
e used for sound shooting in conjunction with a blimp, but a far better
amera to use for sound work is the Arriflex BL.

When the BL was introduced the film and television industries
vere taken by surprise. For years a sound camera had meant using a
eavy blimp to deaden the noise of the camera drive motors and
nechanism. The BL changed this situation for good. It is so silent in
peration that it can be used without a blimp. And the results produced

are well up to the high Arriflex standards. I have used BL cameras or countless jobs and always found them reliable. The BL is a very easy camera to handle. The magazines are small and flat and contain their own take-up motors. They are easy to load. There is a notch on the edge of the magazine casing to indicate the amount of film needed to form a loop between the supply side of the magazine and the take-up. The loop size has to be correct, for the BL, unlike the earlier Arriflex cameras, has no drive sprockets. The magazine clips on the top of the camera and the film loop is fed straight into the camera gate. It then passes directly back to the magazine where it is wound on the take-up film centre or core. A magazine can be changed in seconds. No time is wasted lacing up. But the film loop must be exactly right. If it is too generous, the spare film will rub on the bottom of the camera casing. If it is too small, the film will move jerkily and may well snap. If the loop size is correct, and by using the notch on the outside of the magazine during loading there is no reason why it should not be, the film will run smoothly. Results on the screen will be steady and evenly exposed.

The BL has been designed for ease of operation, especially for television cameramen who often have to work at speed under difficult conditions. The industrial cameraman, too, often has to work in difficult conditions and he will find the BL has much to recommend it. It has the same mirror reflex viewfinder system to be found on the other cameras. There is no lens turret. The camera is supplied with a zoom lens already fitted. This does not mean other lenses cannot be used. They can, though the camera is not designed for easy interchange of lenses like the turret cameras. The zoom lenses are of very good quality and should be suitable for most industrial purposes. If, however, a particularly wide angle shot is required, the zoom lens can be removed quite simply and another lens put in its place. The camera can be hand held though, again, a shoulder pod is helpful. All the controls are easily reached and the camera body has a built-in hand grip with the starter button conveniently situated. A motorised zoom can also be controlled from the same position though a zoom motor is an extra and not part of the basic camera outfit. The lens housing includes a matte box useful for special effects work and for keeping surplus light out of the camera lens. A filter holder for glass filters is set behind the matte box. When a filter is not in use, a panel of plain glass slots into position to protect the elements of the lens. And the lens itself is fitted into the camera body which acts as a self blimp and cuts camera noise to a minimum. I have seen interviews shot in the back seat of a Rolls Royce and still not hear the noise of the camera motor, even though the camera was only a few feet away from the microphone making the recording. The standard camera magazine takes 400 ft of film. Magazines taking 1200 ft can also be provided. The camera is normally powered by rechargeable batteries

In 1970, Arnold and Richter introduced their first through the
·ns exposure control system for the Arriflex BL. As I mentioned earlier,
utomatic exposure control used to be unsuitable for professional use. It
ill is unsuitable for some specialist applications and many professional
ameramen would rather not use a camera with an automatic device.
'he BL system uses a CDS meter working through the camera lens
ITL). It takes a reading corresponding to one-third of the film area
t the centre of the viewfinder, irrespective of the focal length of the
·ns in use. The exposure indication is visible on a projected scale in
te viewfinder. The meter needle, visible underneath the scene in the
iewfinder, can be centred until the correct exposure is reached by
pening or closing the lens. The outer scale indexes marked with a+
n one side and a— on the other represent one stop over and one stop
nder the correct exposure. Before using the camera the correct film
)eed and exposure time should be set. The meter is adjustable from
5–500 ASA (13–28 DIN) and from 24 or 25–50 fps. The power for the
xposure system comes from the same main camera battery so that
hen the camera is connected the system automatically comes into use.
˙ you are using filters with the BL exposure meter, you do not have to
take compensating adjustments for the filter factors. As the filters are
tted in front of the lens, the exposure meter, too, will make its own
djustments. And for close-up work, too, the system has many advan-
·ges. Just set the meter with the correct film speed and refer to the
idicator in the viewfinder.

The Arriflex system overcomes many of the traditional problems
;sociated with automatic exposure devices. It indicates the correct
xposure, but it does not automatically set the camera lens, so the
tmeraman is still really in control. With the reading being taken
trough the camera lens, there is every hope of an accurate reading and,
hereas many cheap built-in attachments give a general wide-angle
·ading of the scene immediately in front of the camera, the TTL system
; more accurate. If you are using a zoom lens and want to move from
t wide shot of a factory to a closer view of a piece of machinery, you can
nmediately get an accurate reading on the new shot, viewed through
te lens. And if the foreground is brighter than the area you intend to
100t, the exposure should still be correct because the meter sees only
hat the lens passes to it. This is one of the most important characteris-
cs of any successful exposure system.

)rmat and the future

So, industrial film makers, using 16-mm film, have a number of
titable cameras to choose from. The 35-mm producer has a choice too.

Apart from the Arriflex, there is the Mitchell range of cameras and for ultra portability the well established Newman Sinclair is still in use. The Arri BL is only one of a new breed of cameras developed largely to meet the needs of television. A few years ago, when 35 mm was the only gauge used by professionals, 16 mm was dismissed as spaghetti and equipment available for serious use was extremely limited. Today, television thrives on spaghetti and in recent years more developments have taken place on 16 mm than on 35 mm. There are now a few people who feel that 35 mm will die out altogether and the trend towards miniaturisation will lead us to use 16 mm as *the* professional gauge and super 8 mm as an alternative. If these people are correct I look forward to an early retirement!

The aim of the manufacturers of the new 16-mm cameras has been to bring 16-mm performance as near as possible to that of 35 mm. It will never be quite the same. The physical characteristics of the film and its size prohibit the same degree of picture and sound quality. But results have been very much improved. I have already outlined the variety of different film stocks available to the 16-mm user. Ten years ago, half the stocks now available were not technically possible. With cameras, too, the same rapid development has taken place.

Eclair 16 camera

Among other equipment widely used by industrial film units is that made by Eclair International Diffusion of France.

The Eclair 16 is a self-blimped camera, designed for ease of holding and for simplicity of use, again, largely conceived for the television cameraman. It is portable and can be used for sound and mute shooting. The camera is very quiet when running because the motor and shutter operate from the same drive shaft with no gears in between. Noise level is thus considerably reduced. The shape of the camera enables it to be rested against the shoulders for maximum steadiness when shooting is in progress. Like the BL, it is a reflex camera with a viewfinder providing ten times magnification. The viewfinder of the Eclair can rotate 360 degrees and can be swivelled for left- or right-eye viewing. That is a useful device when filming in awkward factory corners. The camera takes 400-ft magazines which can be changed very quickly because the camera does not require lacing up at all. Threading takes place in the magazine instead of in the camera body. You simply slot the magazine into position and press the starting button. 100-ft and 200-ft spools can also be used. Lenses on the Eclair fit into a two-lens turret. So a zoom can be used in conjunction with another lens, possibly a very short focal length. The turret is well built and strong enough to hold a heavy lens firmly in position. This is a good, reliable camera particularly suitable for industrial filming off-the-cuff, when scenes have to be shot with the minimum time loss. When a major sponsored film was produced about the Olympic Games, 106 of the 120 official cameramen used Eclairs. As television has proved, they are quite capable of running 6000 ft a day, five days a week, without trouble, if they are properly looked after.

Bolex 16 Pro

Bolex, an old established name in filming, make two cameras which are of interest to industrial producers. The newest of these is the Bolex 16 Pro. The Bolex 16 Pro is designed to give the same type of performance as the Arriflex BL and the Eclair. It is portable, though heavy, and is self-blimped and quiet. Though Bolex have had years of experience making other 16-mm cameras this model is an entirely new design.

The Pro takes a coaxial 400-ft magazine using up to 400 ft of film. It is a remarkable design, for like the camera drive motor it works in forward and reverse directions. The magazine is divided into two separate chambers. One must be loaded in darkness or a changing bag. The other, being self contained, could be opened in daylight at the start of filming. There are two separate footage counters showing the amount of film in each chamber. The magazine is very compact and fits on to the back of the camera in a way that makes the camera quite easy to hold for short periods against the shoulder. Film passes from one side of the magazine to the camera and it is at this point that the first revolutionary point of the Pro becomes apparent. With a loose end of film hanging out of the supply side of the film magazine, all you have to do is place the end of the film in a slot at the back of the camera and press the start button. The camera then laces itself up. The film not only laces itself round the gate and camera mechanism but it also feeds itself into the take-up side of the magazine and winds itself on to the take-up core. That is a real time-saver. There is a light beneath the viewfinder, indicating when the film has been threaded and is ready for use.

The Pro also has a built-in automatic exposure meter which sets the lens reading by using a servo motor. If you pan from a light scene to a dark one the camera makes its own exposure adjustments. The exposure control is coupled to the camera speed control so if the running speed is increased or reduced, the exposure will adjust itself automatically. If there is insufficient light a buzzer sounds. The meter contains provision for filming with film speeds in the range of 12–1600 ASA, and the lens setting is always visible in the viewfinder above the viewing area. The lens can also be set manually by the cameraman.

The magnification of the Pro viewfinder is ×20. Unlike some

professional cameras, the viewfinder always gives a clear uninterrupted view. On some cameras, the shutter can cut off the view between takes and an inching knob has to be used to restore the image in the viewfinder. With the Pro this cannot happen because the mirror shutter automatically stops in the correct position. The camera is normally supplied with a 12–120-mm zoom lens. Power focusing and zooming are also accomplished by servo motors. The lenses can be changed quite easily and the control motors, like the main camera drive motor, are relatively noiseless so sound shooting can continue. The controls are all admirably grouped together, on two pistol grips at opposite sides of the camera. By holding these grips and resting the camera against the shoulder it is possible to shoot hand-held takes. The right-hand grip contains controls for power zooming. There is a separate rocker switch and a speed control for focusing and power zooming, and a camera release which can be locked while running. The lock has a safety device which makes it impossible to run without film. There is also a switch for overriding the automatic exposure and totally closing the diaphragm, a control which is intended for use when making camera dissolves and double exposures. A further control on the right-hand grip enables camera and zoom to be controlled remotely if necessary. On the left-hand grip there is another switch for the power focusing. There is a camera running speed control, and a control for automatic or manual lens diaphragm settings. Push buttons control the opening and closing of the diaphragm settings, and there is also an outlet for remote focusing. The focus and zoom controls, though power operated, can also be used manually. Frame and footage counters complete the controls and the camera is silent enough in operation to be used with confidence with sound equipment.

Some of the older Bolex designs still in production are perfectly suitable for industrial use. One of their cameras is of special interest to small internal units wishing to buy their own equipment but not being able to afford one of the sound cameras we have discussed.

Bolex H.16 cameras have been made for a number of years. The H.16 was originally produced as a semi-professional camera with a clockwork motor and a three-lens turret. It took 100-ft spools of film and could be loaded in daylight. It was, and is, an excellent camera. It has recently been adapted to meet the needs of the small budget professional. The Bolex H.16 RX5 is basically the same as the original camera. It can still use 100-ft spools and can still be powered by clockwork. But it can also be used with 400-ft magazines powered by an electric motor. It is not in the same class as the BL, the Eclair or the Pro but it can be very useful to the small industrial film unit. In the course of a test, I once ran film shot on two different cameras, side by side, on the same screen. I asked five professional cameramen to examine the results and tell me which film had been shot on the RX5 and which had been shot on a far more expensive sound camera. One gave me the right answer. Though the RX5 is not nearly as sophisticated as the Pro, picture quality and steadiness are still remarkably good.

The RX5 is not really suitable for sound shooting. Its main purpose is for shooting silent film and it is quite suitable for general industrial work. The magazines have separate, attachable take-up motors. Film has to be laced round a drive sprocket, through the camera gate and round a further drive sprocket out to the second part of the magazine. It is not very complicated and the results are good. The camera is quite versatile and, by professional standards, cheap. It is nothing like as expensive as the other models we have examined.

The RX5 is very portable. The camera can be used without a magazine. If you detach the magazine and fit a light trap in the top of the camera body, 100-ft daylight loading spools can be inserted. You then only have to carry the camera body and the electric drive. For ultra portability, the electric drive can be detached and the built-in clockwork motor can be brought into use. This limits the amount of film which can be run through in any one take but it does ensure complete portability. For shooting industrial tests under field conditions and for filming in very awkward places, the Bolex RX5 can have great advantages. I once had to shoot from the top of scaffolding surround a new cathedral being built in Liverpool. The prospect of taking a heavy camera to the top did not appeal! To be honest, the idea of going to the top at all did not have much appeal! However, the journey was made, and the film shot on a hand-held Bolex. The material was later cut into film shot on an Eclair.

From time to time I have mentioned hand-holding cameras. Some cameramen are experts at hand-holding. There are many who think they are experts but who, when seeing rushes, discover they are not. It is best to use a tripod whenever possible. At least one tripod should always be included in industrial filming equipment. Sometimes long and short tripods may both be needed. Always make sure that a tripod is really sturdy. A pan and tilt head should be part of tripod equipment. For work where very fine control of camera movement is necessary, a geared head may be worthwhile. Geared heads fit on to the top of a tripod. They consist of a number of gears and handles enabling the panning and tilting movements of a camera to be controlled with complete smoothness and accuracy.

Lighting equipment

What lighting equipment is best for industrial filming?
The largest, most powerful lamps used by film makers are carbon

arcs. Arc lights will probably only interest the producer of a high budget industrial film shooting large areas where a lot of light has to be provided. They are not easy to use for they operate off DC current which often means bringing in a generator. They are very bulky and heavy to handle. The recent introduction of high-speed colour films has done much to make arc lights unnecessary. It is now often possible to shoot large factory scenes by available light where a few years ago, arc lights would have been essential. For lighting large dark areas, arc lights still have much to recommend them, but the cost of providing generator, lights and a full lighting crew will be beyond the means of many industrial film makers. Incandescent lights are far more widely used.

Incandescent light

Incandescent lights fall into two main categories: floods and spots. Floodlights set out to give a pool of flat light. Spotlights can be focused on a particular point or area for, in addition to light source and reflector, spotlights also have lenses. There are many kinds of spotlight. Some are small. The smallest uses only a 100-W lamp. It is known as an "inkie dinkie" and is only useful for lighting a very small area. Slightly larger is the "pup", which is quite often employed as a modelling or key light. The beam angle can be varied between 12 deg. and 60 deg. and the lamps give out 500 W. Larger still is the 2000 W (2-K) spotlight, known as the "junior". The beam angle can be adjusted from 12 to 44 deg. Another kind of 2-K spotlight is the Dualite. The lenses in front of the light source are interchangeable. The standard lens is 12 in diameter, giving an even light which can be varied from 18 to 60 deg. A wide angle lens will give a softer illumination from 30 up to 90 deg. A third alternative lens will diffuse the illumination still further and given an even field over 100 or 120 deg. The "senior" is a 5000-W (5-K) spotlight useful on small colour sets and for many black and white types of film work. More powerful still is the "tenner", giving 10,000 (10 K) over an area variable from 16 to 46 deg.

In addition to spotlights, lights designed to flood large areas are also required. Three single bulb floods are often used on industrial locations. The "basher" is the lowest powered. It covers a fairly small area with a very soft light. The "scoop" is a more powerful light. It can be fitted with either 500-W or 1000-W bulbs and will cover an area of 120 deg. There is also the "broad", using a bulb of 500 or 750 W and giving a soft, diffused light, useful for filling in subjects near to the camera. Floods, unlike spotlights, do not have lenses. They consist of a lamp, reflector and sometimes a diffuser. The floods I have mentioned are handy for lighting small areas with a soft light. For larger areas more powerful units, using two or more bulbs, are needed. The smallest of these is the "lollo". It uses two bulbs of 1000 W fitted behind a diffuser. Where still more light is required, "quads", using four bulbs, are brought in. Each of the four bulbs can be controlled independently. For the largest areas, banks of Tenlites may be needed. As the name suggests, ten separate bulbs are enclosed in one housing which is about 6 ft square. A frame is fitted to the front of the unit and diffusing material can be fitted into the frame. This unit is particularly useful for industrial work. It can be placed on a stand or suspended, and the light can be tilted to angle the illumination wherever it is required. These are all conventional lights. In another ten years they may have disappeared altogether for the conventional bulb is fast being replaced by a new kind of light, the tungsten halogen lamp. Perhaps the best-known tungsten halogen lamp is the quartz iodine (Q I) type of lamp. Q I lamps are smaller and more portable than the conventional type. They have other advantages too, for the life of a conventional lamp is comparatively short. With use, ordinary bulbs tend to discolour and light output and colour temperature tend to change. The tungsten halogen light output remains strong and the colour temperature constant throughout its life. And the lamps are far more portable than a conventional kit.

For industrial use, a Colortran outfit is good basic equipment, and there are two kinds. One uses conventional bulbs, boosted to give a high intensity light output. The other uses Q I lamps. Colortran equipment is normally supplied in kits. A full Colortran kit consists of two control boxes known as converters, and eight lights with stands. A half kit is enough for many industrial jobs. In the conventional Colortran system, each light is supplied with a boosted voltage producing a very bright light. The control boxes make it possible for lights to be switched on at a low voltage before boosting. The elements are thus not subjected to a high voltage until they have first been warmed up. When the lights have been turned on for several minutes, at a low voltage, they can be stepped up gradually until they reach a high operating voltage. After a scene has been shot, they can be turned down again to reduce heat and preserve the lamps. Boosting raises the colour temperature, increases the brilliance of the lights and shortens their lives as well.

A Colortran kit can be fitted into the back of a car. A full kit consists of eight lamps, though it is not always essential to have a full kit. With a full kit you will have a good choice of different types of lamps to use for key, background and fill-in work. The total capacity of the two converters is 80 amps and they can be used with either 200/240-V or 110/115-V supplies. In fact, the eight lights supplied do not use all the power available and further lights can be added if necessary, though not when running off a normal 240-V 13-amp supply! Colortran bulbs consist of a combination of floods and spots with names like "Super Kicker" and "Cinelight Kings". Floods are supplied in either 500-W,

1000- or 2-K size. Spots are normally 500 W, and you can choose between wide or narrow beam. With a combination of the different types of bulb, in conjunction with the Standard Colortran control converter, it is possible to light many industrial sets and locations. The colour temperature of the lights can also be controlled, a temperature meter being built into the converter. Colortran lights are, of course, incandescent and are designed for work with artificial light film. When used with daylight film a blue filter must be put in front of each lamp. Glass filters for daylight conversion are available. They are known as Macbeths and they fit on to the front of the lamps. Diffusing material too should always be carried, together with plenty of spare plugs, cables and fuses.

Modern QI lights are more portable and easy to set up. They can be used on stands or they can be attached by clamps and brackets to suitable supports on location. A wide range of quartz lights is available, suitable for practically every type of industrial use. Here are some suggestions for small basic lighting units.

Basic unit A (Total capacity 3 Kw)
    Colortran 3-kW Kit. (Conventional boosted bulbs)
    2 Super Kickers. 1 Cinelight King. 1 Kicker.
    Barn doors (for complete control of direction and shading)
    Diffuser holders (4) and lightweight stands (4)
    Extension cables (4)
    Spare bulbs for each lamp
    4 Macbeth daylight conversion filters
    Converter with mains cable
    Twelve spare fuses. Screwdriver. Two universal "Fitall" plugs.

Basic unit B (Total capacity 5 Kw)
    Colortran 5-kW kit (again, conventional boosted bulbs)
    2 Super 80s
    2 Cinelight Kings
    2 Kickers
    Filters, stands, cables, barn doors, diffusers
    Spares
    Converter(s)

Basic unit C (Quartz Iodine) (The most portable and practical)
    2 × Lowell quartz lamps heads with control for spot/flood adjustment
    2 × 120-V 1000-W quartz bulbs fitted
    Barn doors. Interchangeable soft/hard reflectors
    Stands

Accessories:
  Wall fixing brackets
  Spare stands, cables and barn doors
  Junction box(es)
  Filters daylight/artificial
  Diffusers
  Fuses and plugs

With a camera and lights suitable for shooting an industrial film, all you need now is a suitable sound recorder. One name immediately comes to mind: Nagra. Nagra recorders are used by many professional film teams. They have a reputation for reliability and quality performance. The Nagra 4 and the Nagra SN are both suitable for industrial purposes.

The Nagra 4 is a portable recorder designed to work either from batteries or from a mains supply. It can be carried on the shoulder quite comfortably, and the construction is rugged and entirely suitable for location use. The Nagra 4 has two input sockets for microphones and two separate inputs for line and mixer use. The microphone and line inputs each have separate volume controls but the mixer input has a set level. The two microphone inputs are connected to preamplifiers which can easily be changed. A complete range of preamps is available and each of the models has been designed for a particular kind of work. Some are particularly suitable for dynamic microphones. Others are better for use with condenser microphones. There is a complete range. The Nagra 4 is a very easy recorder to use. It can be set up quickly and is not complicated to operate. Elementary errors are automatically taken care of. A device compensates for resonance and corrects any errors made by speaking too close to the microphone. The automatic level control, which employs 27 transistors, is very useful for industrial filming where unexpectedly loud noises can occur at the most unlikely moments. The equipment can be recommended. Separate controls are provided for all the main operations, and the recorder can be used for sync. or wild recordings. Two simplified models, designed for use by people with limited technical experience, are also produced.

The Nagra SN measures only 5·8 × 4 in and weighs only 1·3 lb. It looks like a toy, though a very professionally made one. Its performance is far from a toy; it is near studio quality. It works on batteries and with continuous use one battery lasts over 7 hrs. It can also be used with an external power unit. It takes tape 3·81 mm wide and the normal tape length accommodated is 525 ft, enough for 27 minutes of recording at $3\frac{3}{4}$ ips. The machine will also run at $1\frac{7}{8}$th giving 54 minutes run or $\frac{15}{16}$ths for 108 minutes. There are separate microphone and line inputs and an output socket for external playback.

The SN drive motor was originally pioneered for use in a military project. Tape tension is servo-controlled to ensure stability, and the movement of the tape is governed by gears and not belts. Power rewind is also gear operated and the heads are moved out of position for safety when tape is being rewound. There are three heads. The first erases. The second records and the third plays back. As in the Nagra 4, the recording can be monitored as it is made by listening to the playback head. You thus can immediately hear exactly what has been recorded on the tape. An automatic level control, similar to the one used in the Nagra 4, is incorporated. The Nagra SN is a unique piece of equipment. It is portable and thus suitable for many types of filming where access is difficult. It is handy for recording wild tracks and can be used where space is at a premium. It literally slides into the pocket.

Two other recorders may be of interest to small industrial units. The Uher and the Tandberg can both be applied to synchronised sound shooting or for recording wild tracks. They are both quite good and versatile recorders. Uhers can be powered by U2 batteries or by using a rechargeable battery pack. They will also work from the mains power supply. They record at speeds ranging from $\frac{15}{16}$ to 7 ips and the usual controls for forward running and high speed rewinding are incorporated. On the 4000 Report L, there is a microphone input on the front of the machine and line inputs on the side.

Tandberg recorders are quite ruggedly built and work well for general industrial purposes. Again, sync. sound can be recorded and the equipment can also be used for recording wild tracks. One control lever governs forward and reverse movement at normal and double speeds and the equipment is solidly built. Tandberg recorders normally work on U2 batteries which seem to last well. A mains power unit is also available. They are worth examining when equipping a small industrial unit.

5

In Production

When all the necessary preparations have been made, you can set off for the first location. For an industrial film, this may mean travelling by air or sea or spending several days on the road. Or it may just mean going upstairs in the film unit's own factory. Preparations made in advance will now prove their value. If you are shooting a film and have not made the necessary preparations, you may arrive and find that you are not expected. "You've come to make a film? Oh, I haven't heard anything about this. Who are you with? Of course I'll have to check all this."

Setting up

If all has been planned, you should arrive and find your executive contact man ready for you and a local electrician waiting to be called. Instead of listening to a commissionaire complaining that no one ever tells him anything, you will be able to set up your first scene. Industrial filming requires some skill, patience and enthusiasm. Shooting in a studio is very much easier. All the lights and equipment are readily available and everyone knows filming is going on and is there for that reason only. Filming on location is a completely different matter. You often have to shoot under conditions which are far from ideal. Even a simple street scene can become complicated when equipment has to be kept out of sight and members of the public keep asking "Is it for television?" Factory filming presents other problems. In studio shooting, everyone is in some way connected with the filming. In factory shooting, this is not the case. People are working and very often cannot be interrupted. They have to go on working while the filming is taking place. Film equipment has to be set up and used without disturbing their work.

It is often difficult to rig up lights without causing a disturbance.

Even with a simple lighting set up, cables and control boxes are needed. They must be sited so the lights illuminate the scene properly, and so people working are not disturbed or able to trip over cables. It is easy to cause a serious accident by misplacing a lighting cable. I once saw a man move from one machine to another and trip over a cable knocking over a two kilowatt light. It landed a few inches from another man working nearby. A few inches nearer and the light could have killed him. On another occasion, a bulb exploded and splinters of glass shot out towards a secretary typing at her desk. The desk was covered with glass but, miraculously, the girl escaped. Accidents like these can be avoided by careful setting up.

Lights which might explode should always have wire grilles in front of them. A grille will stop large pieces of glass flying outwards. Lights should always be placed far enough from a subject to allow for an emergency. Never bring a large light close to a person's face. Light the subject from further away and use a focusing directional spotlight. And put cables and light stands in places where they cannot endanger people working near by. Cables should be slung overhead, where they are out of harm's way. If they are left on the ground they should be covered by specially shaped wooden covers. Do not take risks.

Setting up involves rigging lights and connecting them to the power supply. A local electrician will often prove invaluable as he should know where the best connection points are located. Try not to run a long cable from the power source to light heads. A long lead can produce a voltage drop and that may affect the quality of the colour from the lamps. Check the colour temperature of the lights before shooting any colour scene.

When the lights are plugged in, they should be turned on at a low voltage and allowed to warm up gradually—five or ten minutes should suffice. This is particularly important with Colortran lights. Never turn them full up straight away or you will shorten the life of the bulbs. The warm-up period also gives the people who are to be filmed the chance to get used to the unaccustomed brightness. Here, too, care is needed. Dazzle can be dangerous, particularly for people manning machines. Warn anyone who is likely to be affected before the lights are switched on and make sure they can see what they are doing when the lights are working.

Lighting a scene is the responsibility of the lighting cameraman. He decides exactly where he wants each light to point, and how much light he wants to shine on each part of the scene. Lighting a film shot is rather more complicated than lighting a scene in a still photographic studio. Movement is involved, and you have to light so that anyone moving in the course of a take moves in fields of light which are always

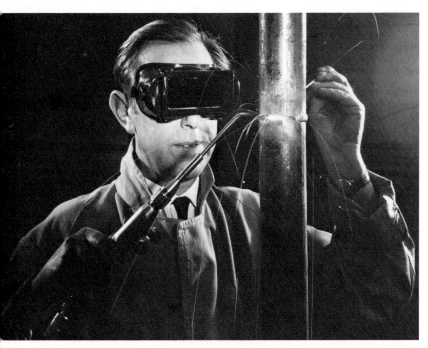

The correct method of welding with Saffire equipment is demonstrated in *Oxy-Acetylene Welding: Part 2* produced by the British Oxygen Film Unit. The film is one of a series produced by a successful and efficient internal unit. Picture: British Oxygen.

photographically acceptable. It is no use lighting a man working at an office desk on one side of the set and forgetting to light the charts he walks across to at the start of the take. His movements must be carefully plotted and lights must be placed in a way that ensures that his walk from desk to charts is along a path lit with lights of similar intensity, falling from the same general direction. If the lights are carefully placed, there should be no objectionable alteration in the lighting. If they are misplaced the man may walk from light into darkness or he may suddenly acquire three shadows, all pointing in different directions. If the man's move is to be photographed as one shot, these basic points are worth remembering. If, however, the script covers his move in two separate shots, the same problem does not arise. If, for instance, he walks from the desk out of view in one shot and into shot and up to the charts in another, the lighting cameraman is faced with a different situation. He can light the man at the desk, taking care to ensure that when he stands up he does not lose his head in any shadows. His move out of shot must also be accounted for. But there is no need to light the move across the room. The camera is stopped after the first shot, and the second shot can then be set up and lit. As films are not photographed in one continuous take, the cameraman can arrange his lights very precisely, knowing that at the end of each shot he can alter his lighting arrangements to meet the needs of the following scene.

Lighting for day or night

When lighting an industrial film set or when on location, take care with the direction of the light. It should appear as natural as possible so first take a look at the set. Are there any windows? Or lights which will be seen in use on tables, or elsewhere? If there are, the light should appear to be coming from these sources and the set must be lit accordingly. Consider a kitchen set, with a window in front of the sink. The window looks out on to a backcloth, but the audience will think it is a real window, and will expect light to be shining through it. If the scene is a night-time one, when all is dark outside, the scene should be lit to look as if the artificial light in the middle of the room is

By building up tension, the audience interest was maintained in the road safety film *Night Driving*. A drunk staggered out of a pub and audiences were encouraged to think he might walk out in front of an approaching car. Picture: Sorel Films.

loing all the work. First make your most powerful light shine from the most natural direction. This will be your key light. You can now position your other lights to fill in and soften the shadows thrown by the key light. Care must be taken not to flatten the scene completely. Shadows must be watched to ensure that they always fall in a credible direction. Lights placed too low will be over-dramatic. Normally, the majority of lights are positioned high up. With key and side lights positioned, you can now fill in the general illumination required for the rest of the scene. Batteries of floods suspended immediately above the set are very useful for this purpose. The back of the set must also be lit, otherwise the scene will lack depth.

Setting up a camera is comparatively straightforward. The lighting cameraman sets his scene and arranges the lights in the way he thinks best. At the same time, the sound recordist selects the right microphone for the scene to be filmed. He assembles his recorder and loads a reel of tape and finds the best position for the microphone.

When the camera and recorder have both been set up and the lights are turned on, the cameraman can shoot a few feet of colour test or grey scale on the head of his reel. He can also shoot a clapper board with the name of the production, the production company and the roll number chalked on it. The grey scale, or step wedge as it is often called, is a piece of card containing patches of different colour and different densities of white, from peak white to grey and through to black. It helps the laboratory to assess the printing exposure when printing a cutting copy. And it provides an accurate test for colour. The clapper ensures that the roll will not be lost. Laboratories process thousands of feet of film daily. From time to time, a reel is lost. By having the production name and company on the head of the roll the reel will be permanently identified. So if it is sent by a laboratory to the wrong customer, eventually its real ownership will be easy to trace. This kind of identification should also be recorded on the head of every sound tape roll mentioning the reel number, the tape speed and the production.

Rehearsals

When a scene has been set up, the action should be rehearsed. This sounds very professional and visions of Elizabeth Taylor and Richard Burton going through complicated lines of dialogue and numerous gestures come to mind. Alas, they are not usually involved. Yet even for a thoroughly mundane industrial film, scenes should be rehearsed, whenever possible. It may not be possible to carry out any rehearsal at all. If the people appearing in a scene are working on a continuous production line in a factory, it may not be practical to hold up their work by staging a rehearsal. Yet it may still be feasible to hold a camera rehearsal to practise all the camera movements without running the film. If the script calls for a panning shot, rehearse the pan. If the shot describes what someone on a production line is doing, make sure the camera can see exactly what has to be recorded on film. Then, when you have practised the shot, shoot it. It is rarely worth shooting without a rehearsal, however limited that rehearsal may be.

Why should an industrial film maker ever bother to rehearse a scene? The script may perhaps call for a shot of a man working a bottle capping machine. The scene has to be photographed at the end of a production line and the man featured in the shot is seen performing the job he does every day. He is used to the job and will no doubt do it very satisfactorily. Or will he?

To assume that because someone is used to doing a particular job in the course of his everyday work he will also be able to perform it satisfactorily in front of a film camera is to take much for granted. Put yourself in the same position. If you are paid to operate a machine putting caps on bottles, you do not expect to have lights shining on you from all sides and people worrying about every move you make. Filming is intimidating.

But much of the worry and anxiety can be overcome by a good film director, and he will probably want to rehearse the action. There are two reasons for the rehearsal. He will want the man appearing in the scene to get used to the lights and to feel relaxed when photographed If he has already run through the action several times, he will be more confident and relaxed when it is actually shot. The cameraman, too, will need a rehearsal. In the course of shooting even a simple shot many things can go wrong. This is particularly true when the scene calls for any kind of movement. As the bottling machine operator moves from place to place, he may cast a double shadow or move out of an even pool of light. Or he may move too close to camera that the top of his head moves out of the picture. With rehearsals such errors can be detected before film is run through. So check first, rehearse second and, when you are sure all is well, shoot.

Other factors in rehearsal

From a director's point of view, a camera rehearsal is invaluable There are many questions he must ask himself while it is going on. I the performance all right? Is it realistic? Is the person appearing in the scene looking the right way? Will the start of this shot and the end of i cut on to the preceding and following scenes without a jolt in con tinuity? Does the dialogue sound right? Are the right words being emphasised? Are there any nasty shadows or distractions which the camera might include? All these questions must be asked and answered before any film is exposed. The director can then correct the errors and run the camera for a take.

In a large film studio, the start of a take is itself quite dramatic. The large soundproof doors of the studio are closed and bells ring while lights flash to warn anyone passing near by to be quiet while a scene is being filmed. Anyone entering the studio when a red warning light is on has to be very careful not to make the slightest sound. Everything is done to enable the film crew to record with perfect sound quality and shoot excellent pictures. Industrial film makers are never so fortunate. Occasionally, a few high budget films include provision for studio filming. More often, films have to be shot entirely on location, often under conditions which are far from ideal. Yet professional results must still be obtained. The procedure for shooting is basically the same as for standard studio work. There are, however, far more hazards. Professional equipment is being used, but not in surroundings designed for shooting film. There is more noise, and there are fewer facilities and probably less time too.

After a rehearsal the director asks for the camera and recorder to be run. When both are running up to speed and the recorder is receiving a satisfactory synchronising pulse, the action can be filmed. As mentioned above, each scene should start with some form of identification and the normal method of identifying a scene is to use a clapper board, often called a slate. The clapper board is not an elaborate piece of equipment but it is a useful one. It consists of two pieces of wood hinged together so that the two parts can be banged together. The top part is a small narrow arm of wood. Below is a small blackboard with space to write the scene and take number being filmed. There's also room to write the title of the film and the production company. Sometimes the names of the cameraman and directors are also included.

Not only does the slate mark make permanent loss of the film rather unlikely, but the clapper board when banged in front of the camera makes a simultaneous sound and picture record of a fixed point—so that synchronism can be easily re-established between the sound and picture components at the editing stage.

Sound and picture are shot and edited on separate pieces of film or tape. When synchronised sound scenes are photographed the camera shoots the action on mute film stock and the sound is recorded on a tape recorder locked to the camera by a synchronising pulse. The tape is later re-recorded on perforated magnetic film. When the film reaches the editor there are two separate pieces of film to deal with: one of sound and one of picture. The two must first be synchronised, so they exactly match. The easiest way of synchronising sound and picture is to find the point on the picture where the two parts of the clapper board first touch when they are banged together. The same point can then be found on the corresponding reel containing the sound for the take. When these two points of sound and picture have been found and united, synchronism of sound and picture should be assured.

Sometimes it is not possible to shoot a clapper board on the start of a scene. At other times it is possible, but not desirable. In industrial filming this is particularly true for people who are not professional actors can easily become nervous. It takes a good director to make them relax and forget they are being filmed but if a clapper board is thrust in front of them, when the cameras are run, it will do little to help them relax or improve their performance. For this reason, scenes are sometimes "slated" on the end of a take, i.e. the clapper board is used at the end of a scene instead of at the start and held upside down to tell the editor to which scene the slate belongs and prevent him from trying to synchronise sound with the picture of the following scene. Slates should be held the right way up at the start of a scene or upside down at the end of it. If synchronised sound is being recorded, the scene number and take number should be read out before the two parts of the board are banged together to produce the clap. If no sound is recorded, the board should not be banged together but merely have the top held open. This is generally accepted practice. If you clap a silent take the editor may tear his hair out trying to find sound which doesn't exist! The clapper board has been replaced by automatic synchronising systems for some types of filming but it is still in very wide use for industrial and other work.

Clapper boards are all part of the formality of filming. Some modern film makers like to do away with convention, hand-hold the camera and shoot at random. I personally do not believe in this sort of approach. It may be all right for arty crafty technical college student exercises, but it is not much use for commercial purposes. Rules can sometimes be overlooked but only by people with enough experience to know what they are overlooking. Filming needs planning, and the plan, once made, must be carried out carefully. The surgeon who performs an operation knows what he is going to do before he cuts up the patient. He assembles his instruments and staff and follows a carefully planned programme. The programme is planned to safeguard the life and safety of his patient. The industrial film maker, too, assembles staff and tools for the job. He should also follow a planned programme. The programme will not save a life but it may save a subject by safeguarding the points made and the actions described in the final shooting script.

Shooting a film is, in many ways, a mechanical operation and it often has to be carried out with limited resources.

Shooting without sound

Many good films are shot on simple equipment. Films shot on low cost clockwork cameras have often won awards and achieved high technical standards. Ideas and professionalism bring success to a film. Elaborate equipment helps but does not, in itself, guarantee success. If a film does not include scenes of synchronised dialogue it is perfectly possible to shoot without a sound camera. Sound can be added when editing is in progress. The film can be shot on a silent camera and a commentary added later. Music and sound effects, vital to every industrial film, can also be recorded later in production. In this case the whole job of building up a soundtrack is left to the film editor. He edits the picture first and then finds all the necessary sounds. He arranges for a commentary to be recorded and will add all the incidental sounds which bring a film to life. A film soundtrack needs more than commentary. A commentary on its own will do little to bring a scene to life. Look at shots of any industrial scene. And see them without sound. A factory looks dead if you cannot hear the background noise of the machinery. A car driving past is only half there without sound. An aeroplane looks much less impressive without sound. Sound suggests reality and, for an industrial film, reality is essential. A film must capture reality as well as it can. Pictures must be supported by a full and detailed soundtrack consisting of commentary and incidental sounds—the sounds of the scenes shown in the pictures, sounds which bring the scenes to life.

If you are shooting an industrial film on limited equipment, always try to record as many location sounds as you can. You may be using a small clockwork camera to shoot the scenes. Try and obtain a suitable portable tape recorder and use it to back up your pictures with authentic location sound. You do not have to shoot and record at the same time. Indeed it is probably a good idea not to if you are using low cost equipment. Clockwork cameras are noisy and a recorder will probably record the whirr of the camera and ruin the authentic sound. It is best to shoot the scene first, then record the background sounds. The sounds you record will not match the pictures you shoot at this stage so the matching is done later in the film-cutting room. But the sounds you record make it possible to reconstruct each scene properly in the final edited version.

Location work

Many industrial films are shot entirely on location, and many locations are far from ideal for shooting film. Location filming can be pleasant, and it can be a nightmare. Careful pre-production planning can do much to ensure that the film unit enjoys the best possible conditions, but there are still many industrial locations where work will always be difficult. I have had the misfortune to film next to blast furnaces and on scaffolding high above a number of incomplete buildings and cannot really claim to have enjoyed either experience. Sometimes nothing can be done to improve a location. Sometimes it is possible to find an alternative but, in industrial work, this may not always be possible. Some shots may just be difficult to photograph. Reflections often present problems and much patience may be needed when filming objects which are shiny or reflective. Various sprays are available to help with this kind of photography, and pieces of putty can be very useful for taking the shine off when photographing highly polished metal surfaces.

Sometimes, the cost of lighting a particular location may be prohibitive. You may perhaps need an establishing shot of the interior of a large building. To light the place thoroughly would take hours and cost a small fortune, yet there may not be enough light for a daylight exposure. If you are shooting on black and white, there may be sufficient light to shoot with a camera running at reduced speed, perhaps as low as four frames per second. But remember, you cannot do this if there are people in the scene, for, when the film is shown at normal speed, the action will be speeded up considerably. If there are no people in view, this method of getting slightly longer exposure time may be a last resort. If the scene is free of movement, you can of course shoot the exposure with a still camera using flash, and then re-shoot the still on film at a later date. If you shoot the still on a large format camera, it will be perfectly possible to track into the still or to pan round it at a later stage. These techniques should only be used in emergencies. The latter method of using stills can be used when filming with colour. The former method, involving alteration of the speed of the camera motor cannot really be recommended for colour use as it can affect colour balance.

Poor lighting conditions

Lighting is one of the greatest problems facing the industrial film maker when on location. Offices can become very hot when lights are used and there is rarely enough room to work in. Factories are often busy and ill lit. Many factories have not only poor lighting but a mixture of daylight and artificial light. Flickering fluorescent tubes and naked light bulbs near skylights can give a cameraman many problems. Filming with a mixture of daylight and artificial light should be avoided whenever possible. If it is inevitable, the quality of the two different light sources should be matched by using filters. If you find your location contains a mixture of daylight and tungsten consider first the intensity of the daylight. Is there enough to make a reasonable lens aperture possible when making your exposures? If there is, look at the way the light falls on the subject you are to shoot. Are there any harsh shadows which cannot be lost by judiciously positioned white reflectors. If you can use the daylight it will save time, but you may not necessarily get the best results. Alternatively, you can black out the daylight completely and use your own lighting equipment. If you do this you will at least ensure that the lighting is exactly what you require. Sometimes, you may find the daylight comes from a window which is too high to reach. If the intensity of the light is sufficient for filming to go ahead you will indeed be lucky. Probably it is not. You will then have to augment it with artificial light, taking care to match the temperatures of the two different light sources. You can either filter the daylight, by placing large sheets of filter over all windows, or you can filter your artificial light to match the daylight. The latter course is often simpler. Non-photographic blue filters should be placed over all lights and a suitable filter for balancing daylight exposures should then be placed in the camera. Use glass filters for your lights whenever possible. Glass does not melt like gelatine and you do not have to keep a glass filter cool.

The type of light you use depends on the power source available and the type of film you use in the camera. At this stage we should consider the basic film stocks we discussed earlier to see how they might be applied under difficult lighting conditions.

High Speed Ektachrome is very useful for filming colour scenes in dimly lit locations. You will remember that there are two types of Ektachrome EF, Type 7241 for daylight and 7242 for artificial light. If you are shooting in a factory or an office where daylight is most prominent, 7241 will be the right stock to use. If there is not enough daylight to give satisfactory exposures, you can augment it with tungsten lights with the correct blue filter in front of the lights and no filter on the camera. Arc light, without filters, can also be satisfactory. Alternatively, you can blot out the daylight altogether or place special orange filter sheets over all the windows. When this has been done tungsten lighting can be used to light the location properly. Exposures could then be made on Ektachrome Tungsten light film Type 7242, or Ektachrome Commercial Type 7252, also balanced for tungsten illumination. So it is possible to balance two different light sources and get a satisfactory exposure on the Ektachrome reversal stocks. What happens if you use colour negative film? Is the same compromise possible?

Eastmancolor negative film is balanced for tungsten exposures. The colour temperature of the light should be 3200 K. The colour temperature of daylight is much higher. So, again, daylight must be filtered by placing the special orange filter sheets over the windows.

Fill-in illumination can then be used without a filter. Or alternatively, the daylight can be blocked out altogether and only tungsten lighting used. The third alternative is to shoot the scenes with a balancing filter in the camera. If you do this you can shoot with daylight flowing freely through the windows. Tungsten illumination must then be filtered to match daylight.

The colour temperature of daylight is comparatively high. If the day is cloudy it will probably be in the 6500 region of K. If the sun shines from a cloudless sky this figure will be higher. In the early mornings and in the hours before sunset, the temperature is considerably lower and scenes photographed within two hours of sunrise or sunset show how much warmer lighting of low colour temperature is. If you are shooting in colour, first of all ascertain the temperatures of the lights you are using with a colour temperature meter. Make all lights match the requirements of the film as closely as possible. A change of anything in excess of 100 K may be noticeable, although a change this small can probably be corrected in later stages of release printing. If the colour temperature is too low, a reddish bias will appear. If it is too high, blue will predominate. For this reason, regular checks must be made on the temperature of lights in use. The public electricity supply can fluctuate. A long cable from mains to lights can also reduce colour temperature. Regular checks must be carried out and corrections made when necessary. For a drop of about 100 K, a Wratten 82 filter will correct the change when using Ektachrome Commercial. The 82A would be a better filter to use if the drop is nearer 200 K. These filters should be used on the camera.

When shooting in colour, most industrial units only use the light balancing filters I have already mentioned. The fine colour correction of every scene can be undertaken later when the film is printed in a laboratory. The scenes are individually graded and filtered so the colours are correct from scene to scene. In black and white photography, camera filters are more widely used.

Control over monochrome film

Black and white photography is very much easier to work with because for it, colour temperature is of no importance whatever. Daylight and artificial light can be freely mixed. Filters of another kind are, however, widely used.

You will recall that panchromatic film is sensitive to all colours. This is true, but the way in which colours are reproduced in black and white can also be controlled or modified with the aid of filters. Filters have numerous uses in black and white filming. If you are shooting out of doors on a misty day, and want to clear away some of the haze, a yellow filter will help. An orange filter will make a sky more dramatic by darkening the blue and making the white clouds to stand out in contrast. And if you want to make even innocent clouds look really menacing, a red filter may produce an even more exaggerated effect. Sometimes a scene may appear vivid and full of bright contrasts when seen by the human eye yet when photographed in black and white it may appear flat and lifeless. A skilful use of filters can do much to prevent this and make the change from colour to black and white satisfactory. If you want to make a colour darker, use a filter of complementary colour. The general rule is that if you want to lighten it, you use one of the same colour. If you have a red apple in a colour picture, it will look quite impressive. In black and white, much of the impact is lost. But by placing a blue-green filter over the camera lens, the apple will appear black. If you want it to look white, place a red filter over the lens. Blue-green is the complementary colour to red. Blue itself is complementary to orange and reddish-purple to green. Purple-blue is complementary to yellow and orange is complementary to blue. The apple example is rather a drastic one. You do not usually want to show something as either black or white, but are more interested in getting a variety of controlled shades of grey. Filters can help. The lighter the colour you seek to alter, the less the effect of the alteration will be. It is much easier to make a bright colour interesting in black and white.

Sometimes when filming on location, you may find the sky is not as you would like it. Perhaps it is too light, or not light enough. If the sky is a light blue, you can make it white with a dark blue filter, or black by using a red one. Yellow filters of differing intensities increase the darkness of the sky from light grey to dark grey. If a really dark grey is wanted, a pale orange filter will produce the required effect. A really deep red filter can also be used to simulate night conditions when filming in daylight, though do not look for a full range of flesh tones where this method has been applied. An alternative is the neutral density (ND) filter, which is designed to reduce the overall brilliance of any scene without altering any one particular colour. This filter is extremely handy if you are ever unfortunate enough to be caught in bright sunlight with a film which is too fast to use. An ND filter should reduce the light quite satisfactorily. With ND filters exposures would normally be increased from the standard reading by the amount corresponding to the light which the filter has actually cut off—i.e. the filter factor. In the case of over bright subjects, the ND filter brings the exposure down to within the range of the camera-aperture. Every filter has its own particular factor and these can usually be found in the leaflets supplied with sets of filters. Light balancing filters, used to adapt tungsten films for daylight and daylight films for tungsten, do not usually have a filter factor. The exposure adjustment required is calculated in the exposure index recommended for use with the film. Commercial Ektachrome, for example, is rated at 25 ASA for normal use with tungsten lighting. An exposure index of 16 is recommended when the film is exposed in daylight with a Wratten 85 filter. Before shooting, consider the speed of the film and any filter factor which could mean that the lens setting should be further adjusted. It is easy to overlook this kind of thing amid the preparations.

Directing

When filming is in progress the film director is in charge. He is responsible for the finished film and he controls the filming in a studio or on location. Directing an industrial film is full of problems. Problems needing a great deal of patience and a complete knowledge of every stage of film making. "I want to be a film director" is a sentiment often expressed by people trying to get into the film industry. There are people who seriously believe that you can step out of a technical college into a professional production company and direct a film. I

Often, the people appearing in an industrial film are not professional actors, and have never appeared in front of a camera before. The director must make them feel relaxed to get a good performance on film.

An excellent example of a sponsored film which is not hard selling. James Hill's delightful treatment of a sleepy Italian garage made *Giuseppina* a pleasure to watch. Picture: British Petroleum.

do not believe in this policy. I personally feel that before anyone can direct anything he must know all the technicalities involved. He must know about camerawork so that he can understand a cameraman's problems. He must know about sound recording, so that he only asks the recordist to do what he himself knows to be possible. And he must understand editing. It is no coincidence that many top film directors have been editors in their time. Before you can edit a film you must know all about continuity. An editor knows exactly what he needs in terms of sound and picture. A director has to provide what the editor needs. A director should know as much as he can about all the technical operations involved in making a film. Directing an industrial film requires special skills, for the director is often working under very difficult conditions.

Directing for television or the cinema involves working with people who are often used to being filmed. Professional actors and actresses are also accustomed to being directed. Industrial films are different. Often the people appearing in a scene are not professional actors and have never appeared in front of a camera before. And crew conditions are often far from ideal, so no one is very happy when filming begins.

A director can make or break a picture. If he knows what he is doing, he will make people feel relaxed and get a good performance on film. And he will keep his crew on his side. He will show them that he knows what he is talking about and so they respond. A bad director may shoot much material which cannot be satisfactorily put together. And he will often give all taking part a very difficult time.

A young man recently approached me asking for a job. He, of course, wanted to be a film director. He was about 26 and I asked him what experience he had of film. He produced a folder containing press cuttings from his local newspaper collected over a ten-year period. In most of the pictures the young man was clearly featured wearing a jacket with the word "director" in large letters across his back, and carrying a Hollywood style megaphone! That was his idea of a film director. The other side of the pictures usually showed a small amateur film unit working with a clockwork 8-mm camera. Out of curiosity, I agreed to see one of his films. It was quite indescribable. The man had no idea whatever about the techniques of making a film. He just wanted to be a director.

A good film director is totally unlike the man with his newspaper cuttings. This is particularly true of the director of an industrial film. Tact and a sound technical knowledge are the two most important qualities. An ability to get on with people and make them feel they matter is also essential. If people feel they matter, they will usually work well. And if a crew see that the director knows what he wants and what he is doing, they will know their time is not being wasted.

Once a director has made known what he wants a shot to show the crew rig the scene themselves. The lighting cameraman arrange the lights and the recordist places the microphone and his recorder in the most suitable position. The director can then rehearse the action. The recordist can check his sound recording levels and the cameraman his camera movements while the director watches the fine points of the action. A rehearsal does not waste film, so the scene can be rehearsed over and over again if necessary, while the director checks the rehearsal with the script. He asks himself if the action taking place is what the script requires. Then he will consider the preceding and following scenes and ask himself if the shot he is currently preparing will fit into its allocated place in the final edited film. Continuity is one of his first considerations.

Continuity

Continuity is an important word in film making. You have probably seen scenes in badly made films where continuity requirements have been forgotten or disregarded. Continuity means smoothness in ransition from scene to scene. It is particularly important when the ame subject is observed in a number of consecutive scenes. Consider n example taken from the Lifton film I outlined earlier.

Lifton: Script (Extract)

1. Int. Day. CMS. We see the whole of the Lifton equipment. The fore-man painter takes a tin of Lifton from the shelves in front of him and stirs the paint with the built-in stirrer.

Cut

2. Int. Day. CU. The tin is stirred. We see how the built-in stirrer makes the job easy.

Cut

3. Int. Day. CU. The paint, now stirred, is poured into an empty tin on the Lifton scales.

Cut

4. Int. Day. CU. Paint flows freely from the pourer, built into the tin.
5. Int. Day. CU. The paint reaches the required level and the pouring stops.

Cut

6. Int. Day. CMS. Foreman painter replaces tin on racks.

Here we have six very simple shots all forming part of one sequence nd all showing one operation carried out by one man. The foreman ainter is seen in all scenes. In ordinary language the work he does in he scenes can be described in one sentence. He removes a tin from the ack in front of him, stirs it, fills an empty tin on the scales and then eplaces the tin he has poured. But, on film, this action is shown in six eparate shots. Six shots designed to hold the interest of an audience uring what is basically a very dull operation. The scenes have been lanned to show the action in a reasonably interesting way and to focus ttention on two Lifton sales points: the stirring handle, designed to nake stirring easy, and the pourer, designed to eliminate drips. Both are hown in close up. There are six scenes in the sequence and each is to e filmed separately. The director will be responsible for each scene. Vhat does he have to do?

When the first scene has been set and lit he rehearses the action. Ie watches during the rehearsal to see if anything needs alteration. There are no camera movements, so one possible source of faults is liminated. He can focus his attention on the action being rehearsed. The rehearsal starts. The foreman painter takes a tin from the rack and tarts to stir it. He holds the tin firmly and turns the handle built into he lid. Then he pours the paint into an empty tin on the scales. He ours the correct amount, then replaces the tin in the rack it came from. The director decides to shoot the whole operation as a close medium hot. The script does not ask for this. The scripted sequence does lowever start and end with a CMS and the director feels it would be good idea to take the whole sequence through from this camera osition. He then re-sets and shoots the closer views as inserts. He shoots

like this for two reasons. He feels the painter will be more at ease if he
does the whole job right through, in the way he is used to. And the
editor will have more cutting freedom if he has one master shot which
he can cut into, and out of, at the points he thinks best.

After the rehearsal, the director has a few quiet words with the
painter. A few quiet words do far more good than instructions shouted
across a room. They make the man appearing in the scenes less self-con
scious, and ensure that he knows what he is supposed to do and what he
must not do. The director noticed several points he did not like during
the rehearsal and he is now sorting them out with the painter. At the star
of the scene, he took the tin out of the rack and started to stir the
paint. The first part was very good, but when he started to stir, the
name on the tin was hidden by the painter's hands. Could he hold i
slightly differently so that the Lifton name could be seen? The director
and the painter try various ways of holding the tin. The painter want
to find a way that is comfortable so that he can stir with ease. The
director wants to ensure that the way the tin is held looks natural. He
does not want it to look pre-arranged, even if it is!

When the paint was poured, the director noticed that drips crep
down the outside of the tin and covered the painter's fingers. It looked
messy, and made the product look difficult to use. So he asked the
painter if there is another way of holding the tin when pouring, so tha
drips would not fall in the wrong direction. The problems are sorted ou
and the action is again rehearsed. Everything seems to be all right, so
the director prepares for a take. The camera runs, the scene is identified
and the action begins. All goes well at first. The tin comes out of the
rack and the painter holds it and stirs it correctly. But he is having
difficulty pouring. The paint splurts out too fast, and covers the outside
of the tin. The scene will have to be taken again. On the second take
the paint flows smoothly but at the end of the shot the painter puts the
tin back in the rack with the label facing away from camera. So take
three is shot. This time everything goes well.

The director now asks the crew to reset for the second scripted
shot: the close-up of the stirring in progress. This is a much tighter
shot. The editor will cut it into the master shot which has just been
photographed, so it is vital that the director exactly matches the action
of the two takes. The man must hold the paint tin exactly the same way
and stir it at the same speed as he did in the last take. The camera must
be carefully lined up. Last time we saw the whole working area. This
time we only see the one can being stirred, so the camera must be lined
up with great precision.

The cameraman asks if the painter can go through the action again
so that he can find out exactly where the tin will be positioned. The
point is traced, and the director again rehearses the action. He watches

the tin and makes sure it is held in the same way. Again, he starts with the tin in the rack. Only this time the camera starts without the tin in view. It is concentrating on the area where the tin is stirred. The director is shooting the first part of the scene again as an overlap to give the editor more cutting freedom. When cutting from mid-shot to close-up, he can either cut to the closer view before the tin comes into shot or he can stay on the mid-shot until stirring begins, and then cut to the closer view. The camera runs, and the action is photographed. This time the director notices that the man is stirring the paint more vigorously than he did when the mid-shot was photographed. So the scene is shot again. This time he stirs at the same speed so the two shots could be cut together. Or could they? No. The painter has his thumb rather too far across the label. In the last take it was alongside the last of the letters on the label. This time it half obscures the letter "L" on the tin. A small point, but one which would immediately be noticed if the two takes were cut together, and one the director has to notice and retake.

So, directing an industrial film needs tact and powers of observation. There are many aids to help maintain continuity in filming. None of these is a substitute for a director with a good memory and well developed powers of observation. On a major film set, a girl is employed to look after continuity. She watches for the sort of unintentional differences which can occur from scene to scene. Industrial film makers are rarely fortunate enough to have a continuity girl. There are, however, two other aids which can sometimes prove useful. A Polaroid camera makes it possible to take a photograph and produce a print within seconds. This is very handy when shooting as you can shoot the end of a take and make sure that the positions are matched when filming the start of the following scene. Closed circuit television can also be helpful, though the equipment needed often makes it impracticable. If time and space allow, a scene being filmed can be recorded simultaneously on videotape. The tape can then be replayed and the results immediately assessed. This is, however, rarely done when shooting an industrial film.

Continuity involves matching the action from scene to scene. Continuity of appearance is also very important. Where two people appear in two consecutive scenes, their appearance must be the same in both shots. If they are wearing blue boiler suits and white shirts in one shot, they must wear the same in the next shot. That is pretty obvious, but other smaller points are easily overlooked. You will remember that one of the main differences between shooting a film and recording a television presentation is that filming is a discontinuous process. One scene is prepared and shot, then everything stops while the next scene is lit and made ready for filming. Now, if a sequence of shots is being photographed, particular attention must be paid to the continuity requirements of each scene. I have already explained the need to match the action from shot to shot. Let us now turn our attention to the people appearing in the shots. Do they look exactly the same at the start of Scene Two as they did at the end of Scene One? Or has someone ruffled his hair or removed his tie. It may not look very different when the scenes are being filmed. But when the shots are cut together, the differences will be very noticeable.

An industrial unit called on the head office of a bank to film an interview with the managing director. They spent two hours in the morning shooting the basis of the interview and the managing director then went away to keep a lunch appointment.

In the afternoon the same unit reassembled to shoot some more of the interview. The director decided that, having shot all the morning material on a close mid-shot, they would shoot all the afternoon shots from a closer viewpoint. Then in the cutting room, the two filming sessions could be cut together. The afternoon session seemed to go well and the film unit sent the film away to be processed. When it came back they had a very unpleasant surprise. In all the morning material the managing director wore a plain white shirt. In the lunch hour he must have changed it, for all the afternoon shots showed him in a shirt with a deep blue stripe. No one had noticed when the scenes were shot, but the difference was so obvious on film that the two sessions could never be cut together. The director had not paid enough attention to continuity.

This kind of mistake is easily made in industrial filming. Only care will avoid it. There are other continuity errors which can present problems too. In our Lifton film, the level of paint in the tin being poured has to be carefully matched in the long shot and in the closer view. When showing a machine in two adjacent shots, make sure the machine is doing the same job in the same way at the same speed at the cutting point. When filming shots designed to form part of a sequence, always ask yourself if everything is the same at the beginning of the second shot as it was at the end of the first. Then, if the two are identical at the editor's cutting point, there should be no problem in putting the shots together.

Continuity of action

It may sometimes seem impossible to achieve smooth continuity in an industrial scene. Perhaps you do not want to show the whole of an operation. If you are filming a man fitting a new windscreen to a car, the script may call for shots showing the start and the end of the job. Perhaps the first shot is designed to show how a windscreen first slots into position. The second shot shows how the last length of reaining rubber is sealed. But fitting a windscreen takes several minutes, and no one wants to watch a film of the whole job. Yet if you start the camera and shoot the first part of the action then stop and restart again, when the last part of the job is taking place, the scenes will never cut together satisfactorily. When the two are shown together, the man fitting the windscreen will be in one place one moment and in a completely different place for the second take. He will appear to jump from place to place. This kind of jumping is not good filming. It is disturbing to view and is only seen in shoddy film making.

There are two ways in which the two parts of the window fitting job can be shown without watching the whole operation. You could start with the first part of the job and use an optical dissolve to the second part. It is better to use optical effects than to jump from shot to shot, though even this is not very good. We will examine how optical effects can best be used later.

The alternative way of telescoping the time taken fitting the window is by using what is known as a "cutaway". A cutaway is an intermediate shot showing something other than the main theme of the action. It could be a close-up of the fitter's face or his hands. It must not show the window or the position of the man alongside the car. First shoot the start of the window fitting, on a wide shot. At a suitable point, cut and position the camera shooting only the man's face. Do not show what he is doing. Make sure he is looking in the same direction as he was in the last scene and get him to run through the action again. You are only shooting his face but, if he carries out the same familiar action, he will move in the right way at the right speed. Then, after filming this intermediate shot, you can line up the second wide view, showing the window fitting being completed. Again, match the position of the man's head and make sure he is looking in the same direction at your cutting point. When the film is assembled later, you can start with the wide shot of the window being inserted, hold that shot for a few seconds so that the audience can see what is going on and then cut to the shot of the man's face: the cutaway. Finally, after a brief pause on the cutaway, you cut to the shot of the window completion. You now have a sequence which shows what the script requires without making the action visibly jump. The cutaway has acceptably excused what would otherwise have been a bad jump in picture continuity.

Shooting without a script

Sometimes you may have to shoot without a script. This should be avoided whenever possible, but it is not always possible to plan in advance. Internal film units are particularly liable to get a phone call asking them to work at short notice. The calls usually come from the sort of people who imagine that films flow out of a tap!

What is the best way to set about shooting without a script? Again, cutaways are essential. Most subjects can be covered satisfactorily by shooting long establishing shots. Closer views can then concentrate on the detail of the action. And cutaways, for editing purposes, should always be filmed. Every subject demands different treatment, but the need for cutaways is always the same. Always remember that a script calls for a variety of different types of shot. If you are shooting without a script you have to remember the need for long shots, medium shots and close-ups, and shoot what you can. Always try and establish a scene with a general view before you go into detail. Make sure that the theme of your subject can be followed from what you record on film.

Shooting synchronised dialogue

We have already discussed the equipment needed to shoot and record synchronised sound. And we know that the sound and picture of each scene must be identified by using a clapper board on either the start or the end of the take. Now let us consider the ways in which a simple dialogue scene can be set up and photographed—a sequence featuring a discussion between two people. It could be part of a training film, or it could be the managing director answering questions put by an interviewer. How is this action best put on film?

There are a number of different ways of observing every kind of scene. If two people are holding a discussion the camera can show both people at once or one after the other. It can take a wide view, showing both people from floor level to the tops of their heads or it can take a closer view and show them both from the waist upwards. There are other alternatives too. The camera can shoot at right angles to the two people, so one is on the left of the screen and the other on the right. This way they are both given equal prominence. If you move the camera further round until it gives you one person's view of the other person you have another alternative for the camera position. This position can be reversed. For example, in the first shot the camera shoots over the shoulder of the interviewer, including him on one side of the picture with his back to the camera, and showing the subject being interviewed facing the camera, on the other side. The reverse approach would give a general view favouring the interviewer. From this position the camera can be moved in closer, to concentrate on one person only or such a shot can be cut in directly, following a shot of the other person.

If you have to shoot an *unscripted* dialogue scene, and there are so many alternatives when working without a script, what are the best positions to use?

iroup dialogue scenes are often centred on one individual, with shots of other participants
itercut here and there through the sequence. In these shots it is essential to have the person
eplying looking in the right direction relative to the questioner. A still from *A Tale Out of
School* Picture: British Transport Films.

With interview sequences, you can adopt a simple formula
although there are many ways of shooting any interview and each
producer has his own ideas and preferences. One of the simplest to set
up and carry through quickly uses three basic shots. It is often employed by television producers and is ideal for industrial films. First,
position the interviewer and the person being questioned. When they
have been satisfactorily placed, move the camera up for a close-up of
the person being questioned. Do not show the interviewer, just con-
entrate on whoever is providing the answers. Run the camera and
ecorder and let the interviewer ask the questions and film this person
hroughout all the questions and answers. Make absolutely sure that
he man answering is looking in the right direction. He should look
t the interviewer and, if the camera has been correctly positioned, will
ppear through the viewfinder to be looking almost centre screen. When
ll the questions have been asked and answered, stop shooting and re-
et. Move the camera back to get a wide two shot of the interviewer and
he person being questioned. Show only the back of the interviewer and
he front view of the other person. Shoot enough to establish the scene.

And let the interviewer say a few words. Run the camera, but not the recorder, and shoot off a minute or so of this introductory material. Make sure the interviewer is talking. You will not see his lip movements but you will be aware that he is talking because there will be a very slight movement of the chin perceptible even from the back camera view. Do not let the interviewee answer or open his mouth at all. Make him keep his eyes on the man asking the questions. The object of this shot is to provide a cutaway and an establishing shot. When the film is edited the interviewer's first questions can be placed over the shot. Then when the man starts to answer, the editor can cut to the close shot filmed first.

One further shot should be filmed if time allows—of the interviewer, seen from the subject's viewpoint. Known as a "reverse" shot, this must be carefully lined up so the eyelines of interviewer and subject are the same. You do not see the subject in this shot but the interviewer must still look in the right direction. So if the subject looked right to left in his close-up, the interviewer must now look left to right at the same eye level. This time you can run both picture and sound. Let the interviewer ask again the questions he asked before. This time no one will answer, and the questions can follow each other one by one. The camera will record the action and sound will record the questions. Later, all three shots can be edited together to make one version. The change of camera angle will preserve the pace and interest of the film.

Importance of pace

Pace is vitally important in an industrial film. A film which appears to drag will seldom prove successful. To preserve the pace, a number of shots must be photographed from carefully thought-out camera angles. And the camera positions must be planned so that the shots can be cut together. Every scene must be observed in terms of film. A man demonstrating a crane can be observed from one position using a camera giving a general view of the whole demonstration. But if the shot lasts for more than 30 seconds, an audience may lose interest. It is extremely dull to watch any one shot for a long time. The human eye tires quickly and constant changes of view are necessary if audience interest is to be maintained. The man demonstrating a crane in my earlier example should be observed from a number of different camera positions. Long shots immediately establish the location and show what is being demonstrated. Close-ups show how it works and how it is controlled, and cutaways show the man in charge of the demonstrations. In the final edited film scene follows scene and audience interest is maintained throughout.

Value of close-ups

Industrial films can sometimes benefit from the extensive use of close-ups. This is particularly true when a film is shot on 16 mm. If the film is to be shown on a large screen, close-ups usually look better than long shots though I am certainly not suggesting that a film should consist only of close-ups. Long shots and medium shots also have their place. Close-ups can be particularly advantageous in training films as they focus attention on detail. In the Ford tractor training film

Comparative close up pictures from the Unilever film *Fluid Flow* showing the relative viscosity of fluids by direct comparison in close up. Picture: Unilever Films.

I have already mentioned, close-ups were used to concentrate attention on the key pieces of equipment and *all* points needing close examination were studied in close-up—how to drain a fuel pump, how to change an oil filter, how to find the correct oil level in a gearbox and so on. By using close-ups, the work being carried out could be very easily seen. But the whole film was not shot in close-up. Each sequence began with a wider view because it is no use knowing how to drain a fuel pump or change an oil filter if you do not know where it is. After the general view the camera then directed attention to the appropriate point to study the details.

Shooting record

Whenever you shoot, always keep detailed sound and picture report sheets. A camera sheet should list the name of the production unit and the title of the film. The names of the cameraman and the director should also be listed at the top. The type of film stock must be clearly marked together with detailed laboratory instructions. At the end of each day's filming the top copy of the sheet should be sent with the exposed film to the laboratory. Details of the type of film must be precise, so list the type of stock as well as the speed at which it has been rated, and make a note of any processing instructions necessary.

A camera sheet is divided into a number of different columns. The columns should be used to list every single scene and take. Alongside the scene and take number, space is left for comments. The second copy of a report sheet is usually sent to the film editor, and comments likely to help him can often be written in this space. There may also be an instruction printed on the top of the sheets telling the laboratory to "print only circled takes", or sometimes "print only takes marked 'P' ". There is a chance here to save money, for although the laboratory will have to process every foot of the film exposed in the camera, it is not necessary to print every scene. If several takes have proved a disaster and are not worth printing, the letters "NG" should be marked alongside the scene and take numbers on the camera sheet. Where a scene is satisfactory, the letter "P" should be marked, or alternatively, the take number should itself be marked round with a circle. The laboratory will process all the original film, but when the original is printed, and a cutting copy is produced for editing purposes, it will only print the takes you have circled or marked with a letter "P". The cost of making prints of useless takes will thus be saved.

Although this method of printing selected takes can reduce costs it is sometimes misused and, if used in the wrong way, can prove very unsatisfactory. There are a few points worth remembering. A laboratory can only print selected takes if the scenes and takes are clearly identified by a clapper board. It is not worth missing out short "NG" takes but only long takes running for several minutes. If there are a few short "NG" takes, it is cheaper and quicker to print up the whole of one roll. But if you have shot 400 ft and only one 100-ft take is any use at all, it may be worth asking the laboratory to print only that take. But make sure that the take is clearly identified. If the 400-ft reel consists of 300 ft of good material and 100 ft of doubtful scenes at different parts of the roll, it is better to print the whole roll and throw away afterwards what you do not want. Printing selected takes involves extra handling of the master and some laboratories also make a special charge. It is only an economy, and only worthwhile when large "NG" footages are involved.

In the Dunlop film *New Concept* a new total mobility tyre was tested under different conditions. A film camera was mounted on the front of a car in a similar position to the stills camera shown here. Eastmancolor 16mm film was exposed at normal speed and in slow motion. The results showed the contrast between a total mobility tyre and a conventional tyre when both were run without air. The conventional tyre came off the wheel at 3 m.p.h. The total mobility tyre could still be driven at speeds up to 100 m.p.h. Film is extremely valuable in carrying out tests of this kind. Pictures: Dunlop Film Unit.

Slow motion

Some industrial films call for special techniques. One of the most widely used special effects is slow motion photography. It can be of great value in an industrial training film. Slow motion can be used to check the operation of a machine or to analyse a working procedure. Many factories use the technique for work study and research purposes. It is also used when testing prototypes of new plant. When Concorde was being designed, scale models were extensively tested and the results were analysed by using slow motion film. Britax, manufacturers of car seat belts, carried out extensive laboratory tests to find out exactly what happens to a driver of a car when he crashes into an obstacle. They used dummies and special equipment to simulate the effects of crashes at 30 and 60 miles per hour. Seen in the test shed, the crashes occurred and passed in a split second, far too fast for any worthwhile lesson to be learned. But the tests were filmed in slow motion and when the results were replayed the real value of the tests could be seen. Slow motion has many applications. And it should not present any major technical problems.

The slow motion effect is achieved by increasing the filming rate from the normal 24 fps, i.e. more film must pass through the camera in the same period of time. When the extra footage is then projected at normal (sound) speed the action appears to take place more slowly. Material shot at 48 fps (twice normal speed) when projected will slow the action to half its normal rate. At 100 fps the action is a quarter normal speed, and 400 fps gives a very good impression of slow motion. I recently saw some scenes of a golfer driving off, shot at normal speed and at 400 fps. At normal speed the golfer could be seen preparing to hit the ball, addressing it and carrying the stroke through. It all happened quickly, and the ball was on the tee one moment and then nowhere to be seen. At 400 fps, the same operation took 350 ft of film. The camera was noisy so it had to be run before the golfer made his shot, so the noise didn't put him off. The actual stroke took nearly 200 ft of film. But it was a remarkable shot, and it showed far more than the normal speed exposure. The club bent with the stress as it was brought down to hit the ball and the ball itself changed shape as the club hit it and drove it off the tee. The follow through was almost poetry! Slow motion showed much more.

So, to get a slow motion effect you have to speed up the camera. But slow motion does present some problems. Many cameras will run at up to 64 fps but few run above this speed. Slow motion cameras for really slowed down effects are specialist pieces of equipment. Filming slow motion is similar to ordinary filming except that you need plenty of light. This is because film passes through the camera so fast that exposure time is drastically shortened.

Stop motion

Another type of specialised camera effect of interest to industrial users is stop motion. High speed filming and slow motion work both involve moving film continuously through the camera at either slow or fast speed. Stop motion work involves exposing the film one frame

In *Motorway* the results of trying to brake on a wet road in a car with worn tyres were illustrated dramatically. The film received a very wide showing and is used by most UK police forces. Pictures: Sorel Films.

at a time. One frame is exposed. Another is moved into place. Time passes, then a further, individual frame exposure is made. The time lapse between exposures can be controlled. Time lapse photography is a very specialised activity and the main application is in research and work study. By telescoping time, long term events can be made to happen quickly and their action can be more easily observed in this fashion. The most familiar example is of a flower being filmed from bud to bloom. By exposing frame by frame at predetermined intervals, the development of the flower can be followed. When the frames are projected one after the other continuously at normal speed, the flower will appear to grow and bloom in a matter of seconds. Industrial film makers may not film flowers, but they may well use stop motion. By setting a camera up overlooking a factory floor, and exposing one frame every minute throughout the day, the exact pattern of movement of people working on the floor can be seen and future layout and developments can be planned with the results in mind. There are many other industrial applications for stop motion and it involves little expense. It is easy to operate and you do not need bright illumination though efforts should be made to keep the light consistent throughout the exposures.

Keep it simple

The small internal unit, working with very limited equipment, will often find it has to overcome seemingly insuperable problems. It is important for a small unit to avoid being too ambitious. Do not attempt to tackle big scenes and light big areas, but settle for a simple film You can still make it interesting and still make it pacy. Concentrate on getting good quality raw materials. Shoot, shoot and shoot until you are sure it is perfect.

Perfection is sadly lacking in too many industrial films. Standards are abysmally low and there are several reasons for this. Too many sponsors are prepared to settle for second best. Often they do this because they do not know what best is, and do not set themselves a high enough standard. Too many producers are ill equipped or inexperienced. There are hundreds of small breakaway film companies and though a few are very good indeed, many are struggling without enough capital, with inadequate equipment and keen, but inexperienced staff. Shooting an industrial film is never easy. But if a film is to be made at all, it should be made properly.

Subject and camera movement

There are still some companies who insist on thrusting a film camera into inexperienced hands. At a recent showing of industrial films, three films were presented by one internal film unit. One had been shot by a stills photographer loaned to the films officer to cut salary costs and save money. The scenes were beautifully exposed but they should never have been presented to an audience. Having been given a movie camera, the cameraman decided to move. And move he did. Every shot was a pan round one way or another and the violent movements were always carried out too rapidly for anything to be seen or appreciated. Zoom shots were carried out at lightning pace too, and accompanied by loss of focus.

Panning and zooming

When shooting a film with a movie camera, some people, like the man who was just mentioned, feel that they have to move the camera all the time. This, of course, is completely untrue. The camera should be held as still as possible. The *action* moves, not necessarily the camera. I would advise a still cameraman using a film camera for the first time to set it on a tripod and shoot each scene from a static position. Start the camera long before the action and keep it running after the action has finished for a few frames. It is difficult to shoot too much film but it is very easy to shoot too little. If camera movements are essential, it is best to pan *with* a subject, holding it in the middle of the picture. Always pan slowly and hold the beginning and the end of the pan before and after the camera movement. Start the camera running and hold it still long enough for an audience to see and appreciate the reason for the shot. Then pan, slowly, again letting the audience see what is going on. End the pan at a point which is, itself, an interesting shot. Again, keep the camera running for long enough to see what is happening. Then stop. The same rules apply to zoom shots. If you have a zoom lens on the camera and you are not used to shooting cine film, do not zoom on every shot but use the lens at different set points. Use it to get a long shot, then stop and tighten up for a mid-shot. When it is composed and focused, shoot, then stop and reset again. Do not zoom unless you are used to the correct camera movements. Zooms must be smooth and well planned.

Sound recordings

Recording sound for an industrial film also requires skill. Even if there is no synchronised sound, wild tracks should be recorded. Basic sound equipment consists of a recorder, a supply of $\frac{1}{4}$-in tapes and a selection of cables and microphones.

There are several types of microphone and it is important to select the right one for each job. Some are more directional than others and can pick up sound from one area only and will hear selectively what they are aimed at. Omnidirectional microphones, as their name suggests, pick up sound from a much wider area. There are large microphones which have to be mounted on stands and radio microphones so small they can be hidden behind a tie.

Cardioid microphones are quite suitable for general industrial use. A uni-directional cardiod microphone can pick up dialogue or record sound effects some distance from the subject. A small condenser microphone is often suitable for the same kind of work though both types must be used with care. In industrial work they are ideal for recording the general sound of a scene or for picking up dialogue spoken by several people in a small area where there is no heavy background sound. Always beware of background noise. It can drown important details. Filming in a workshop or factory for any length of time, it is easy to get used to the general level of background noise yourself and forget about it. But, when you record, the background will be very much in evidence. Always record a track of general background noise. Then move in close to any detailed sounds featured in the action and record them with as little background as possible. If you go close, you should be able to make an individual sound stand out on its own.

Background sound can be a serious problem when recording synchronised dialogue on location. If you use an overhead microphone, the background noise may obscure the sound of the voices you wish to hear. In cases like this it is often best to give the speakers individual chest microphones. They can hide them under their clothing and the voices should then be clear to hear. A separate background noise track can be recorded later. When the two tracks are dubbed together the sound mixer will be able to make the voices clear and add just enough of the background noise to make the scene look and sound authentic.

Chest microphones can give good results. They can also present a few problems. As the microphone is resting against the person speaking, every sound he or she utters will be picked up, and every rustle of clothing will also be heard. Try not to put a chest microphone on top of a pure nylon shirt or tie as the sound of microphone movement on the shirt is very objectionable. Silk ties too can cause trouble.

Chest microphones can also be used without an attaching cable. Instead, a small frequency modulated transmitter can be placed in the speaker's pocket and a receiver near the sound mixer. Here again, check for trouble. As the sound travels through the air, other extraneous sounds can be collected. Clicks and bangs are very easily picked up when filming near industrial equipment. Police messages and radio cars can also be recorded accidentally. Wherever possible use a separate microphone mounted on a boom held over the scene. It should be as near the source of sound as possible, and of course, out of the camera's view. And beware of boom shadows, particularly if there are camera movements in the course of a shot. When filming out of doors, wind can prove a hazard. It can completely ruin a recording and there is not very much you can do with an ordinary microphone in a howling gale. A wind gag will reduce wind noise considerably and can make a light wind inaudible by keeping air currents away from the microphone. A small piece of foam covering the top of a microphone can also be very useful for the same purpose out of doors.

The cast

One of the main problems in shooting an industrial film is that of finding a suitable cast to appear in front of the camera. Some industrial film makers use actors, but many find the cost of employing professionals too high. Is a cast of actors essential? Many producers feel it is impossible to shoot anything worthwhile without actors who have been thoroughly trained. I have never found this to be the case, though if dialogue scenes are involved, actors are usually able to produce better results quickly. Many completely inexperienced people can give first class performances if they are properly directed and not asked to attempt the impossible.

Consider first, three types of industrial film. One type consists of factory and office scenes showing the production and use of a company's products. Another, like the Lifton film described earlier, shows two fictitious companies manned by staff whose characters have been planned to project a particular image of their work. And a third type of production, a training film, where long dialogue scenes are scripted. Now, do we use professional actors or not? Look at the first example.

Factual scenes

If a film shows the company's factories and products in production and in use, it usually has to be shot on location in the company works. Sometimes additional scenes may be needed and some may have to be staged. I personally always prefer to shoot factory scenes with the people who normally do the jobs appearing in the film. It does not seem practical or worth while replacing a machine operator or a draughtsman with an actor. Shoot the man who is accustomed to doing the job and he will usually look right on film. This is a general rule, to which there are some exceptions. And the exceptions can sometimes be embarrassing.

It is obviously better to show someone reasonably good looking or smart in any close shots. When filming on a production line this can

The Groundnut, an industrially sponsored film for school use. Hard selling techniques would have made such a film unacceptable in the classroom. Picture: Unilever Films.

The films *Antarctic Crossing*, and its predecessor *Foothold on Antarctica* both got cinema and television showings. Films of this kind, though not cheap to produce, do much to promote a good company image. Picture: British Petroleum.

lead to trouble. For example, when filming in a whisky bottling plant recently, I had to shoot various stages of the main production line. The line was staffed by girls who operated various machines controlling the filling of the bottles, the sealing of the caps and labelling for despatch. One shot, specified in the script, was a close-up of the operator using a labelling machine. When I visited the location to reconnoitre, I noticed that the machine was being operated by a very presentable blonde. Good, I thought, on this occasion I'm in luck—as far as the film shot was concerned, of course! When I returned with the crew three weeks later, the blonde had been replaced by a woman who was quite unsuitable. I was rather worried about this, for to show this woman operating the labelling machine would have been a great mistake.

While the crew set up I had a quiet word with the factory production manager. I should have explored the staff problem on my earlier visit for I soon discovered that the production line worked on a rota basis, so no one girl stayed on the same machine two days running. I explained my problem and the production manager immediately agreed to move the girl when I wanted to shoot. The idea seemed all right to him, but not to me. To move the girl just before a take would make her shortcomings very obvious and would cause a lot of embarrassment. It is this sort of thoughtless action that can easily lead to a full scale

strike. Moves have to be made more subtly. I explained this view to the
production manager and together we rearranged the order of shooting
so the required labelling scene would be shot in the girl's lunch hour.
Filming went on without delay or embarrassment.

Actors are not essential for this kind of location filming. Indeed
they almost invariably have to be taught how to do every job and
they never give as convincing a performance as the person used to doing
the job every day. Ordinary people can be very good on film, if they
are handled in the right way. Again, every producer has his own
methods. I always have a word with the person due to appear in a scene

Scene from a film aimed principally at school audiences. *Surf Boats of Accra* is a useful teaching
film although industrially sponsored. Picture: Unilever Films.

before the crew set up the shot. I just explain what we are going to do
and how long it will take. I do not at this stage tell him (or her) what
I want done. I just explain that we are going to take a shot of the
bottle capping machine, or whatever it is, and we shall be moving in a
few pieces of equipment. Just before the lights are turned on I return to
have a further chat. By keeping a person occupied and distracting them
when the lights are turned on, nervousness can be quite effectively
combated.

I usually ask what the operator normally does to operate the
machine. It helps the operator to explain and makes him feel that I am
interested enough to know what he does and how he does it. And it is
often possible to learn from the explanation. I then ask the man not

to look at the camera or to take any notice whatever of what is going on and I ask him not to do anything until he hears me say "action" and then to proceed in the normal way without doing anything special. If something goes wrong on the first take—and it often does—I always begin by saying "Good. We are nearly there. Now this time I wonder if you could . . ." Then together we work out what went wrong and how it can be put right. With care and cooperation ordinary people can be excellent on film for this kind of shot.

Planned character-scenes

The second type of film I have outlined is like the Lifton film. There you remember we planned to show two rival garages, one, very efficiently run by a manager using the Lifton system and another, run down and losing money, managed by a haphazard character called "Fred". The script featured two people. Both demanding parts. The budget did not encourage the use of actors. So I tried to find two suitable people who could do the job. The efficient manager had to be familiar with the Lifton system. So I went down to the Lifton factory and asked if I could spend a morning walking round the different departments. The company agreed and I was given a circular tour. One of the departments visited was the training school where new staff are taught how to use the company equipment and products. The training manager was a smart efficient looking man with a sense of humour. He immediately appealed to me as a possible candidate for the Lifton garage manager in the film. Fred I found in another department of the factory. He was sixty and I first saw him lighting a cigarette. It had been in his pocket for some time and was bent in the middle. He looked untidy, though he turned out to be a brilliant paint technician! On film, I thought he could be made to look exactly right. Both characters were approached and both agreed to appear in a screen test. When the film was produced the two characters were perfect.

"Amateurs" must never look amateur. They should never be used unless you are absolutely sure they will prove a success. Shoot a test first to confirm your first impression. People always look different on film. If there is any doubt at all, keep looking, or increase the budget and use professional actors.

Dialogue scenes

The third type of film I mentioned included dialogue scenes. Dialogue really sorts out the professional from the amateur. Very few inexperienced people are any good in dialogue scenes. This does not apply to interview work. When someone is being interviewed, hesitation or a lack of emphasis may appear quite natural. But there is a difference between answering interview questions or speaking *ad lib* and acting scripted dialogue scenes. Actors can cope because it is their job. Non-professionals may sound fine until you surround them with lights, recorders and cameras. Then they may dry up completely or come out with a totally inexpressive performance. Of course, this is not always the case. Some amateurs can manage dialogue scenes. But in my experience most cannot, though they often think they can.

Some film dialogue scenes call for people to talk into the lens of the camera. The script normally states something like this:

Script (Extract)

1. Ext. Trafalgar Square. Day. LS. Camera concentrates on Peter Mason who is walking towards Camera. He approaches, stops in CU and talks to Camera.

Talking to the camera, as it is generally known, is something of an art. If the person concerned can learn his or her lines, the work will be easier though not necessarily better. The alternative is to use an Autocue device which provides a continuous prompt. Managing directors introducing company films often like to spend a few minutes talking to camera. Where this idea cannot be discouraged, it should be put on film in a way as technically perfect as possible. Managing directors are busy men and often do not have time to learn a complete script by heart. Some have a unique knack. Mr. Jefferson, managing director of the British Aircraft Corporation G.W. Division, holds my own record for learning a script. Presented with a two page script at 5 o'clock in the evening, he knew the whole thing, and recorded it without the script, half an hour later! Alas, few people have the knack. They have to be prompted and here, again, there are techniques to be employed.

Prompting

Autocue consists of a motorised machine taking a reel of paper on which the words of the script are typed in bold type. The type is large enough to read at some distance from the machine. The script is typed on yellow paper and the paper is wound on a reel in the lower part of the prompting machine. It then unwinds and passes upwards, across a light box which enables the words to be read. The paper is wound on to another reel at the top of the machine. The speed of the take-up reel can be controlled by the operator, so it can be adjusted to the individual reading speed of the person appearing in the picture. That is the basic equipment. There are two variations. The equipment I have outlined can be placed alongside the camera. Or, by using an additional hood of glass and a mirror, it can be reflected on to a sheet of glass immediately in front of the camera lens. What advantages and disadvantages do the two systems have to offer?

If the prompter is set alongside the camera, the subject does not appear to be looking into the camera lens when seen on film but appears to be looking slightly off camera. But the camera will be free to zoom or pan if necessary. If the prompting words are reflected on to glass in front of the camera lens, camera movement is restricted by the prompter hood. Zooms may still be possible but pans and tilts are not. For an ordinary static shot the reflected method is undoubtedly the best to use. It enables the subject to look directly into the camera lens. If movement is essential, the side technique should be used.

VIP visits

You may be called upon to shoot VIP visits. Openings of new plants and visits by important company executive or heads of state are often filmed for company purposes. In England, when the Queen visits a factory, many companies like to film the event for later reference. In the USA the visit of the President is likewise an event which may be worth preserving on film. Industrial sponsors often leave arrangements to the last minute. The ceremony is probably planned weeks ahead but at the last minute someone thinks it would be a good idea to shoot some film. If you are called upon to shoot a VIP visit, what are the best steps to take?

VIP visits are always surrounded by a lot of fuss and organisation. Protocol is a dirty word to anyone trying to get a film of a royal visit and sometimes everything seems to be done to make the occasion as difficult as possible to record. Most Heads of State have press secretaries responsible for liaison with authorities wishing to shoot film at VIP events. In the UK, coverage of royal visits is always permitted to the two main television networks and the Central Office of Information. Anyone else wanting to join the official press party with a film unit may have to spend weeks making the necessary arrangements. They may well be told "Oh, no, we can't let you film. It's already being covered by television."

Television coverage of important events is very little help to the producers of an industrial film. Often the events are recorded on video-tape and a film copy is expensive to obtain and of poor technical quality. If film coverage is provided by the TV networks, it may simply be news coverage. A camera team is sent out, often without sound, to record the event for a news bulletin. Often the original negative is cut and the film may be force-processed to get it on the air quickly. Quality is not usually the first consideration. In news coverage, speed often takes precedence. So an industrial unit trying to obtain coverage

rom a television network may find it gets less than it requires. The
alternative is to film the event first hand.

Whenever permission can be obtained it should be sought with
every effort. Usually officials are keen to help and, if you put up a
sensible plan, will do all they can to assist you. They will limit the size
of your crew to one or two people and may restrict your use of lights,
but otherwise they will help on most occasions. There are, however,
a few petty officials who seem to get pleasure from denying every facility
to everyone whenever they get the chance. In England, steeped in his-
ory and occasionally creaking in official quarters, permission to film is
sometimes quite difficult to obtain quickly. Where it is impossible to
ilm as one of an official press party, other arrangements may have to
be made.

The first thing to do is to visit the location. Get a copy of the official
programme of events and see how they can best be covered in terms of
ilm. Plan your camera positions. You will probably need more than
one camera. Always carry a spare camera and recorder when shooting
an event which cannot be retaken later. Plan your shots and a complete
programme of events for yourself. When the day of the VIP visit comes,
get to the location early so that you avoid the traffic jams and allow
yourself time for any unexpected hazards. Barriers and other last minute
drawbacks may have to be negotiated. Take up your position and make
sure the camera is working. If you are shooting a VIP arrival, cover
he event and shoot cutaways. The ideal situation is to cover each stage
of the event with a different camera crew. The official arrival and welcome
can be covered with one camera and the tour of inspection by another,
preferably as part of the official press party. The official opening ceremony, or whatever the main event is, can be covered by a third camera
or by the first one again, if it can move to the second location quickly.
And the departure can be covered by another camera or by the second
one suitably redeployed. Always allow time to move from one location
to the other. And allow more time than you expect to use. You may have
to go a long way round to avoid crowds or to comply with an official
diversion. And always ensure that you have enough film in the camera
and a spare magazine nearby.

The new high speed films have done much to make this sort of
filming easier. Equipment is now more portable and film can be used
in conditions which not long ago would have been considered impossible. So, from a technical point of view, there are fewer problems
in filming a VIP visit than there were a few years ago. Other kinds of
problem have increased. Since the death of President Kennedy,
security at official events has been drastically tightened. This is an
excellent move, but it does tend to restrict the number of places from
which an official event can be observed. Buildings are now sealed off

and high vantage points cleared. The worst job of all falls to the police and security forces. I have always found them very helpful. But they must be consulted in advance. If they know what you want and what you would like to do, they will do all they can to help. Help them, and you too will get all the assistance you need.

Equipment security

When shooting any industrial film on location, arrangements must always be made for the equipment to be kept under lock and key whenever it is not in use. People who leave film equipment in cars are extremely stupid. I have only done it once! A very expensive camera disappeared in five minutes when someone smashed the car window. If you are shooting on location, arrange with the local security officer or management representative to leave equipment in a locked store or office when it is not in use, and make sure no one else has a key. When filming anywhere, always keep the equipment you are using under observation. When moving from one set up to the next, make sure that all the equipment is moved from place to place. Someone should be made responsible for checking that everything is moved. If it is not, it may be forgotten or stolen. Film equipment is stolen in the most unlikely places. When producing a film about artist John Hutton, I shot several scenes in Coventry Cathedral. The authorities, trying hard to preserve the Cathedral as an ecclesiastical building and not a railway station annexe as some of the visiting crowds suggest, only permitted us to film in the early hours of the morning. We set up, shot scene one and moved to reset for scene two. We then tried to find our box of filters. We knew exactly where it had been, and could see that it was no longer there. No one in the crew had touched it and no Cathedral officials had been near. One of the visitors has probably now learnt how to use them. Wherever you film, keep your equipment together and the cases locked up when not in use.

Checking of equipment

To ensure that the right equipment is delivered to a location in the first place and transferred from location to location, a check list can be prepared. Copies of this list can be duplicated and kept with the camera. Alternatively, one copy can be fixed to a piece of board and covered with a transparent sheet of plastic. The items can be crossed off on this sheet with a wax pencil each time they are moved from scene to scene. When all the equipment has been accounted for, the wax pencil marks can be cleaned off the plastic sheet and the list cleared for use at the next move. A list should take into account all equipment and film possibilities. Here is the sort of list you could use:

Camera (35 mm)

Arriflex 102S blimp
2C Arri. +mag.
1 × universal base
1 × 24v 50c motor sync
1 × 10-1 Angineux zoom
Nos. 1 & 2 diopters
Set 9 filters
Blimp matte box
2 × Op. handles
Remote/off/on switch
2 × pulse leads
2 × mains/batt. leads
3 batteries

18-mm lens
25-mm lens
32-mm lens
40-mm lens
50-mm lens
75-mm lens
100-mm lens
Set of 8 filters
3 × 400-ft magazines
Changing bag
Measuring tape
Groundsheet

Camera (16 mm)

Arriflex BL
10-1 Angineux zoom lens
2 × 400-ft magazines
Mag barney blimp
Matte box and filter holder
Zoom lever
2 batt/camera cables
2 sync pulse cables

Remote control cable
Filters set
Changing bag
Measuring tape
Carrying handle
10-mm lens
2 × 100-ft spools
Shoulderpod
3 batteries

Sound

Nagra 4 recorder
12 tapes
2 × mike stand bases and sticks
2 × AKG windgags
Headphones
Mixer unit
Mains unit
24 U2 batteries

5 mike leads
AKG D 25
2 neck mikes
1 × 13-amp adaptor
Mains leads 2
Rifle mile sennheiser 405
4 leads
2 control units

Lighting

Colortran converter
3 × 1000-W heads
3 × 500-W heads
6 extension leads
4 stands
Mains extension lead

13/15-amp adapter
Fuses
Filters. 4 glass blues
2 french flags and arms
2 Rls filter
2 Rls window lite

Tripods

Long
Short

Moy geared head
Spreader

Accessories

Tool box	Camera tape
Camera sheets	Stills camera
Sound sheets	Film stock ...... ft.
Slate	

The best part of location filming is the time when the last take of the last scene has been satisfactorily shot! The unit dismantles camera, recorder and lights for the last time and equipment is loaded aboard the camera car for the journey back to base. Filming has been completed. But the film is still very far from complete. Half the work of making a film has been done. And the other half remains and, if it is not done efficiently, all the work so far carried out can be completely wasted. Industrial film sponsors often tend to forget that when shooting has been completed there is still so much work to be done. They think that because the film unit is no longer on their premises everything except making copies of the finished film has been accomplished. Alas, this is not the case.

Rushes and daily routine

At the end of each day of shooting the exposed film should be sent to a laboratory for processing. It is unwise to keep all the exposed film together until all the scenes of a film have been shot and then send it off in bulk for processing. Send the film in day by day. Most laboratories can process original film and produce a cutting copy overnight. This cutting copy should be viewed each day before filming begins to see if anything is wrong with the previous day's efforts. You then know if you have to reshoot. Also, if there is something wrong with the camera or with a batch of film stock, the fault will be apparent after the first day of filming and not when it is too late because you have shot deep into the production.

It's not always possible to view film each day especially when shooting on location. A portable projector may prove useful, and rushes (or "dailies") are often screened at night in hotel rooms! If it is quite impossible to arrange a showing, be sure to telephone the laboratory each morning to obtain a verbal report on the state of the previous day's master material. When film is processed, the laboratories usually produce a report on the condition of the master. This report should be taken very seriously. If your material is scratched or out of focus, the faults will be noted on the laboratory report. And if there is a camera or stock fault, it too should be apparent. Check and make sure. You can then continue filming with confidence.

Identifying and ordering rush prints

When sending film to a laboratory for processing, it should be accompanied by an order. Never send cans of film without clearly identifying them. Mark the production company and its address on the top of each can and note the film title. You should also list the footage of each reel and the type of stock. These facts should normally be written on a printed label, but when this is not possible, strips of camera tape may suffice. Copies of the camera sheets must always accompany the cans to the laboratory. A laboratory order should be incorporated in the camera sheet or enclosed as a separate item. Again it should list the vital information marked on the cans. Tell the laboratories what you are sending them and tell them what you want them to supply. If you are sending in colour film and you want it processed and printed, it is not enough to simply say "Please process and print colour film supplied". There are several types of colour film and several different kinds of print. You can send in reversal colour film of one type or another and you can want a colour or a black and white cutting copy. There are many possibilities. To eliminate those which do not apply, you must give detailed instructions on your laboratory order form, such as "Herewith three reels of Ektachrome EF 7241, rated normal. Please process and produce one 16-mm black and white cutting copy on pan. stock of all takes." If you state the facts you will get what you want.

It is equally important to be precise when ordering sound transfers. You will remember that sound is often recorded on ¼-in tape. It has to be re-recorded on perforated magnetic film for editing purposes. This method of re-recording is known as "transferring" sound and a sound transfer order has to be sent with the tapes at the end of each day's shooting. Again, list the facts and say what you want the transfer suite to provide. Tell them your film title and tape speed. If it is a synchronised sound take, make the point clear on your sound sheets. And tell them what you want the sound re-recorded on. "Herewith six ¼-in tapes recorded at 7½ ips, 48 cycles. Please transfer takes circled on the attached sound report sheet to 16-mm perforated magnetic film (centre track) at 24 fps." List the basic facts. Other information should be covered on the sound report sheet accompanying the tapes to the transfer suite.

When the film has been processed and the sound transferred, the work of putting the scenes together can begin.

6

Post-production

WHEN AN INDUSTRIAL film has been shot, several stages of production still have to be completed. I have already said that shooting is only part of the story. What remains, and why is it so important? The film exposed each day must be sent off to a laboratory and as soon as it has been developed and dried, it can be printed. The first print from a master film is often produced in a hurry for viewing the following day. Hence the term "rushes" (or "dailies" in the USA). This print is never a technical masterpiece and is intended only for the film editor to work with and for the production team to inspect. On the edge of a rush printed cutting copy are a series of consecutive numbers—one number for every foot of film. These numbers are present on the original film exposed in the camera so, when a copy is produced, they appear on the copy too. When the film editor has completed his edited version of the film, the numbers are used as a permanent reference point to match the edited cutting copy with the original negative. The scenes can be matched, shot for shot and cut for cut. Negative cutting (producing an identical version cut in the original negative material) is a critical job and one requiring mechanical accuracy rather than creative ideas and abilities. It is one of the few production stages at which the master material is physically handled.

I have spoken about two types of film: master materials and cutting copy. Why doesn't the editor cut the master film and miss out the cutting copy stage? This question is easily answered, but is one which in-experienced industrial film sponsors sometimes fail to understand. Master film is a general term. It can apply to negative or reversal film in colour or black and white. The master film we are talking about here is the film actually exposed in the camera. It is sometimes known as the camera original and it is very valuable, because all the efforts involved in staging and producing the film depend on the results produced on the master. If it is damaged, the damage is there for ever. If on the other hand a cutting copy is damaged it does not matter very much. By going back to the master, another cutting copy can be produced.

In the course of editing a film, the cutting print will be run through various machines many times. It will be marked with wax pencils and will get dirty and scratched. Again, it does not matter. The cutting copy is intended for this rough work. If the editor makes a cut and does not like it, he can change his mind and alter it. Only when everyone is completely happy with the final version of the film will the master be matched to the edited cutting copy.

Negative cutting is always done with almost clinical care. Unlike editing a cutting copy, the negative cutter often works in an air-conditioned room and wears gloves. He or she only touches the edges of the master film and handles every scene as carefully as is humanly possible. When the master exactly matches the cutting copy, it can be sent back to the laboratory and a new print of the edited version can be produced. The print will not contain any of the dirt or scratches to be found on the cutting copy. And it will be "graded" ("timed" in the U.S.A.).

Graded prints

When film is exposed in a camera, the cameraman selects the lens aperture and filter he wishes to use for each shot. In the course of printing a copy of an original film, the laboratory will also make an exposure. They expose the master on a reel of new stock. This is done with a motion picture printing machine which is very like a camera. It takes two reels of film, on one side the processed master, and on the other a reel of new stock. For printing, the film, from the two reels, is run through the machine in contact, and at speed. At one point, light is allowed to pass through the original film on to the reel of unexposed stock. The original is thus printed on to the new stock. Like the cameraman, the laboratory technician can assess the exposure and determine how much light is allowed to pass through the original film on to the copy. This assessment of printing exposure is known as grading. When printing colour film, the grader also has to choose filters to balance the colours from scene to scene. This is highly skilled work. There are, in fact, special grading machines but they are never as good as the experienced man who has spent years grading in a laboratory. A badly graded print will never look really good, and that is why cutting copies always lack the impeccable quality of show prints. Cutting copies are often printed "at one light". With limited time at his disposal, the grader winds through the reels of processed master and selects a printer light which will give an average exposure to the maximum number of scenes. The scenes are then printed at that one light in the cutting copy. On the other hand when the final prints are made, each scene is separately assessed.

Industrial film sponsors often tend to forget that rush prints are not designed for quality. They sit and look at the final edited version of a film and the cutting copy churns through a projector with tape joins, grease pencil marks and cues written all over it. They may have been warned that a cutting copy is not a guide to the quality of the final film but they still often seem to miss the point. They must be told never to expect good picture quality from a cutting copy. It is a good guide to film content, and to the way the finished film will flow along. But it is not a guide to the capabilities of the cameraman or the laboratory.

Production of cutting copies

There are several ways in which a cutting copy can be produced. If you are working on a high budget sponsored film you may be shooting on 35-mm colour negative and decide to have a 35-mm cutting copy in colour. This can easily be made. But if you have spent more money than you anticipated shooting the picture, you can economise by making a black and white cutting copy. The process is quite simple. If you make a colour copy the laboratory printing machine is threaded or "laced" up with your reel of 35-mm colour negative on one side and 35-mm colour positive on the other. The original is then re-exposed on the copy. For a black and white cutting copy, the same re-exposure method is used though the reel of new colour stock is replaced by one of un-exposed monochrome material.

Remember also that when ordering black and white prints from colour material, there are two more alteratives to choose from. If you ask simply for "a black and white cutting copy" you may find your original is printed on a reel of black and white film which is not sensitive to all the colours of your original. This often does not matter, as the resulting print is clear and often contains enough detail for editing purposes. To ensure faithful reproduction of all the scenes of the colour original in a black and white cutting copy, the copy should be made on panchromatic stock.

These are the main ways of producing a cutting copy from a colour original.

> *35-mm colour negative originals* can be printed on 35-mm colour positive *or* on 35-mm black and white positive.
> *16-mm colour negative originals* can be printed on 16-mm colour positive or on 16-mm black and white positive.
> *16-mm colour reversal originals* can be printed on 16-mm colour reversal or on 16-mm black and white reversal.

When printing a black and white cutting copy of a colour original, it is a good idea to print up colour test sections from each roll. Make sure that you do not have a bad reel of stock, and study the laboratory reports carefully. On 35-mm film, "colour pilots" can be ordered. Pilots are test frames printed in colour from the original film. If there is any doubt at all about the quality of a scene, print the entire take in colour.

We have so far explored the production of colour and black and white cutting copies from colour originals. Making cutting copies of black and white films is very similar in principle. One piece of film is re-exposed on another. Black and white 35-mm negative can be printed on 35-mm positive. Negative 16-mm film can be printed on 16-mm positive, and that is all there is to it. Later on, when the film has been edited and the master has been matched to the cutting copy, other laboratory procedures can be used, as we shall see later. A 35-mm film can be printed on 16 mm. A colour reversal film can be printed on colour negative.

There are other variations, too, which are useful in the later stages of production.

Initial editing stages

When a cutting copy has been printed and the sound transferred to perforated magnetic film, the two raw materials are passed to the film editor. Now, one of the most important stages begins—a stage where many films are ruined, and where others are turned from mediocrity to brilliance. Editing an industrial film is a creative and vital job and one which is usually completely misunderstood. Sponsors have no idea whatever about what a film editor does. Yet the work he carries out has a tremendous influence on the shape of the finished film and on its success or failure. Even a superbly shot film can be ruined if it is put together in a slow or boring manner just as a film shot without any particular skill can be made very much more interesting by skilful editing.

Many sponsored films are ruined by bad editing. Often this is because a small film unit has an excellent cameraman who is also expected to be his own editor. Frequently, internal film unit editors have to work without adequate equipment or without sufficient professional editing experience.

The editor and his job

The first job of an editor is to synchronise the sound and picture as they are received from the laboratory. The scenes can then be broken down into individual takes and reassembled in the order dictated by the script. This may be done while the film is still being shot, or later when all material is at hand and shooting is complete. The first assembly is not meant to be a masterpiece. Its sole purpose is to get the scenes in the right order and to give a rough idea of the final shape of the film.

The "rough cut" version can then be fine cut until the film moves along smoothly from scene to scene. When the picture and the tracks of synchronised sound have been cut, the editor can start to prepare his final film soundtracks. You will note I said soundtracks, in the plural, for in preparing the final film sound the editor produces a number of separate soundtracks, all recorded on perforated magnetic film and matching the final edited version of the picture. The tracks are all different. Some consist of music, others of sound effects and still more of dialogue. There may be three, there could be thirty. In fact there should be as many as are needed to bring the scenes on the film to life. When all the tracks have been prepared, he goes to a sound dubbing theatre to mix the tracks together in order to produce one single final soundtrack—the sound an audience is to hear on the final prints. After dubbing, the camera master can be matched to the edited cutting copy and prints of the final version can be produced.

I hope the previous paragraphs have shown that there is rather more to editing the average industrial film than simply cutting out the blank scenes and joining up the rest! Many people seriously believe that an editor just "cuts out the bad bits"! It is a far more creative job than that.

Industrial film editing can in many cases often be highly creative. It has to be because some industrial subjects are so pictorially dull that editing has to be skilful to hold audience attention. I have outlined the main technical stages of editing. The editor puts the scenes together and builds up the sound. These are technical processes and the creative industrial film editor must be sure that he understands them thoroughly.

He must also have a feeling for the film. He must understand the need for each sequence to proceed at a definite pace. He must know how to make a sequence interesting or exciting by varying the length of each shot, and sense when a shot is too short or too long. He must know when to cut from one scene to another and when to dissolve and he must understand the grammar of film and use the technical processes available to him to produce an edited film which runs smoothly from beginning to end.

Industrial film editors often have to work with inadequate equipment. Some internal units are expected to produce masterpieces with an animated viewer and two rewind arms. This is a very common and extremely stupid situation. Animated viewers, though fine for basic elementary assembly editing, can never be used for really creative work. It is essential to have equipment on which picture and separate sound-tracks can be handled together. A motorised editing machine, capable of running at the same constant speed at which the finished film is to be projected, is also essential for anything but very elementary work.

Equipment for editor

Editing takes place in a room known as a cutting room. It has lino on the floor and plain painted walls. An industrial film cutting room should contain a motorised editing machine, a synchroniser and a synchroniser bench.

Rewind arms and a reasonable supply of spare spools are also essential and an animated viewer can be added to the basic equipment. It is sometimes useful for finding shots in a hurry and for making the first mute assembly of picture.

Editing machine

The first essential is a motorised editing machine. An animated viewer is very much cheaper but cost should not be the first point to consider. If it is too expensive to set up a cutting room properly, do not set one up at all but just hire the facilities when they are needed.

A motorised editing machine is essential for a fully equipped cutting room. It enables the editor to see his film at constant speed (the speed at which an audience will see the finished film projected) and to run picture and separate magnetic sound together. Most editing machines run both at normal speed and at increased or reduced speed in both forward and reverse directions. Double speed is not essential, but it can save time. When you have finalised the early part of a film and want to make adjustments to the end, you can race through the completed part at double speed. Motorised editing machines can usually run one reel of picture and at least one soundtrack, recorded on perforated magnetic film. Some can run two or three pictures with separate soundtracks.

A number of machines can project one reel of picture and two or three soundtracks. There is a variety of models to choose from with differing sound and picture combinations.

The German Steenbeck company make some excellent editing machines. The ST 600W model is designed for 16-mm editing. Picture and sound pass from left to right across a horizontal table. The picture is back projected on to a back projection screen, and a quartz iodine light gives a very clear picture measuring 7 × 9 in. It is sharp, clear and easy to see. The film path is simple and can be laced up quickly. One reel of picture and one reel of separate magnetic sound can be run in forward or reverse directions at speeds varying from 2 fps to 100 fps. The speed controls are all operated from one central switch. Normal sound speed is essential for normal editing. The 100 fps speed is useful for running down quickly to a part of a film needing adjustment and by moving the picture frame by frame it is possible to make minute adjustments or check precise points of synchronism. Picture and sound can be locked to run together or can be separated and advanced or retarded individually. The quality of sound and picture is excellent.

A smaller and less expensive Steenbeck machine likely to interest the industrial film unit where space is at a premium is the ST 1600. It is similar to the ST 600W. It too, gives a bright back projection picture even though the screen size is 6 × 8 in. The same motor control switch operates slow speed, normal speed and a high speed of 120 fps. Steenbeck also make excellent models for 35-mm work. The ST 400W and 400C are similar in many ways to the 16-mm machines I have outlined. In addition to normal picture and sound projection, they can handle Cinemascope.

The above editing machines are all table models. The American Moviola Company make one of the world's most widely used editing machines. Indeed, it is so widely used that in the USA the word "Moviola" is generally used to describe any kind of motorised editing machine.

Unlike the Steenbecks which are table models, the old established Moviola models that are in such wide use have a completely different layout. Film passes from front to back and the picture is projected on to a small screen immediately above the film path. Many major studios are equipped with Moviolas. They are rugged and ideal for running short pieces of film and perfect for cutting individual shots. There are take-up and feed spool spindles and reels of film can be run through quite easily.

It does, however, take rather longer to lace up film on a Moviola and place the film on split spools than it does to drop a couple of reels on a flat table editing machine. The standard Hollywood Moviola is undoubtedly an excellent machine, though for general industrial use I personally feel a table machine is more handy. Besides the normal editing duties it can serve for viewing prints and showing rough cut versions to sponsors. It is particularly interesting to note that the manufacturers of original Moviolas, having for years made what many people consider the ultimate editing machine, are now introducing a table model.

The smaller industrial film unit, may find that the machines I have outlined are too expensive. I am often asked if I can recommend a good cheap editing machine. I have used many different kinds of editing machine and have come across only one low-cost machine which is completely satisfactory in my opinion.

The Acmade Miniola is less than half the price of most table editing machines. It is not in the same class and its performance should not be compared with the Moviola or Steenbeck table models. It is, however, a good machine for the small unit. It is not a luxury product, but it is reliable and gives quite good quality reproduction of sound and picture. On the basic Miniola, picture and sound are run above and below each other from left to right. The picture is back projected by a rotating prism on to a screen. A separate magnetic soundtrack passes underneath the picture. The two can be run together or separately by disengaging the drive mechanism of one of the drive sprockets. Take-up plates with motors are situated at both ends and the machine will run at normal speed or double speed in forward or reverse directions.

There are quite a number of manufacturers of editing machines. The Italian firm of Prevost also make good equipment and if you are equipping a new cutting room it is worth inspecting their range. Kem editing tables are also well known and tested. They are quite well built, though I have found the controls are often situated in an inconvenient place for me.

The Swedish firm of Atema also produce a range of machines at various prices but, for me, the Steenbeck has no rival.

Synchroniser

The second vital piece of film editing equipment is a synchroniser. It consists of a number of sprockets locked to a common shaft so when one turns the others also turn in exactly the same manner, starting and stopping at precisely the same point. Synchronisers are not usually motorised. To pass film through a synchroniser, you turn a small handle on the front or take up the tension on the film passing through. The film itself will then turn the sprockets round. A synchroniser is essential for editing anything but the simplest sequence. It enables sound and picture to be edited and held together in synchronism. Some of the latest synchronisers include a small back projection screen. This allows the editor to see the picture projected and to run soundtracks at the same time on the other sprockets.

The Acmade picture synchroniser is an excellent example of a synchroniser with its own picture screen. Many editors cut entire films using a synchroniser and little else.

Synchronisers are usually positioned on the middle of a bench.

Rewind arms are fixed to either end and bags are set into holes at either side of the synchroniser. The bags are essential, for when using a synchroniser, it is often necessary to wind first one way and then the other to make adjustments to a short length of film. If you run loose film into the bags you do not have to spend time winding from one reel to another again and again but you can just let the slack film run into the bags while adjustments are made. Then, when all is ready, take up the tension on the film and wind on. The editing machine, synchroniser and synchroniser bench are the three most important pieces of equipment for editing an industrial film. Film trims bins, wax pencils, cement and tape joiners are also essential. When these have been purchased, or a fully equipped cutting room has been hired, the work of editing can begin.

Editing

You will recall that an industrial film can be shot with or without synchronised sound. If synchronised sound has been shot, the editor receives separate cans containing picture and sound. The first job is to synchronise the cutting copy action with the sound which has been re-recorded on perforated magnetic film. This is easily done by using a synchroniser.

First find the sound and picture report sheets. They will tell you which scenes have been shot and printed and which have been left out and any comments made on the sheets should also be noted. If a scene has been identified at the end instead of the beginning, the cameraman or sound recordist should have noted the fact on the appropriate sheet. To synchronise sound and picture, first place the reel of picture in the synchroniser and wind down to the first slate. Note the scene and take number and wind down to the point where the two parts of the clapper board are banged together. Find the exact frame where the two parts first touch and mark it with a cross. It can only be one frame. The two parts may remain together for several frames but that does not matter. The important frame is the one where the noise occurs and that is where the two parts of the board first come into contact with each other.

The scene and take number can be written alongside the marked cross. Having done this you can take the picture out of the synchroniser for a few moments and place the reel of sound in on one of the synchroniser soundheads.

Again, wind down until you find the same scene and take number and hear the bang. Mark the exact frame where the bang starts, with another cross.

Now place the two crosses opposite each other in the synchroniser. From here on sound and picture will match each other exactly.

Breaking down rushes

Sound and picture normally have to be synchronised each day so the production team can view the previous day's takes. If there is no synchronised sound, the rushes may remain in the order in which they were shot until the shooting schedule has been completed and the main part of the editor's work begins. After viewing the rushes, the director will usually know which takes he wants to use. The reels of picture and sound can then be broken down into individual shots. If takes are long, they can be coiled on a small film bobbin and held together with an elastic band. If they are short, the normal procedure is to hang the shots in a film bin (or barrel in the USA). Film bins are usually made of either fibre or metal. Above the bins are racks with clips or pegs from which individual shots can be suspended. Rushes should be broken down and hung in these bins at the start of editing. You write the scene and take number on the start of each shot. A wax pencil will do the job satisfactorily. It is worth writing these identifications because film can fall out of the clips or off the pegs and drop into the bin. A single unattached shot is much more easily found if it is clearly identified at the start.

First assembly

When all the shots have been broken down you can start making the first assembly. The purpose of a first assembly is simply to put the shots in the order dictated by the script. This can be done with an empty reel and a rewind arm but an animated viewer can be useful too. And the work can be done on a motorised editing machine, though it is rather a slow way of doing what is a very simple job. At this early stage it is a mistake to cut scenes together too tightly. It is sometimes difficult to make a fine cut straight away and a rough assembly shows you at a glance what raw materials are available. It is also easier to shorten a scene later than it is to find a trim and then put it back again.

If the shots are left long the fine cut can be planned to make the best possible use of all the material there.

Assembling an industrial film is not a complicated job. Scenes should be joined together and the slates and blank pauses removed. Where there are obvious action cutting points these should be used. In all other cases where the exact length of a shot is not dictated by the need to avoid a repetition of the action or an unnecessary pause, scenes should, as I said, be left long. Later, when the film commentary has been recorded, this rough assembly can be fine cut so that the commentary fits exactly with the words and pauses occurring in the most advantageous places.

Tape and cement joins

Two kinds of film join can be employed to make joins between pieces of film. One is made with film cement, the other with tape. Tape joins are ideal for cutting copy use. They are easy to change, for if the editor wishes to alter a cut he can simply peel off the joining tape and re-cut the scene. But they should never be used for joining master material.

Tape usually discolours with age and if you are joining show prints or any kind of master material, always use the cement method which gives a solid, welded splice.

If you're equipping an industrial cutting room you will find there are several different types of joiner to choose from. One very widely adopted model is the Italian Incollatrici. It gives a strong join with ordinary unperforated tape. It has at least one film-cutting blade. After cutting, the two pieces of film to be joined are laid end to end across a joining block.

Tape is then drawn across the two pieces of film. By lowering a handle and pressing it down, sprocket holes are punched through the tape and the film is immediately ready for use.

There are a number of other tape joiners in use, but before making a purchase it is worth looking into not only the capabilities of the joiner, but the cost of the tape. Some machines work only with per-forated tape and they may give an excellent join, if you can afford the time to make it. Pre-perforated tape is a major drawback as it is very expensive. And on one machine I saw demonstrated, the holes on the tape and on the film had to be aligned by eye. Making a join was a slow, laborious process, and unless the editor had two steady hands, often inaccurate too. Joiners like that are cheap to buy, but expensive to operate.

There is a wider selection of cement joiners to choose from. Bell and Howell make a large pedestal joiner which is operated by foot controls.

It is first class and makes a very strong join. Acmade, too, makes several excellent joiners. And Robert Rigby have long produced one of the best hand-operated cement joiners which is quite inexpensive. But for cutting copy tape joins are best.

Matching action cuts

The correct point at which to cut from one scene to another is

Any scene can be observed from a number of different camera positions. The positions used must be carefully planned when an industrial film is scripted. When cutting, continuity must always be safeguarded so

often made clear by the need to avoid a repetition of the action. If, for example, we see a car arriving, stopping and someone getting out in a long shot and then have to cut on a medium shot of the same person getting out, the actual cutting point will be dictated by the need to avoid letting the car door open twice, once in the long shot and again in the mid shot. The name given to this kind of repeat action is a "double take". When making a first assembly double takes should be avoided at all costs. Let the car draw up and stop in long shot, then cut to the closer view before the car door opens. Or let it open in long shot and cut to the closer view when the door is already open. Whatever you do, do not let the same action happen twice.

In a factory sequence, you may have to cut together a number of shots showing a man operating a particular machine. Start with a long

that the action is properly matched when cutting from scene to scene. For example, cutting from shots right, top, to right, centre, would work, but to cut to right bottom could be misleading. The girl would appear to turn round.

shot and choose your cutting point carefully. Make sure that the machine is doing the same thing in both shots at the point where you make your cut. And watch the machine operator. Are his hands in the same position and is he looking exactly the same at the start of your closer shot as he is at the point at which you have cut out of the longer view? Or is he looking down at one point and ahead in the other?

Assembly editing of shots forming part of a continuous action sequence is largely a matter of common sense—a case of studying the scenes carefully, finding exactly the right point and cutting where the action matches exactly.

Unlike an entertainment feature film, where the same characters appear in shot after shot, industrial film sequences may be made up from shots which do not show the same people or subject in consecutive scenes.

Making a fine cut

In the Painton film to which I referred earlier, one sequence consisted of views of different parts of the paint production line. A different part of the line, and different people too, were seen in each shot.

Now, as I emphasised earlier, when putting scenes like these together, in a rough assembly, it pays to leave them overlength. They are easy to cut down later and you have complete freedom of choice when selecting a cutting point. In the Painton film, the shots were left long until the fine cut was made. The sequence was then cut to music. We will see how this is done later. Other scenes in the same film had to be cut accurately from the start. They featured the same people in a number of consecutive shots. A girl painting a wall was shown in four shots. The script showed the action like this:

Painton: Script (Extract)

1. Int. Living Room. MS. Margaret is painting the wall. She takes the brush away from the wall and dips it in a tin of paint.

Cut

2. Int. Living Room. Day. CU. The brush emerges from the tin. We see the paint does not drip.

Cut

3. Int. Living Room. Day. CMS. The brush applies paint to the wall. Paint flows on freely.

Cut

4. Int. Living Room. Day. BCU. The paint flows off the brush on to the wall. There aren't any brush marks.

This is a very simple sequence of shots and it is typical of many similar sequences to be found in industrial films. The shots are all part of one sequence dealing with one subject: Margaret painting a wall. And the shots all form part of one continuous sequence. So the cutting points must be chosen to avoid a repetition of the action. There's no room for error. This is how the sequence was cut:

We started with the first mid shot. It showed Margaret, the wall and the tin of paint at the bottom of frame. After a few seconds, Margaret took the brush off the wall and dipped it in the paint tin. There was a choice of cutting points here. We could cut to the shot showing the tin before the brush was dipped in it, or after it had been immersed. We chose the latter and cut to the close-up of the tin as the brush was being dipped in the tin. The position of Margaret's hand on the brush was exactly matched and the position of the brush in the tin was also carefully matched.

We stayed on the close-up until the point where the brush was taken out. The director, keen to emphasise that Painton does not drip, had asked Margaret to hold the brush above the tin for a split second so the point could be made clear without emphasising it in commentary. So we stayed on the close-up of the tin until the brush had been held up and then whisked out of shot. Then we cut.

The next shot was a close medium shot showing the brush being re-applied to the wall. Here, too, there was a choice of cutting point. We could have cut away from the tin with the brush still hovering above it and cut into the CMS just before the brush came into shot and was applied to the wall. In the event, we let the brush go out of the close tin shot and cut the CMS when the brush was on its way to the wall.

Here, too, there was no room for error. We had to consider the whereabouts of the brush at the cutting point we had chosen. It would have been easy, and wrong, to cut from the brush in the tin to the brush already on the wall, or from the brush out of the tin to the brush emerging from the tin. Continuity and smoothness of action are the two points to consider when cutting scene to scene. When we cut from the CMS to the BCU of the brush on the wall, we again had to match the position of the brush at the cutting point. Margaret was painting with short strokes and we cut at the end of one of the strokes in the split second when the brush was stationary between strokes. We made quite sure that her hand was in the same place on the brush at the cutting point. The shots then ran together smoothly.

Cutting moving shots

As you know, cameras do not necessarily shoot scenes from a static viewpoint. They can pan round or up and down and zoom in and out. When cutting shots involving camera movement, particular care is needed. Industrial films are often marred by bad editing and the most frequent causes for annoyance are cuts made in the middle of camera movements. Never cut in the middle of a pan or a zoom. It is disturbing to view. The mind concentrates on a shot and expects it to reach its conclusion and if it is cut off in the middle or started too late, the smoothness of the action is violently disturbed. I have already mentioned that zooms and pans should always be planned and shot as carefully composed shots. You will recall my recommendations that the camera should start running on a shot which is itself an interesting shot. It should then pan steadily and end at another position which shows a view which is itself an interesting shot. For zooms, the same basic rules apply. Never ruin the smoothness and pace of a scene by cutting into the middle of a camera movement. When you cut to the scene, allow a few moments before the camera movement begins so that the audience can see and appreciate the reasons for the shot. If you cut and then immediately zoom or pan, the purpose of the shot will be wasted and the audience confused.

Hold both ends and never cut in the middle. If you have to get out of a camera movement, use an optical effect.

Opticals

There are a number of ways to move from scene to scene in a film. You can cut from one shot to another making an instantaneous change. Or you can fade out one shot and fade in another. Or, you can dissolve and let one scene gradually merge with the other until it re-places it.

These optical effects, the fades and dissolves, are all a part of the grammar of film. They are another reason for using an experienced film editor, for there is a right place and a wrong place to use optical effects and the choice of place is often a matter of instinct and ex-perience.

It is most infuriating to see a film where scene after scene begins and ends with a fade. Dissolves in the wrong places are also very an-noying and cuts used where dissolves would be better are wasted opportunities. There are no hard and fast rules about the right and wrong place to use these opticals. It really depends on the pace of the film and the way in which it moves along from sequence to sequence. Each situation must be separately assessed. A fade out at the end of the film and a fade in at the beginning is almost standard practice. Other fades should be confined to the beginning and end of the main sequence, and then used sparingly.

The end of a chapter in a book is marked by a full stop and a fresh page. The end of a main sequence in a film can be marked by a fade out or a dissolve. It does not have to be marked by either. A cut can still be used but there are some occasions where a cut is disturbing to the eye.

In the Ford tractor film I mentioned earlier, some of the live action was interspersed with diagrams. To cut from diagrams to live action might have been disturbing, so dissolves were used. They were carefully lined up so that the relevant parts of the diagrams dissolved to the same parts in reality and diagrams and live action were thus closely related. Dissolves giving a gradual transition from scene to scene, can be very effective. A slow dissolve slows down the pace of the film. It can be revealing or restful. In a travel film, a few dissolves in the right places can be very effective, but do not overdo it. Dissolve after dissolve is maddening.

Amateur photographers sometimes make their optical effects in the camera. This is not a good idea, except in the course of animation or bench photography where the length of each scene can be precisely determined before it is shot. The best place to fade or dissolve will often not be apparent until the film is being edited. Camera opticals are very limiting and often technically unsatisfactory so this work should be entrusted to a laboratory.

Marking and ordering opticals

Laboratories can produce fades in the course of printing release copies and dissolves too can be produced in printing, if the edited master is assembled in A & B roll form, as we shall see later. Optical effects should always be marked on a cutting copy. Use a wax pencil and mark the film with the correct optical sign. An optical effect can be one of several different lengths. The time during which the effect takes place, is calculated in numbers of frames. A fade or a dissolve can be 8, 16, 24, 32, or 48 frames long or longer still if required. Some laboratories use printers capable of producing opticals in multiples of 8 frames.

Other labs work on a footage basis. The cutting copy should be cut so that the two scenes are joined together in the centre of a dissolve or at the beginning or end of a fade in or out. And the correct optical sign should always be marked on the print. For a fade in, the correct sign is an upturned letter "V" starting with the narrowest point at the start of the frames where the fade begins and ending with the "V" wide open at the end of the frame where the fade in ends. For a fade out, the "V" is reversed starting at the widest point and ending at the narrowest. Dissolves should be marked with a line starting on one side of the picture at the start of the dissolve. The line should then be drawn across to the other side of the picture reaching the other side at the centre point of the dissolve.

At this point, the two scenes should be cut together in the cutting copy. The line can then cross back to the other side, along the other scene, to mark the end point.

In a dissolve, one scene gradually merges with another and the two overlap for a short period. In fact, one scene is gradually superimposed on the other until it eventually replaces it. To make a dissolve, the first scene must be faded out and the other faded in and an overlap of these two scenes produced. When you join your cutting copy you make the join in the middle of the intended dissolve. When the master is matched to your edited cutting copy, the negative cutter allows an overlap on the end of one scene and the beginning of the other. He does this by using A & B roll assembly technique. You must ensure that he has enough spare film to overlap. You should allow half the overall length of the optical effect on each side of your join. If you have a 40-frame dissolve, allow 20 extra frames on each side of the point where you join the cutting copy.

Do not join the extra frames into the cutting copy. Just make sure that they are available, so that the negative cutter can provide the necessary overlap. The overlap will not affect your cutting point. When the two reels of assembled master are sent to the laboratory for printing, the printer will start to fade out one reel and fade in the other at exactly the right point. The length of the dissolve effect will depend on the marks you put on the cutting copy and the length of the overlap indicated.

A and B rolls

As we shall see later in this chapter, there are two main ways of matching a master to a cutting copy. A master can be neg. cut in two separate rolls (A & B) or it can remain as one. In a two roll assembly, the first scene must be put on one roll of master. If the second scene follows the first with a cut it may also be on the same roll, but if scene one dissolves to scene two, the second shot must be placed on a second master roll. The first roll must be built up with spacing to keep the two strips of film the same length. At the next dissolve, the incoming scene must be put on roll one and spacing must be joined on to roll two. Where a dissolve occurs, one scene is placed on one roll and the master left overlength. Half as much spare film as the length of the dissolve must be left on each side of the join. On the second reel the incoming shot must also overlap the outgoing exposure by half the length of the dissolve. For a 48-frame dissolve, 24 frames overlap on each roll is needed. When the laboratories print the two rolls of master on one reel of printing stock to make copies of the final film, they start to fade out the outgoing shot on one roll of master at one point and they start to fade in the shot on the second roll at exactly the same point. Both fades will be timed to end at the end of the dissolve length and the optical effect will thus be produced on the print. This is one way of producing optical effects.

Opticals from single roll

Optical effects produced from A & B roll masters are a relatively straightforward matter. Industrial film makers using 35-mm film often have to use a single roll of master. As it is impossible to overlap two separate pieces of film on a single roll of master, optical effects have to be produced on a single strip of duplicate film which can be cut into a single roll of edited master. You still mark up your cutting copy and you still need an overlap. When you have marked up the cutting copy, turn to the uncut reels of master. Note the edge numbers of the scenes where the optical effects occur and find the scenes in the reels of master. Take out the complete shot of both the scenes needed to make the optical, and send them off to the laboratory with an optical order sheet. The laboratory will make a single duplicate piece of film incorporating the optical effect. Tell the laboratory where you want the duplicate to start and end, where you want the optical to take place and how long it should last. You can do this by referring to the number on the side of the film. You will remember that there is one number in every foot of film and the numbers are all different. By using these numbers it is possible to pinpoint an individual frame. Simply note the number and indicate the exact frame required by marking plus or minus the appropriate number of frames. Edge numbers often cover more than one frame. To pinpoint an exact frame, the frame from which the count must start must be indicated. This is normally done by putting a small box round the part of the edge number occupying one individual frame: (6JT $\boxed{430}$ 47). In this case, the 430 part of the number occupies one individual frame. By pinpointing this frame it is possible to be accurate to a frame when ordering opticals. Tell the laboratory where you want the duplicate shot to start. Always duplicate the whole of both shots in which an optical effect occurs. "Start dupe at 6JT $\boxed{430}$ 47 + 12″, might be the instruction noted on your optical sheets. This tells the laboratory to start their duplicate twelve frames after the frame on which the figures 430 occur. If a start before this point is required, a minus sign should appear in place of the plus. Also tell the laboratory where the duplicate should end and where the optical should start and finish. It is also normal to note the centre point of a dissolve. All these points can be indicated by using the numbers on the edge of the film. When the duplicate has been obtained it can be cut into a single roll of edited master.

Edge numbers are vitally important. If they are not clear and easy to read, it is very difficult to match a master to a final edited cutting copy. Before even breaking down rushes, check and ensure that the numbers are clear to see. It is quite possible for a laboratory to miss them out and mask them off when printing a cutting copy. If you find the numbers are missing, before breaking down the rushes return master and print to the laboratories. Numbers printed in a special ink can then be added.

Cutting pace

Editing is, as I have already pointed out, one of the most important stages of industrial film production. An editor is concerned with giving a film a definite pace. If all the shots are put together in the same way, a film will lack visual appeal. If every shot is held on the screen for ten seconds many opportunities will be lost. By varying the cutting pace the whole mood of a film can be altered. When cutting a major dramatic film, an editor can make a sequence more dramatic by shortening his shots as the drama reaches its climax. In a car chase, he may make his shots progressively shorter as the tension mounts. By cutting quickly, he will increase tension. By cutting slowly from shot to shot, tension can be relaxed. Industrial film editors seldom have to produce a mood of tension, but the techniques used in feature film editing are still relevant. Cutting pace must be varied and used to maximum effect.

Cutting speech and dialogue scenes

Slow cutting tends to be relaxing. For a peaceful holiday film, shots of boats sailing on the sea can be cut together slowly to appear relaxing and restful. Shots of speedboats charging along can be cut much more quickly; the cutting pace can be matched to the mood of the situation. By cutting quickly the boats will appear to be going fast and the excitement of the scenes will not be wasted.

There are many opportunities for creative editing in every industrial film. They are often thrown away. The most mundane production line can be made interesting by a skilful juxtaposition of shots. A sales talk can be made more interesting by skilful cutting. And a managing director's long-winded introduction can be made less boring by inserting suitable cutaway material at relevant points. Cutaways can do much to make a film interesting. Where a sponsored film has to include lengthy shots of people talking into the camera lens, the speeches can be considerably enlivened by cutting away from the speaker to suitable illustrative material at various strategic points. Keep the voice going, and cut the picture. The shots must, of course, be chosen to tie in with what is being said on the soundtrack. After a suitable break, the action can be cut back to show again the man who is talking.

Cutting to music

Scenes free of dialogue can sometimes be cut to music. This kind of cutting can be very effective. Cutting to music simply means cutting action scenes to match the beat of a particular piece of music. The Painton production sequence was cut to music. It came at a point in the film where the director felt a break from commentary was needed.

The rushes showed hundreds of tins being filled and moving along a maze of production lines. The director spent most of a day listening to different tapes and discs and eventually found a jig which appealed to him. He arranged for the music to be re-recorded on perforated magnetic film and the transfer was passed to the film editor. The editor viewed the rushes and listened to the music. Then he sat down and marked the beat of the music on the back of the track of perforated magnetic film. After that he broke down the production line rushes and re-assembled them to match the beat of the music. Where there was a definite beat on the track he cut from one picture to another. By skilfully selecting the beats and cutting at exactly the right point an interesting and pacy sequence was produced. The whole sequence relied on editing for its success.

I hope in outlining the basic facts about editing an industrial film I have shown how very important this stage of production is. Look at a badly edited film—there are plenty to be seen. It is probably boring and slow moving. It is not pleasant to watch. Then look at a well edited film and, subconsciously perhaps, you will be aware of the difference. You may not be able to pinpoint a reason unless you are in the film business. But you will notice that the film keeps you interested and moves along in a logical way at the right speed. There are no long pauses or embarrassing silences and your eye is not constantly distracted by unexpected cuts made at the wrong points. The film has been well edited. Badly edited films do little for a film sponsor or producer. It is easy for a low budget sponsor to give his film commission to a one-man band because he knows he can shoot good quality pictures. For a stills photographer, the ability to shoot good pictures is qualification enough. For a film maker it is not. All the efforts of the cameraman can be wasted if the editor does not do a good job when he puts the scenes together. Making an industrial film is a team effort. The editor is part of that team. On page 209 there is a full summary of the main production stages.

You will notice that the word "commentary" is listed among the editing stages. Most industrial film soundtracks include a commentary. Commentary, unlike synchronised dialogue, is spoken by a person or persons out of view of the camera. An industrial film commentary can be recorded when editing is in progress or when the final edited version is being dubbed. When is the best time to record and why are there two alternatives?

"Commentary over" final version

If you record when the final version is being dubbed you are working at the last moment possible in the production schedule. You

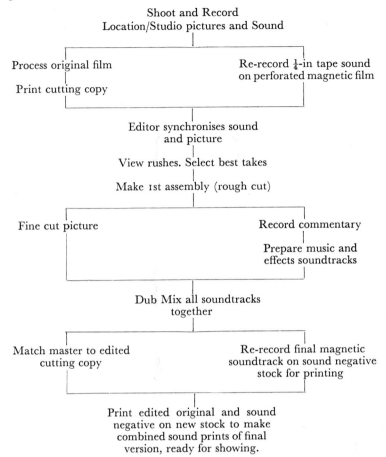

Shoot and Record
Location/Studio pictures and Sound

Process original film

Print cutting copy

Re-record ¼-in tape sound
on perforated magnetic film

Editor synchronises sound
and picture

View rushes. Select best takes

Make 1st assembly (rough cut)

Fine cut picture

Record commentary

Prepare music and
effects soundtracks

Dub Mix all soundtracks
together

Match master to edited
cutting copy

Re-record final magnetic
soundtrack on sound negative
stock for printing

Print edited original and sound
negative on new stock to make
combined sound prints of final
version, ready for showing.

seat your commentator in a soundproofed commentary booth from which he can see the screen where the final edited version of the cutting copy is projected. He can also see a film footage counter located under the screen and there may be a cue light in front of him. He is given a script alongside which is a series of numbers. Each number corresponds to a particular film footage. For example the figure 18 may appear opposite his first paragraph of dialogue. That means he should start to read his first paragraph when the footage counter under the screen shows 18 ft. As he reads, his words are recorded on a new reel of perforated magnetic film, running in synchronism with the edited picture. When the whole commentary has been recorded, this reel of commentary is mixed with the other soundtracks prepared by the editor and the final composite recording is then dubbed.

Recording at this late stage of production can be perfectly satisfactory. Success depends on the abilities of the commentator, the editor and the script writer. But if you are recording to match the final edited version of the film and the editor has cut the scenes too tightly the commentary writer may not have enough room to say what he wants to say over a particular shot. If he has been left too much room there may be an embarrassing silence at the wrong point. Now, if the commentary writer is used to writing film commentaries, there should be little problem as he should know exactly how many words are needed for a particular length of film. He will know the reading speed of the commentator and will adjust the length of the commentary accordingly. This ability to write to length is part of the art of writing film commentaries. If you plan to record during a dub, it is essential to have a commentary writer with this kind of experience. The alternative is to record earlier in production, as I suggested in the diagram of the main stages of editing.

Pre-recorded commentary

If you record before the edited version of the film is finalised, you allow yourself much more freedom. You can still use a dubbing theatre to record. But this time instead of running the picture you make the commentary recordings before the film is fine cut. You do not need film footage counters—just an unnumbered script and a reel of new magnetic film. Let the commentator read the script and record it, if necessary again and again until it is exactly right. Then go back to the film-cutting room and break down the recorded roll into individual sentences. The sections can then be edited to match the picture. If the commentary is too long in one place you can extend the picture. If it is too short you can cut the picture or make sure other sound is available in the pause between sentences. You can make sure that every sentence occurs in exactly the right place and that sound and picture really do complement each other.

Never be afraid to allow a pause between sentences. Nothing is more infuriating than continuous talk because after a while, people cease to listen. A pause, however slight, breaks the monotony and lets an audience refocus its attention. And, if the editor does his job properly, there will not be dead silence between the sentences, for the commentary soundtrack will only be one of several different tracks, all matching the one reel of edited picture. Where there is no commentary, the other tracks will be heard. The music, the sound effects, the synchronised dialogue—will speak for themselves.

To make a pause in pre-recorded commentary, cut the perforated magnetic film and join on spacing. Spacing does not make any noise as it passes over magnetic soundheads. When you want the commentary to start again, cut out of the spacing and join on the next sentence. An edited commentary track consists of a combination of magnetic film and spacing. The spacing ensures that the sentences are correctly spaced out and occur at the right points. The commentary track will go dead when spacing passes over the soundheads, but it does not matter because the other soundtracks will cover the pause between sentences. When editing commentary to match picture, a synchroniser or a motorised editing machine can serve equally well.

Having completed the first assembly, the reel of picture can be put in the first channel of the synchroniser or on the picture section of a motorised editing machine. A film leader should be joined to the start of the edited picture roll and also to the start of the new commentary soundtrack. Film leaders consist of a series of numbers starting at 12 or 10 and running in descending order down to 3. There are then two feet of black film and a point at which to join the sound or picture. Leaders protect the film from damage and ensure that there is always enough film with which to lace up a machine. With both strips in the synchroniser run down to the first frame of picture. Now, if the commentary starts with the first frame of picture, the first sentence can be joined to the end of the leader. Many industrial films begin with a fade in and it is wise to allow a slight pause before bringing in commentary. Let the picture establish itself and then let the man talk. So, at the end of the leader, join in a short length of spacing. When you want the commentary to start, make a cut in the spacing and join on the first sentence. You can then run on.

Now you can adjust the commentary to match the picture and vice versa. You can ensure that the two work together. Editing commentary to match picture also requires experience. There are some unfortunate mistakes to be made, as many industrial films show. I have already suggested that it is wrong to keep the commentary running throughout without a pause. But also ensure that the commentary is always relevant. Do not describe one scene and show another, and try not to describe the obvious. Inexperienced film makers often tend to describe exactly what the picture shows. "Here the foreman is putting the new metal into the jig and turning a handle to start the lathe." Credit an audience with a little intelligence . . . only a little, but some at any rate! Let the scenes speak for themselves and use commentary to amplify the points made by the pictures. And be careful where you let your commentary occur. If the words come at the wrong point the effect can be a mess. I saw a Swiss promotional film about the city of Basle in which the commentary had been badly matched to picture and many sentences occurred in quite the wrong position. One of the finest examples, thoroughly enjoyed by the audience in the cinema, was the sentence "the citizens of Basle are here seen going about their business". The sentence was supposed to occur over a shot of people travelling to work along a busy street. Unfortunately, the sound was late, and the dialogue was heard over shots of three gorillas in the Basle Zoo! The commentary writer had miscalculated the number of words needed for a particular scene. The Zoo sequence commentary came over the next shot—the interior of a Basle bank. The audience laughed so much after the first sentence I couldn't hear the rest of the dialogue! There are many splendid examples of how not to edit commentaries.

Another film I saw showed scenes of Kew Gardens. Over shots of a coach-load of elderly visitors passing through the entrance gates, the commentator announced, "In Kew Gardens you will find some magnificent specimens."

Choice of commentator

When recording an industrial film commentary, always use a professional commentator. News readers, television and radio personalities will usually undertake the job for a fee. But be sure to choose a voice which is suitable for your particular subject. Do not just choose a name. There is a right and a wrong type of voice for every film commentary. The formal newsreader may not be the right person for a lighthearted film. The well-known TV personality may be quite unsuitable for a technical film. Match the man to the job, and choose someone who has a wide experience of film commentary work.

Some sponsors feel they can do the job of selection themselves. One holiday film I once produced was made for a company promoting overseas package tours. It was quite a long film showing three countries and the budget included provision for a well known commentator, exactly right for the job. Before we could record, the sponsor's managing director wrote to tell us that he wished to read the film commentary! When I spoke to him he pointed out that he knew all about the company's activities and felt that audiences would wish to hear the voice of someone who knew what the company did. We did not record him. His voice would have killed the film. He sounded rather like a dying frog making his last bid for breath, and wasn't quite what the holiday film needed.

But he had to be told, tactfully, and the reasons had to be explained. We did this by showing him what was involved and by showing him what his own voice really sounded like. He then agreed, and has since said how much he likes the commentary used on the final version.

A professional commentator did a professional job. And for film commentary recordings, a professional approach is the only one to adopt.

The commentary

Writing commentaries for industrial films is also a skilled job. It is easy to write mundane boring material and it is easy to describe what the film itself illustrates quite adequately. A film commentary should always add something to the picture and not describe what is obvious. Again, it should be designed to interest an audience. It is only too easy to sound patronising and to say something irrelevant. It is also very easy to be hilariously funny, unintentionally. An agricultural film designed to sell cow food to farmers contained the splendid line, "And if you use our products, you can be sure to get your cows off to a flying start."

Inaccurate commentaries are also very commonplace. Accuracy should be checked before a word is recorded. In the UK, for example, the Trades Description Act makes it an offence to make inaccurate claims for goods or services. Checks must be made. Write a draft commentary, then read it through without the picture. Make sure it reads well and contains facts which are true. Is it interesting? Does it add to the film and help to achieve the purpose for which the film is being produced? Then read the commentary with the picture and make sure you are not stating the obvious or have not left out any vital point. If the film is designed to increase sales, are there any promotional points which could be included? Does the commentary make claims which can never be backed up by evidence? Does it make the film better and more interesting, or does it just plough on in a thoroughly tedious manner? And, are there any unfortunate sentences? Once, in a German tourist film showing scenes of a beer festival, the commentator announced—"on these tours you can drink as much as you like without spending a penny"!

As I have explained, a commentary is only part of a final film soundtrack. Other tracks of music and sound effects also have to be prepared. These tracks are important and the work of preparing them is the responsibility of the editor. What does the work involve? Consider sound effects first.

Effects tracks

If the sound needed has not been recorded by the film unit on location (wild tracks) they will have to be obtained from tapes or discs supplied by a sound effects library. When you have fine cut the picture, sit down, armed with a pencil and paper, and reconsider each scene in terms of sound. Assess each shot and decide what sounds are needed to recreate the original scene shown on the film. Make a full list of all the sounds you need and then contact a library to obtain the necessary recordings. The library will supply tapes or discs which can be re-recorded on perforated magnetic film. You can then start to match the sounds to the edited reel of picture.

Ordering library sounds

Finding the right raw materials is the first part of the job. If the film unit has recorded wild tracks the job will be very much easier and the sounds will be much more authentic. All you have to do in this case is arrange for the tapes supplied by the film unit to be re-recorded on perforated magnetic film. You can then edit them to match the picture. If there aren't any wild tracks you will have to rely entirely on library sounds.

Most general industrial and background sounds can be obtained from library sources, though specialised machinery may have to be specially recorded. If you have to use library sounds, make sure the list of sounds you require is as detailed as possible. It is absolutely useless ringing up a library and saying you want the sound of a lorry. It is equally useless to say you want the sound of the company lorry. You must be much more precise. The library probably has hundreds of recordings of cars, vans and lorries. They want to know what kind of lorry. Is it large or small? Does it start or stop, run forward or in reverse, and at what speed? Are any doors opened or shut? Any gear changes which should be heard, and is the camera shooting inside or outside the lorry? Does the lorry approach and pass, and so on? These questions must all be answered for every individual sound. Describe exactly what the scene shows, then you will get the right sound. If you think I am being unduly fussy, look at a scene with the wrong type of sound. Again, there are some splendid examples. A small television network in one of the African countries produced a prestige film about the visit of their head of state to a number of major countries. The film was cut by an inexperienced editor. The sounds used for the interior of the presidential car purring gracefully along on its ceremonial route would have been ideal for Le Mans. The editor had asked for the interior of a car. And he had got it: the interior of a racing car doing 100 mph. Not quite right for the presidential procession.

Laying effects tracks

When the sounds have been obtained and re-recorded on per-forated magnetic film, you can match them to the edited reel of picture. This process is known as "laying" sound effects tracks. Sounds skilfully laid will recreate the mood and atmosphere of the scenes shown in the film.

A synchroniser is the most suitable piece of equipment for laying sound effects. Several tracks can be laid simultaneously. It is very like editing picture and commentary. Where there is not any sound on a particular track, it should be built up with spacing. You will need several tracks. There may be three, there could be thirty. There should be as many as are needed to re-create the sounds of every scene.

Consider two scenes from a promotional film about wines. In the first scene the marketing director is talking to the camera. He is standing in the bottling plant and machines filling bottles can be seen in the background. In the second scene, a lorry loaded with crates of the finished wines starts up and moves away from the winery, past the camera.

Both scenes need sound. The first shot was filmed with synchronised sound. No sound at all was recorded for the second shot, so all the necessary sounds for that scene have to be obtained from available library sources.

In the first of our two scenes, the marketing director talks to the camera. The recordist has recorded his voice: that is one soundtrack. But, the scene was shot in a bottling plant which was very noisy. So that the dialogue would be clearly heard, the recordist gave the marketing director a chest microphone. The voice is clear but the scene lacks life. The recordist also recorded a wild track of the atmosphere of the bottling plant. It contains all the background machine and bottling sounds you would expect to hear if you stood where the man stands when he is speaking.

The editor has both these tracks of sound. The synchronised dialogue track and the picture have already been cut. Now he backs up the dialogue track with a second track, containing the general plant background sounds. When these two tracks are reproduced in a dubbing theatre, the sound mixer will be able to control the volume of the two tracks separately. He can ensure that the voice is clear and he will also be able to mix in a little of the background sound—just enough to bring the scene to life.

The second scene has been photographed without sound, so the editor has had to assess the picture and work out what sounds he needs. The action shows a lorry driver walking out of the winery and climbing into a lorry. He starts it up and drives towards and past the camera.

The whole scene is observed from one stationary point. The editor has listed the sounds he needs. As the man comes out of the winery we should hear his footsteps. He is walking in a concrete yard so the sound of footsteps on stone will be needed. The lorry door opens and closes and the engine is started. It is a two ton truck made in about 1972. It starts and moves slowly up, past the camera and away. For one shot, six sounds are needed to bring the scene to life. Footsteps, door open and

shut, engine start and approach and pass, and a background atmosphere track too.

Having obtained the sound effects from a library, and having had
them re-recorded on perforated magnetic film, the editor's next task
is to match sound and picture. How does he make the footsteps, supplied
by a sound library from a master effects recording, match the movements
of the man in the picture? First he uses the synchroniser and winds
down the picture and marks it up. He finds the exact point where the
driver's feet touch the ground at the start of each footstep and marks the
appropriate frame with a wax pencil cross. It can only be one frame for
each footstep. The feet may be on the ground for several frames but
that does not really interest the editor. The frame he is concerned with
is the one that actually makes the sound and that is always the first
frame where the foot hits the pavement. When these frames have been
marked up on the reel of edited picture, the editor can take his reel of
re-recorded footsteps sound. Again, he can wind through the synchroniser and mark the back of the soundtrack with one frame cross
each time a step occurs. When all the steps have been marked, he can
put the first cross of the sound opposite the first cross of the picture and
then wind down.

The first two crosses match: they are exactly opposite each other
in the front and second track of the synchroniser. But the others are not
such a perfect match. The man in the picture was not walking at the
same speed as the man who made the sound recording, so adjustments
must be made.

The first two footsteps are going to be all right so they can be
joined into the soundtrack. The third cross on the sound is late as it
comes after the third cross on the picture. The track must be cut after
the second cross on the picture.

The procedure can be continued until every picture cross has a
sound cross exactly opposite it. The sound will then exactly match the
edited picture.

Sometimes the sound may be early. The man making the master
library recording might have been walking faster than the man on the
film. The crosses would then have to be separated and dropped back by
inserting spacing between the paces, until the picture and sound crosses
exactly matched. The footsteps track would go dead when the spacing
came up, but that would not really matter because the other soundtracks passing through at the same point would cover the deadness and
loss of background sound. This is the standard way of laying what are
known as "spot effects". Spot effects must be accurately synchronised.
For the lorry door, exactly the same procedure should be followed. Mark
the point where the door opens and closes and put the appropriate

sound opposite the right cross, and then build up the gap between with spacing.

That is one track of sound for our scene. Others are needed to complete the same shot. We have our spot effects sounds. Now we can think about background noises. The scene shows a lorry in a yard immediately outside a winery. Standing by the camera you would expect to hear not only the lorry, but some of the plant machinery clanking away in the background. So, a further track must be prepared dealing with the background atmosphere sound. It is important, for it too adds authenticity and it covers the joins and pauses in the spot effects track. When spacing and joins are passing through, the pauses will be covered by the continuing track of background sound. So there are now two tracks. More are needed. Track three should contain the lorry starting up. It must be carefully laid at exactly the right point. The driver gets into the cab, shuts the door and looks down. That is the right point for the starter motor. It can be laid on track three. The background track continues and spacing can now be joined to the end of the spot effects track. The lorry moves off.

It may be possible to find a track of the starter motor and lorry moving off recorded as one continuous sound. The lorry may start and move on at the same time in the picture as it does in the sound recording, or it may not. Perhaps the lorry starts and moves off almost immediately on the film whereas on the library sound, it starts off, ticks over for half a minute and then moves away.

Adjustments will thus have to be made, and another soundtrack must be introduced.

The lorry starting can go on track three and the tick-over of the engine can be allowed to run. Shortly after the engine has started, the sound of the lorry moving off can be laid on track four. When the sounds are reproduced in a dubbing theatre, the sound mixer can mix from track three to track four at the point where the lorry moves off in the picture. Sound and picture will then match each other exactly. When laying sounds to be mixed together, it is important to allow an adequate overlap.

Always provide more sound than you are likely to need if two or more tracks are to be mixed together, or if a scene is to start and end with a dissolve.

This may all sound a very elaborate way of adding sound to a film. It is reasonably elaborate but it is also standard practice for any film maker worth employing. There are many sponsors who give film editing and dubbing no thought at all. There are some film makers who are prepared to settle for whatever they can produce at speed with maximum profit at minimum cost. Such producers often edit their films in the quickest way possible. They then contact a commentator and ask him to come along to the dub. They record their commentary and play a few records and call the finished result a soundtrack. This is a shoddy way of turning out films. Any film producer worth employing should take the trouble to produce the best possible results and he will spend time finding the right sound for each shot. He should ensure that each commentary sentence occurs at the most advantageous place, and make absolutely certain that the message of the film is put across in a clear and interesting manner. He should not take short cuts and when he goes into a dubbing theatre to complete the last stage of film editing, he must take with him the best possible raw materials for the sound mixer to use.

In the film dubbing theatre, the material that has been prepared by the film editor is seen together for the very first time. Dubbing is the last major technical stage of film production. Few industrial film production companies possess their own dubbing theatre. The normal practice is to hire a theatre on an hour to hour basis. The hire fee includes the use of all the projection, reproducing and recording equipment, and the services of a sound mixer and his staff. It does not include the film stock used for recording or any fees payable to commentators. These should always be negotiated separately. Most professional commentators have a set fee per reel for reading commentaries.

If the film runs for 400 ft of 16-mm film or 1000 ft of 35-mm, they will charge for one reel. If it exceeds these standard reel lengths you will be charged more.

How long should a dubbing theatre be booked for mixing an industrial film? There is no firm rule, for some films are more complicated to mix than others. It is, of course, quite useless booking half an hour to mix a half hour film. Two hours is just enough for a very simple half hour film. If it is complicated, you may need a day. And if you are recording commentary as well, you should allow extra time. The commentator will want to go through the script before recording it and he may well make mistakes which have to be corrected and time must be allowed.

Pre-mixing, too, takes time. It is always far better to overestimate dubbing time than to find yourself running out of time in the middle of a dub.

A dubbing theatre consists of a projector locked to a recorder and a number of machines capable of reproducing separate magnetic soundtracks. All the machines are locked together to run at exactly the same speed, usually 24 fps. The sound output of the reproducing machines is fed through a mixing console. The console contains individual volume controls and sets of filters for each track. The sound mixer sits at the console and blends the different sounds together. He can alter the volume of each individual track and can also alter its quality by using filters. If a sound is too loud, he can lower it. If it is too quiet he can amplify it and if there is too much bass, he can use filters to adjust the pitch. The output of the console, all mixed together, is recorded on a separate recording machine. It, too, uses perforated magnetic film and runs at the same speed as the projector and the reproducer.

The recorded track is generally referred to as the final mix master recording.

Preparing a dubbing cue sheet

The soundtracks to be dubbed are prepared by the film editor but he does not actually mix them together. That is done by a sound mixer supplied by the sound department. He does not know your film or your tracks and he cannot be expected to know what results you want to achieve. You have to tell him what you want done with the tracks supplied. The normal way to do this is to use a dubbing cue sheet. A cue sheet is divided into columns. There is a column for the action (cutting copy) and one for each track. At the top of the page you should mark the name of the film, the reel number and any other relevant facts, like the date and the production company. The rest of the information on the sheet depends on the contents of your tracks. List each track and tell the mixer how you want it to be mixed together. The normal way to do this is to plot each track with the footage at which you wish it to start and end. Sounds can cut in or out or can overlap and be mixed together. Or they can be faded in or out.

When drawing up a dubbing cue sheet you have to let the mixer know which of the ways of moving from sound to sound you want to use. Plot each track and tell him where and how you want it to begin and end. You can indicate the precise point by listing the starting and finishing footages of the tracks you have prepared. Starting footages should go on the top left hand side of the sound concerned and finishing footages on the opposite side underneath. A straight line indicates a cut.

A "V" placed the right way up means a fade out. The footage at which you wish to start fading the sound should be listed at the top of the "V". The fade will be completed by the footage listed underneath. If the "V" is placed upside down the sound will be faded in. If two "V"s occur at the same point the mixer will fade out one and fade in the other simultaneously. This is known as a cross mix.

If you are recording commentary during a dub you will not want to mix and record simultaneously as there would be too much to look after at once. It is better to record the commentary on a separate reel of stock and then do the mixing later. There are several reasons for this procedure. Mixing takes time and can be a trying job. It is often a matter of running through for a rehearsal and then doing the take scene by scene. Commentators do not usually like to hang about. They want to do their recording straight through if possible and then go away, so it pays to record without keeping them waiting too long. There is another more important reason too.

Preparation for foreign versions

Many industrial films are dubbed into foreign language versions, so when the tracks are mixed together the mixer will first of all make a pre-mix track containing all the music and effects tracks except the English language commentary. It is known as an M & E (music and effects) track, and is sometimes called an international sound band. It very much simplifies the production of foreign versions, for when another language version is required the foreign commentary can be recorded on one track and the combined M & E track can then be mixed with it quite simply. There is no need to go back to all the original tracks and remix the whole film. Pre-mixes save time and money.

Foreign versions of industrial films can be prepared quite easily if an M & E track is produced when the original language version is prepared. If it is not made at this stage, the preparation of foreign versions may involve remixing or relaying all the original music and effects tracks before a final soundtrack can be produced. With an M & E version the commentary can be recorded and edited to match the picture. The edited commentary track can then be mixed with the final M & E recording. Alternatively commentary can be recorded to picture in the dubbing theatre in the same way as the original language version.

There are several points worth remembering when recording foreign language versions. English is not a difficult language to dub. Some languages are more long-winded and when an English commentary is translated, ensure that the translation takes the same time to read as the English original, otherwise the sound will not match the edited version of the picture. Always try to get the person who reads the foreign version to do the translation. Foreign radio correspondents can usually do a good job. They can translate well and are also used to reading expressively in front of a microphone. If a recording is being done to picture, an English transcript should first be prepared with the starting footage of each paragraph marked alongside the dialogue. The script can then be sent to the commentator to be translated to length and the foreign script checked and recorded. For this the commentator is seated in a booth and the picture run through. The English final mix soundtrack can be used as a guide and monitored on headphones and the commentator can take his cue from the sound of the original English version, or from a film footage counter. At the footages listed on the script he can start to speak. If the translation is carefully prepared, it will fit the slot allowed for it. An alternative method is to pre-record the commentary and edit it to match the picture. The latter method requires more recording and dubbing time and is thus usually more expensive. With careful planning, and an experienced commentator capable of preparing his own translations, recording to picture can prove quite satisfactory.

Some languages are very un-technical. Arabic is an excellent example of a language where anything technical has to be explained in detail. This all takes time, and more words are needed to make the explanations. When editing a film which has to be dubbed into several foreign languages the length of the foreign dialogue should be remembered and allowance made when the pictures are cut. Do not leave long pauses. Leave *some* pauses, but prepare them in a way that ensures that they do not look like obvious pauses. It is not difficult if the film is properly planned. Sound effects and music can cover the gaps well, and when a long winded foreign track has to be prepared, there will be room for the dialogue.

Rock and roll dubbing

Many dubbing theatres now use a rock and roll system. A few years ago the mixer used to run through the film reel by reel and make copious notes. He then went back to the top of the roll and ran through to do the mix. If he made a mistake or missed a cue he had to stop and go back to the top of the roll. Today, he still runs through to rehearse and find out what the tracks sound like. He then starts to mix. But if he makes a mistake he now can stop, run back a few feet and start to record again without losing the previously dubbed scenes. This stop–go process is known as rock and roll dubbing. If he is mixing a large number of tracks the sound mixer may have an assistant or he may decide to do several premixes. Some mixers like to premix effects tracks, premix music tracks, then blend the two premixes together with the dialogue. Others like to run through in one take from beginning to end.

At the end of a dubbing session you have two pieces of film containing your final edited version. There is the cutting copy—the final edited version of the action—and a final mix master magnetic soundtrack. If you plan foreign language versions you may also have a master M & E track. These two or three materials should always be kept. After dubbing, the individual soundtracks prepared for dubbing can be reclaimed. The spacing can be removed and wound together on a reel for later re-use and the longer sections of magnetic can be re-claimed. It is only worth keeping lengths over 200 ft. The master tracks produced in the dub should be kept for the life of the film. The cutting copy and the final mix master track are still needed for the last stages of production.

By projecting the two separate pieces of film resulting from the dub on a projector capable of handling picture and separate magnetic sound, it is possible to view the film. But the cutting copy may by this time be in a very poor state of repair. It will be scratched and full of wax pencil marks and joins. If the film was shot in colour the cutting copy may be in black and white. Quite apart from these drawbacks, there are not very many projectors capable of showing picture with sounds on separate perforated magnetic film. So, prints combining sound and picture must be made for general showing. The camera master must be matched to the edited cutting copy and the magnetic sound must be again re-recorded.

Negative cutting

Matching the camera master and the edited cutting copy is known as negative cutting. I have already explained that the work is done by matching numbers on the side of the cutting copy with identical num-bers on the edge of the master film. Few industrial films makers do their own negative cutting. It is normally regarded as a job for specialists and the cutting copy can be sent to a negative cutter when dubbing is com-plete. It normally takes 4–5 hours to negative cut an average 15-minute film though the work can take much longer if the edge numbers are not clear or if there are many very short shots. The negative cutter works in a spotlessly clean room. He wears white cotton gloves and works in conditions which are as dust free as possible. Handling the master film is a great responsibility. If one mistake is made the error is there for ever—a cut in the wrong place or a scratch on the master film. So, care is the greatest qualification. The negative cutter first winds through the cutting copy and notes the edge number of each scene used. He then runs through the uncut reels of camera master and logs the numbers of the scenes and takes out all the scenes he needs. He only refers to the numbers—he is not interested in the action, so if there are no numbers on the cutting copy the editor will be in trouble. The negative cutter hangs all the extracted scenes in a bin lined with a clean linen bag. Then he assembles the master using a synchroniser and a cement joiner. Where there is a cut in the cutting copy, he cuts the master until scene matches scene and cut matches cut from beginning to end. Then, if he is good and reliable, he winds through again to make a final check.

Checkerboard cutting

The edited master can be assembled in a single roll or in two or more separate reels. If there are optical effects two or more rolls are needed unless the editor has asked the laboratories to provide a single roll optical dupe (containing the optical effects). Many industrial films are shot on 16 mm and the A & B roll master assembly system is very commonly used. This was explained earlier in the book but is briefly summarised here to aid comparison with an alternative system. In an A & B system, scenes are placed on alternate rolls whenever an optical occurs. Scene one is joined on roll A. If scene two follows with a cut it may also be joined on to roll A with a cement join putting the shot on to the end of the previous shot. But if scene one dissolves to scene two, the second shot is placed on roll B, with a suitable overlap to enable one scene to be faded out and the other to be faded in while both overlap. The centre point of the overlap is the point at which the two scenes have been joined together in the cutting copy. That is why you must always remember to allow for an overlap when optical effects are introduced. Black spacing will complete the rolls between shots.

There is an alternative to A & B roll negative cutting and it, too, is in general use. It is known as checkerboard cutting and closely resembles the A & B rolls method. In the A & B roll system, two or more rolls are used with the action changing from roll to roll when a dissolve takes place. In the checkerboard system, alternate shots are placed on alternate rolls regardless of whether or not a dissolve takes place. The joins are overlapped and they must be made on a frame line splicer with the direction of the overlap always into the black leader film between the scenes. This means that the direction must be reversed for the head and the tail of each shot. The easiest way of doing this is to wind through one way and make all the head joins then wind back the other way and make all the others.

The A & B and checkerboard systems allow optical effects to be printed direct from master film which ensures optimum technical quality. Intermediate duplicates needed for single roll master assemblies lack the impeccable quality of original film. The overlapping splices on checkerboard assemblies eliminate the small white flash which can betray a 16-mm join. When the master has been matched to the edited cutting copy it can be returned to the laboratory for printing. But first a suitable soundtrack for printing must be produced.

Soundtrack for printing

Prints produced for general showing are known as release prints. There are three different kinds of film print in general use. A cutting copy is one type. Release prints for general showing are another type and answer prints are a third variety to be remembered. The first graded print of a final edited film is known as an answer print. It is the first showprint of the final edited version of a film. Release prints normally combine sound and picture on one piece of film. Again, there are two types, one of which is much more common than the other. The difference is in the soundtrack, for you can have combined prints of sound and picture with either optical or magnetic sound.

A magnetic soundtrack on a combined print consists of a stripe of magnetic coating (ferrous oxide) on the side of the film. As with the tape used on an ordinary tape recorder you cannot *see* any sound recorded on the stripe. Sound has to be recorded and re-produced by a magnetic sound system. To make a print with combined magnetic sound you ask the laboratories to produce a show print in the normal manner on single perforated stock. The edge of the print can then be coated with a magnetic stripe. The master magnetic of the final mix sound can then be replayed on equipment locked in synchronism with a recorder capable of re-recording the sound on the magnetic stripe on the edge of the print. This sound stripe system gives excellent results but is not, alas, in very general use. Industrial film users intending to use magnetically striped prints should be aware of two serious drawbacks to the system. For quality magnetically striped prints have much to recommend them. But unfortunately comparatively few projectors are capable of projecting a print with a magnetic stripe. And print production costs and transfer charges are high which is why most release copies are made with the alternative system: optical sound.

An optical soundtrack is easy to recognise—a visible wavy line on the side of the film. Optical soundtracks are produced and printed by a photographic process, rather like the printing of the edited camera original. To make an optical soundtrack you must arrange for the final master magnetic soundtrack to be re-recorded as an optical sound negative. Before doing this, place one frame of 1000 cycle tone on the figure 3 on the leader of the final master magnetic track. When the track is re-recorded this frame reproduces an audible "plop". This is important, for when the sound negative is developed it will appear as a mass of lines without any readily identifiable reference point. Now, before the sound negative can be printed with the edited picture master, it must be synchronised to it. There is no slate this time, and no point that is easy to identify unless you remember to put one frame of tone on the figure 3 of the leader. When the track is developed you can then immediately identify the plop: it has a very easily recognised form. By using the synchroniser, the sound negative can be synchronised for printing, rather like synchronising rushes but with one important difference.

In all the editing stages of an industrial film the materials handled are cut in level synchronism with each other. Sound and picture are opposite each other in the synchroniser, and are laced up at the same point in the dubbing theatre. On prints of the final edited film, the sound must be slightly ahead of the picture. Why is this sound advance necessary? Think of the basic mechanics of a film projector. It consists of a drive sprocket, a film gate and a claw. Under the gate there is another drive sprocket and a sound drum. The sound drum and the picture gate are set apart. This is because movement through a picture gate is intermittent. The film is moved along frame by frame in a jerky motion controlled by a claw. Now if the sound reproducing equipment was near this intermittent movement, the sound would jerk along too, and the sound quality would be unbearable. So sound and picture are separated, and the soundtrack is always ahead of the picture. There is an internationally standard sound advance for both 35-mm and 16-mm films. On optical sound prints of combined sound and picture the sound must be advanced by 26 frames on a 16-mm and 20 frames on a 35-mm film.

To synchronise sound and picture for printing, place the leader of the edited camera master in a synchroniser and find the sync. plop on the optical sound negative. Now, you put the magnetic frame of tone on the figure 3 of the film leader, so if you put the re-recorded plop opposite 3 you will be in level synchronisation. But remember, on combined prints sound must be advanced for printing, so pull the sound up 26 frames (on 16-mm film) or 20 frames (on 35-mm film) and wind back a few feet to the head of the reels. Put a new start mark on all reels and write "16 mm (or 35 mm) print sync. start" on all the rolls. The reels can then be sent to the laboratories for the production of final show prints.

Answer print

In an earlier chapter I explained how a laboratory makes copies of an original film by using a motion picture printing machine to re-expose the processed master on a new reel of unexposed stock. You will recall that cutting copies and rush prints are often produced at speed and given an overall general exposure. When release prints and show copies are made the printing procedure is slightly different, so I will consider here the laboratory's contribution to industrial film making in rather more detail.

In a motion picture printer one piece of film is re-exposed on another. The amount of light which is allowed to pass through the film has to be assessed before the print is produced. You will remember that a printer is like a camera. It consists of a light and a shutter which can vary the amount of light passing from the original film on to the copy. By changing the shutter aperture it is possible to alter the exposure from scene to scene. Assessing the amount of light required is known as grading. When you return your edited master to the laboratory after negative cutting has been completed, the grader winds through the film and examines each shot. He assesses the correct printer exposure for each individual scene. If the film is in colour, he also chooses the right colour correction filters to balance the colours from scene to scene. Colour grading is, in my opinion, a science and an art. An ability to choose the right filter for every scene is the result of experience and a thorough knowledge of the principles and practices of colour photo-graphy.

When a colour film is photographed, the cameraman may use filters to balance daylight film for artificial use or tungsten film for daylight use. He is unlikely to employ fine colour correction filters, for he will rely on the ability of the laboratory grader to balance the colours when prints of the final film are produced. On a modern motion picture printer there are hundreds of different filter and exposure combinations. The aim of scene to scene grading is to obtain identical colour quality and continuity throughout. If you cut from a long shot of someone using a typewriter to a closer view, the grader examines both shots and makes sure that the person using the machine looks exactly the same in both shots. He ensures that there is no more red, for example, in one shot than the other and evens out the colours from one scene to the next. When he has assessed the lights and filters he wants to use he plots the information on a card and arranges a pro-gramme of cues to trigger the shutter and filters of the printing machine as the film passes through. On a modern printer like the Bell and Howell Model C, the information is programmed on a computer tape and fed into the machine. As each scene passes through, the printer selects the right exposure and correction filters taking its programmes from the tape. On some of the older types of printer, notches or clips were placed in the side of the master film.

Laboratories have done much to modernise their equipment and techniques in recent years and industrial film makers should now get a first class service. Printing machines work at an alarming rate. When a film is printed it may pass through the printing machine at anything from 40 ft per minute to 200 ft per minute. When you think that the machines are printing master film full of joins and simultaneously operating scene to scene light and colour change you realise what a complicated and clever piece of machinery a printer really is. When the two pieces of film have been printed, the master is re-canned and the exposed print processed. It can now be viewed and for the first time you can see a combined colour print of sound and picture. There will be no joins in the print and the colour should be properly corrected.

First prints should be good, but they rarely represent absolute perfection. There are usually a few slight changes which can be made when subsequent copies are produced. I normally expect to see two or three prints before I am satisfied. When a really good print has been produced, the next stage can be considered. Technically, the film has been completed, but few industrial film producers or sponsors can stop at this stage. One print may be superb, but many more will normally be needed. More release copies must be made and distribution must be arranged.

Duplicate master

It is extremely unwise to continue to produce prints from the camera master. If you damage it, or wear it out your film will be finished for ever. As soon as a satisfactory print has been made, a duplicate master should be produced. As a general rule it is worth making a duplicate if you expect to make more than five copies of the finished film, and always make one if there is any doubt at all. Many sponsors tend to underestimate the demand for their films. Duplicates are not cheap to make, but they do save money in the long run, particularly if the original is assembled in either "A", "B" or Checkerboard form. It is always more expensive to print from two separate rolls. When a duplicate master is printed the two rolls can be included in one. How is a duplicate master produced?

Again, laboratories use a motion picture printer to expose the master on another piece of film. If the film is in black and white and shot on a negative film, the laboratory will have to make an intermediate print before making a duplicate black and white negative. It is not possible to go straight from negative to negative on black and white film. A low contrast print, known as a fine grain duping positive, has to be produced. The laboratories load the original negative on one side of the printer and a reel of fine grain positive stock on the other. The reel is then printed and the fine grain print processed. After this it is laced upon the other side of the printer and re-exposed on a reel of new negative film. This new duplicate negative can then be processed and used for making further release prints without wearing out the original.

Colour negative can now be copied in one stage. Until 1970 a process similar to that used for making black and white copies had to be employed. The intermediate positive stage was known as an interpositive. Now it is possible to print straight from one Eastmancolor negative to another, known as a reversal internegative. The introduction of this process has done much to improve the quality of many industrial release copies as it is possible to make a duplicate negative of good quality in one simple stage. Again, the printing machine is used. The original negative is re-exposed on a reel of new reversal internegative stock and the internegative is then processed and used for producing further prints.

The masters of industrial films photographed on reversal colour stocks can be copied in two different ways. A duplicate reversal master can be made or a negative can be made from a reversal original. Both methods give satisfactory results and can be accomplished in one printing stage. For economic reasons, many sponsors prefer to make a negative. It is cheaper to make subsequent prints from a colour nega-tive than to continue to print from a reversal master. Look at the different duplication processes in simplified diagram form.

If you shoot black and white negative you can make a duplicate negative in these stages.

Re-expose your
Original cut negative
on
Fine grain duping positive
this can be developed and then you
can
Re-expose the fine grain duping positive
on unexposed negative stock.
The processed duplicate negative can be
used for making further prints.

If you are shooting on colour negative film you can make a duplicate colour negative in one stage:

Re-expose original colour negative
on
Reversal internegative stock. (CRI)
The reversal internegative can then be
printed on colour positive stock to
make further release copies.

If you are shooting on colour reversal you have a choice. On the left is the procedure for making a duplicate reversal master. On the right is the way to make a colour internegative which can be used for making cheaper release prints.

Re-expose reversal master	Re-expose reversal master
on	_or_ on
Duplicate reversal colour stock.	Colour internegative stock.
The processed duplicate can	The processed negative can
then be printed on reversal	then be printed on colour
stock.	positive stock.

Many industrial films shot on colour negative are on Eastmancolor and printed on an Eastmancolor positive stock. Reversal colour films shot on Ektachrome can be satisfactorily printed on Kodachrome or on Ektachrome stock.

When the first show print has been accepted and a duplicate master satisfactorily produced, the job of making the film is complete. Now steps must be taken to ensure that it is put to good use. And there are plenty of distribution outlets to be explored.

7

Using Industrial Films

THE DAYS WHEN a potential film sponsor could dismiss the possibility of making a film because he did not think anyone would want to see it have gone for ever. Today, there should be no difficulty in finding an audience for a well-made general interest film. If a film does not get a good showing, it is probably because the sponsors do not understand the distribution outlets or because the film is badly made and no one wants to see it. It is easy to reach *an* audience but it must be *the right sort* of audience.

Industrial films are usually produced for what film distributors call "non-theatric use". This means they are not principally designed for showing in commercial cinemas or on national television networks. Inexperienced sponsors may feel that if a film does not get a cinema or TV showing, it will not be seen by anyone. This is not true. There is an international distribution network catering for non-theatrical audiences. By using all the distribution outlets, it is possible to reach either a general audience or a specialised one likely to be interested in a particular product or service. The distribution network has been built up over the last twenty years and it is still growing. Although cinemas are still closing, and bingo and bowling have taken over, industrial film audiences remain. Beyond the many millions of people on the home market who see non-theatric films, the world wide audience gives a sponsor access to hundreds of millions of people—people who can be persuaded to buy, who can learn and who can be influenced by a sponsored industrial film.

Some people still fail to understand the size of the non-theatrical audience and insist on cinema showings. A South of England holiday town, famous for its old ladies and toasted tea cakes, asked a production company to quote for producing a short promotional film. The company submitted the quotation and some ideas for a script. It did not get the job, because it would not guarantee a cinema distribution. Another company produced the film and guaranteed a cinema showing which delighted the sponsors. Twelve months after the film had been produced, I checked with the distributors and found that it had been shown in eighteen cinemas. What a vast audience! Before commissioning any film, distribution outlets should be thoroughly explored.

These are the main audience outlets:

Cinema showing
Television transmission
Film library distribution
Direct distribution by a sponsor
Use by salesmen and company representatives
Mobile shows
Exhibition use
Company cinema presentations.

Cinema

Cinema showings are not of much interest to industrial sponsors. To get a cinema showing the film must be shot on 35 mm, for most commercial cinemas can only project 35-mm film. This situation is beginning to change with the trend towards smaller cinemas and a few 16-mm cinemas have now been introduced. If this trend continues, industrial users may be able to make wider use of cinema outlets. It is extremely difficult to get a general cinema showing for any documentary film. Even with a thoroughly uncommercial film of general interest, it is difficult to get a wide showing. The film distribution world is very well tied up and thoroughly out of date. The only effective way for a sponsor to use a 35-mm film is to hire a cinema out of normal hours and throw it open free to an invited audience. A few excellent films with indirect commercial connections, like BP's account of the crossing of Antarctica, have achieved a general cinema showing, but most sponsors will find the medium has little to attract them.

Television

Television is also of little use to industrial sponsors, though in the USA industrial films are used on television more than in the UK where they are almost unknown except for trade test transmissions. Some USA distributors are able to place films for TV showing. There are nearly 800 TV stations in the USA and many sponsored films which are not "hard sell" get a good showing. For television use a film must be of general interest and the product name must be kept very much in the background. Travel and sports subjects are particularly popular. Films for television must fit the regular TV time spots. There is also a reasonable market for short filler films with a running time around 5 minutes, though again, they must not be hard promotional material. Television audiences are difficult to arrange but if a showing is negotiated, a large audience can be reached very quickly. A figure of 45,000 people in one showing has been quoted by one distributor as an average TV audience for an industrial film shown on a local station in the USA. So twenty-five bookings on local stations will put the sponsor's message into over a million homes. But do not expect to walk into a TV station and find they have all been just waiting for your industrial film. They want to sell their commercial advertising time and if your film contains a hint of promoting your product, you will not be made welcome.

Film library

Film library distribution offers far the best way of reaching a specialised or a general audience. No film sponsor can afford to ignore the film library system. It operates on a world wide basis. Every major country has its film libraries and international distribution can be arranged by the Inforfilm consortium. Film libraries supply copies of films to organisations and individuals possessing their own projection equipment. There are thousands of people who either own or have access to 16-mm projectors. A film library can bring a sponsor's film to either a general audience or a specialised one.

Audiences can be divided into a number of different categories. Here are some typical audience groups:

Education

Education authorities	Residential colleges
Schools	Universities
Parent/teacher associations	Teacher training colleges
Technical colleges	Agricultural schools
Evening institutes	

Clubs, social and political groups

Youth organisations	Agricultural and horticultural
Clubs and societies	societies
Athletics associations	Young farmers clubs
Townswomen's guilds	Film societies and cine clubs
Women's organisations	Motor clubs, motor cycling and
Golf clubs	scooter clubs
United nations associations	Cricket clubs
Holiday camps	Football, rugby and hockey clubs
Passengers on ships	Tennis clubs
Church organisations	Fishing clubs
Unions	Sailing clubs
Airports	Young mothers' clubs

Government sponsored groups

Youth employment officers	Government departments
Gas, electricity authorities	Industrial training boards
Railways	Fire services
Police	Hospitals
Museums and public libraries	Armed forces

Industry and business

Professional associations	Business and professional
Scientific societies	women's clubs
Technical and engineering	Local productivity associations
societies	Commercial and industrial
Research associations	companies
Chambers of commerce	etc., etc.

How are these audiences reached and how does the library system work? When a film is completed the sponsor or the producers can contact a library and arrange a showing of the completed film. The library will then say how many copies could be profitably distributed. In the UK, twelve copies is the minimum normally required for a subject of general interest. In the USA fifty is often considered the minimum worth handling. Now it may perhaps seem that a library is being difficult in specifying a minimum number of copies, but this is not the case. Libraries know what their customers want and they know there will be a steady demand for a well made film of general interest. They know it is useless handling a very small number of prints, for when bookings come in there will not be enough prints to meet them. Bookings will have to be refused and audiences, after waiting for weeks for a copy of the film, will lose interest. So, enough prints should be supplied.

It is not of course necessary to supply at least a dozen copies of every kind of film. Many industrial films are not intended for mass audience showing. They are made for more selective use. Again, by using the library system, it is possible to reach a very select audience. A medical film can be restricted to medical audiences. A film demonstrating sales and management techniques can be restricted to industrial audiences and a tractor training film can be sent only to audiences involved in agriculture. The minimum number of prints needed depends on the nature of the subject and the type of audience it is to be made available to.

The library takes a number of prints which the sponsor supplies and pays for. The film is listed in a catalogue which is sent to all library customers. The customers then book the films they wish to see, usually submitting their bookings several weeks in advance. About a week before the date on which a film is due to be presented, the library despatches the film to the borrower. The film is then presented and after the showing the borrower is asked to complete a simple form listing the type of audience and the number of people in it. The borrower pays nothing at all to screen the film and the audience pays nothing to see it. When the film is returned to the library it is looked at by qualified film examiners to see if it has been damaged. The print is rewound, cleaned and if necessary, repaired and sent off to the next booking. At regular intervals, the library sends the sponsor information contained on the sheets completed by the borrower. The sponsor thus knows exactly who has seen his film. The sponsor is charged a small sum each time his film is seen by an audience. The sum charged to the sponsor covers the complete library service. It covers the catalogue entry which normally includes a short synopsis and the name of the sponsor, storage of the copies between bookings and despatch charges each time a film is sent out. Insurance against loss in transit is also often covered. Film examination and running repairs are included, as is the report on bookings and audience statistics. It is a comprehensive service and the charges are very nominal. But is it really worth paying a library to distribute a film? Is a sponsor better advised to despatch prints himself?

Sponsor distribution

It is usually a mistake for sponsors to handle the distribution of their own films. There can be no hard and fast rule, for every film is different and some subjects are so specialised that library distribution may not prove profitable. For most subjects, and many specialist subjects too, library distribution can be unhesitatingly recommended. There is far more to distributing a film than simply wrapping a reel in brown paper and putting it in the post. Travel film sponsors sometimes produce films and send them to travel agents who write in and ask for them. This works well for a while but very few sponsors examine the prints between showings and copies soon get worn and have to be replaced. Replacement print costs can often be avoided if a film is checked after every showing. Small damage can be repaired before it develops into a fault which may be expensive to put right. Libraries are well equipped and staffed to carry out preventive maintenance and to spot faults when they occur. Borrowers do damage prints. Sometimes they damage them so badly that they have to be replaced, but this is not very often the case. The present trend towards automatically threading projectors is doing much to lessen damage caused by incompetent projection. It is now often impossible to lace up a projector in the wrong way. I do not like automatic projectors but would recommend them for use where a projector is used by many different people, most of whom are untrained in the use of film. If a projector is going to be operated by one person only, or by a few people who can be trained, a projector which has to be laced up has much to recommend it. Automatic projectors do not get the attention they need. Dirt collects in the film gate and on guide rollers and can scratch the film. And when anything goes wrong with some types of automatic projector, it sometimes takes a very long time to trace the fault and put it right.

There are other reasons why sponsors are well advised to use a library to handle distribution. The library already has a list of established customers. So there should be little problem in finding an audience. And the monthly report on audience statistics helps to keep a close check on what is happening to a film. Some libraries will arrange for copies of sponsors' publications or publicity matter to accompany the film. It is also possible for bookings to be notified in advance so that a sponsor can send a representative to attend or follow up a showing.

A sponsor handling his own distribution should arrange for the prints to be checked by a film company at regular intervals. Where possible, he should wind through each copy after a booking to make sure the film has not been damaged. Prints should always be insured before despatch. It is generally a mistake to accept telephone bookings which have not been confirmed in writing. There are people who steal films and like to build up their own collections. A booking form stating the address to which the prints should be sent and the date on which they are required is essential. If the availability of the film is advertised in any way, always ensure that the film size is made known. If it is a 35-mm film and is not available on 16 mm, the matter should be made clear from the start so that no one books a copy and tries to run it on the wrong type of projector. It is also important to make it clear that sound films cannot be projected on silent projectors. Many silent machines have teeth on both sides of their drive mechanisms and the teeth make a hearty meal of optical soundtracks printed on single perforated film. Films should never be sent out without a spool and can, and the can should always bear a label giving the film title and the name and address to which the copy should be returned after use.

Some of the sponsors who decide to handle their own bookings make a small charge for handling each booking. This service charge system may be worth while when several films are handled, but I would never recommend it. The paperwork and time spent checking and entering payments usually writes off any financial benefit. It is better to entrust the work to a properly equipped distributor.

We have so far considered some ways in which an industrial film can be presented to audiences with access to film projection equipment. Not all audiences can hire or borrow a projector and many are not part of any organised group. Such people have to be reached by mobile presentations. How can mobile shows be arranged, and how are they best presented?

Mobile shows

A sponsor can present his own show, or he can ask a professional projection unit to do the work for him. Sometimes the two work together and that is probably the best way of ensuring success. It is useless for a sponsor to present a show in a large hall with unsuitable projection equipment. This may sound obvious, but it does, alas, happen. Mobile film presentation standards are often disgraceful and well made films are frequently ruined by villainous presentation. There is no excuse for shoddy work and sponsors who insist on presenting their own shows must ensure that they have the right equipment and staff to do the job properly. Any sponsor who bothers to make a film should have it properly presented. If it is not, the whole point may be lost. Some mistakes are made again and again whenever films are presented. People try to present too large a projected picture. A 20-ft screen is far beyond the capabilities of most 16-mm projectors. Only those with an arc or xenon light should attempt such large screen showing. A 10-foot screen is quite large enough for a normal tungsten lamp machine. It is always far better to present a smaller well lit picture than one where the light output of the projector is stretched to its limits. I recently attended a sponsored film show in a local town hall. It was presented by a travel agent who tried to project from the back of the hall on to an enormous screen. The pictures looked terrible—the beaches were dull and flat and everything lacked colour. If the presenter had brought the projector nearer the screen and thrown a smaller picture, the image would have been brighter and the scenes would have been far more attractive. So, if you have to present a mobile show, concentrate on projecting a well lit picture on a screen of reasonable proportions.

Sound on mobile presentations can also present some problems. Often the major problems are not the fault of the presenter. Some shows take place in halls with high roofs and echoes galore. People and curtains are the best antidotes for echo. The larger the audience, the more people there are to absorb sound and stop it bouncing from wall to wall. It also sometimes helps to cut some of the bass out by using a tone control if one is fitted to the projector. The major problems with sound are often caused by placing the loudspeaker(s) in the wrong position. Often they are placed behind the screen. This is completely useless, unless the screen is perforated to allow sound to pass through. If it is not, and very few screens used for mobile work do have perforations, the sound may be muffled and difficult to hear. Some people place the speaker on a chair under the screen. That too is useless, for the people sitting in the front row will hear all the sound and no one else will get the message. Speakers should be set alongside the screen and above the heads of the audience. The screen too should be situated quite high up. It is not good enough to put a screen on top of a table. The projected picture must clear the heads of the audience. It is often best to place one table on top of another and then place the screen on top of both tables. Another table can then be placed alongside the screen with a chair on top of it. The speaker can then be placed on the chair and pointed to face the middle of the audience. Everyone will then be able to hear properly and the people in the front row will not be deafened. Industrial films often have to be presented in places where conditions are far from ideal. The simple set up I have described can help to solve many problems.

When setting up a mobile show it is important to make preparations and run a test before the arrival of an audience. Make sure everything works and everyone can see and hear before the audience arrives. Also, put cables under carpets or overhead. I have seen someone come in late, trip over a cable and knock the projector over. The dialogue that followed was far more entertaining than the film! A few simple precautions can save trouble and ensure that the film is properly presented. Of course, not everyone will be satisfied. That is too much to expect. There is usually someone in an audience who asks the projectionist to turn the sound up or down because he is deaf or has got a headache. And there is always someone who has seen the film somewhere else before and feels that it looked rather different. "Has it been cut?" he usually asks. Mobile shows can be fun, and can be very worthwhile for they give a sponsor the chance to come face to face with an audience and with customers. But they must be properly presented.

Who attends mobile presentations? A sponsor can invite his own audience or offer to show a film to existing audiences in clubs and organised groups. Both systems are used. Some sponsors prefer to write to clubs and offer them a film show. Others like to advertise in the press or invite individuals to form an audience. Specialist films are often presented to invited audiences. A GKN film on flue linings was produced specially for showing to audiences of builders merchants. The sponsors presented evening shows at regional centres and invited local builders representatives to attend. The film was then shown and followed up by a product demonstration. This kind of specialised showing to invited audiences is widely used by many industrial film sponsors. The sponsor invites the audience. Sometimes he relies on an area representative Or he may advertise in the local press. Or he may rely on direct mail advertising. He may present the show himself or call in a local photographic dealer to handle the technical side of the showing. The shows are often presented as social events. Films are shown, refreshments provided and the sponsor's representatives are available to answer questions.

Some film libraries also handle mobile presentations. They have fully equipped vans and will agree to present any film, anywhere at any time. Some of the larger libraries also arrange their own presentations. Guild Sound and Vision, perhaps the most enterprising European library, present regular shows to audiences of housewives. These shows represent yet another way of reaching an audience. They are organised by the library and all the sponsor has to do is provide a copy of the film and meet part of the presentation costs. The shows are presented in series which consists of about 100–150 shows at different locations. In the case of the housewives' shows, the showings are to women's audiences but similar group showings are organised for mixed audiences in hotels and other places. The sponsor agrees to take part in a series of presentations. The library makes all the arrangements and provides the projection equipment. Two or three films are presented in each programme, often sponsored by different companies. The cost of the show is then divided between the sponsors. The total running time of a show is about one hour. The library also provides advance publicity material. A sponsor's publicity materials can be distributed in the course of a showing.

We have so far discussed ways by which a film can be presented to general or specialised audiences in group showings. There are ways of reaching a different kind of audience, for many sponsored industrial films are never intended for general group use. This is very often the case with films designed to sell at a high level where a general showing may be of no interest at all. The sponsor's aim is to get the film seen by whoever places orders. Often the person concerned does not have time to go to a cinema. So the film must be brought to him.

The days when showing a film in an office meant blacking out the windows and setting up a screen have now gone, as far as small audience showings are concerned. The conventional projector now has an ally, ideal for showing short films to a handful of people—the portable cassette type of projector. The Videotronic, Technicolor and Fairchild machines are perhaps the most widely known examples of this type. They have done much to open up a new audience for the industrial film, for they make it possible to show a full sound colour film to someone on an office desk. They do not need blackout or a screen as they have their own built-in screens and the picture is back-projected. They are portable and can be carried like a briefcase. You just plug them in, switch on and show the film. The man who has no time to go to a cinema will often be sufficiently interested by the machine to want to watch the film. And, as it is in his own office, he does not have to go to any trouble. Many sponsors use these machines and get satisfactory results and firm orders. They are particularly suitable for sales promotion use.

The three projectors I have mentioned take super 8-mm film. Films shot on 35 mm or 16 mm can be copied on super 8 mm so any film can be used on any of the three machines. The Fairchild and Videotronic projectors both use magnetic sound. One Technicolor machine uses super 8-mm optical sound. I personally consider this a very considerable drawback for although the Technicolor machine is well made and gives a good performance, super 8-mm optical sound can be difficult to obtain.

The Videotronic and Fairchild machines use super 8-mm film with a magnetic sound stripe. These are comparatively easily obtained, particularly in the USA where super 8-mm print quality is very much better than in the UK. American laboratories are much better geared to super 8 mm. All three machines use film cassettes—a major advantage. Film is loaded into a cassette by either the film producer or the laboratory. All the user has to do is slot the cassette into the machine, and switch it on. To change a film you simply slot out one cassette and drop another one into place. There is no film to lace up, and the whole operation could not be more simple. It has been designed for use by people without film experience such as salesmen and company directors, and by people who want to use industrial film as a sales aid and not as a technical piece of equipment.

The film cassettes work well though prints have to be perfect. With the slightest imperfection in film stock trouble will follow! The machines work well if they are used with care and not expected to perform the impossible. I don't think they are ideal for continuous running, not because of the machines, but the film. Super 8-mm film is not strong enough to run for long periods without trouble. Two days of continuous running must be considered good for a super 8-mm copy. Some would say it is miraculous but people trying to sell machines would claim it as a minimum. The real answer depends on the condition of the print and the way in which it is used.

Tape joins are best for use in cassettes as cement joins tend to give trouble. Film should be waxed before it is loaded in a cassette. The cassettes, working on a continuous loop principle, run round and round until stopped. There is no need to rewind and on most machines it is impossible. You run through to the end of the film and the beginning comes up all over again. Always carry a spare cassette. Film does break and though it does not happen very often, it usually seems to occur at the worst moment.

These cassette projectors are excellent for sales promotional work. The Lifton film we explored earlier was presented on a Videotronic with conspicuous success. It was shown to garage managers and created such a demand for the Lifton system that showings had to be discontinued until orders could be met! The success has been repeated many times. Hygena produced a film showing their quick assembly kitchen furniture. By using the film and a Videotronic machine the directors could show the equipment and their factory to buyers in the USA and Canada. The 3M company in London produced a film to sell a vehicle marking system. The Videotronic enabled them to show it to people able to place large contracts. There are many success stories, and many audiences waiting.

Portable projectors can also be used to present films at exhibitions, preferably with 16-mm film. A conventional front screen projection can be used on an exhibition stand if the area is large enough and if sufficient blackout can be arranged. Back projection units are often more suitable. There are also 16-mm back projection cabinets rather like the super 8-mm machines I have mentioned. They are not very portable. Most 16-mm BP cabinets incorporate a normal optical sound projector which back-projects a picture via mirrors to a small screen, usually about 24 in wide. Sound is relayed to a built in speaker immediately under the screen. Again, prints should be waxed before they are used and spare copies should always be carried.

Company cinema

Some established film sponsors have built their own company cinemas. It is not always the large companies who take this step. Some very small companies have pleasant viewing theatres. Size does not mean success. The success of an internal cinema depends on whether or not it can be put to good use. In a large company there will be many applications. If the cinema is large it can also be used for meetings and social events. Few company cinemas are large. Most seat fewer than 20 people and quite a number only have room for half a dozen. In a large organisation a company cinema may be used for training and for sales promotion. In a smaller company, it may only be used for showing films to customers. What should a company cinema consist of, and how expensive is it to equip?

Few sponsors are fortunate enough to have the opportunity of planning a cinema as part of a new building. Usually existing areas have to be converted. Offices and store-rooms are sometimes used and can be made suitable if skilfully converted. It is really best to have two separate rooms divided by a solid brick wall. One of the rooms should be small. It can then serve as a projection area. The second room can form the main part of the theatre. It should be long and narrow. A low ceiling is not a disadvantage. If the room is the right shape, the rest can be altered or provided. There must be a separate projection area.

The whirr of a projector in the background ruins any films and hampers concentration. Fire regulations specify a brick wall between theatre and projection room, though, unless nitrate film is likely to be run, this official stipulation can usually be overcome. It is, however, essential to have a reasonably solid wall between the two rooms for sound carries through any sort of flimsy partition. Projection and viewing ports should also be cut through the wall. There should be one port in front of each projector at lens height, and another somewhat higher to give the projectionist a clear view of the screen. Ports should be double glazed with optical glass set at an angle to minimise reflections and light loss. With the walls and projection ports in place, you can plan the rest of the theatre.

Equipment for company cinema

Equipment in a cinema theatre must, of course, include a projector, a loudspeaker and a screen. The projector is probably the most important piece of equipment. One projector may not be enough. If the theatre is only to be used for presenting the company's own films, one machine designed to project the type of films produced may suffice. If the company films are 16 mm with optical sound, a 16-mm optical sound projector may be good enough. But if the theatre is to be used for showing films made by other companies, a wider variety of presentation standards may be needed. A 16-mm projector capable of reproducing 16-mm optical sound and magnetic sound stripe might be an advantage, or a projector which can produce both these types of sound and separate tracks recorded on perforated magnetic. If the theatre is to be used by an internal film unit, this kind of projector will enable rough cuts and early edited versions to be shown in the course of production. It may also be worth acquiring more than one projector. Two machines make continuous running possible and also ensure that there is always a spare one if unexpected trouble occurs. Most industrial theatres are small and a projector with an incandescent lamp will give a clear brightly lit picture of the correct size. If a large picture is needed, or the theatre is designed to hold a large number of people, a machine with stronger illuination should be selected.

When buying any projector rigorous tests should be carried out. Many new machines are supplied without being properly checked and their performance sometimes falls far short of paper specifications. Check the sound and picture quality by running a piece of test film which you know is good. Check that the picture is steady by moving the frame line until it is visible. Make sure the film path does not scratch —a badly aligned gate or roller can cause great damage, and see that all the amplifier and sound controls function properly. Always keep a projector covered when not in use. Dirt quickly collects and spoils performance. Also carry a supply of spare lamps and fuses. Lamp life is difficult to predict. If a projector is permanently fixed in a company theatre the life of the lamps will generally be longer than if it is used for mobile work.

Some people claim that 15 hrs. is the longest life that can be confidently predicted for the average lamp used in projectors. Others say 50 is nearer the correct figure. But lamp life depends on many factors. Frequent switching on and off shortens the life of a lamp in the same way as movement of a machine while a lamp is warm. Life is normally longer for machines operated via a transformer running the light at slightly less than the recommended power.

When equipping a projection room it is important to allow plenty of room on either side of the projectors, so that film can be laced up without difficulty. Spare reels are also needed and can be kept on hooks fixed to the wall alongside the projection ports. If tape and record reproducers are to be incorporated in the theatre equipment, it may be best to keep them in the projection area rather than in the main viewing area. Plenty of storage racks for film cans should also be included. And do not forget to provide a monitor speaker so that the projectionist can hear the sound. Lighting in a projection area should be reasonably subdued. Bright light must not shine on the projection ports and it is important to avoid stray light falling on the soundhead, for excessive light falling across an optical head and on to the photo electric cell will produce a constant hum.

In the viewing area comfort is an important consideration. People who are uncomfortable may not enjoy a film. Site the screen high enough to clear the heads of the audience but not so high that the neck is strained looking up for a long time. Make sure that the picture is evenly lit and the sound is clear. Motorised curtains are a luxury but a large black mask round the screen is essential and should be at least one foot deep all round the screen. Black surrounds emphasise the brilliance of the projected picture and also cover the extreme edges of the film frame where definition is not particularly good. A carpeted theatre improves the quality of sound. Hard walls make the sound hard and curtains deaden the effect—if used on all walls they can prove too deadening. In commercial cinemas the normal practice is to fit either acoustic tiles or fibreglass to the rear wall of the theatre. Flameproof curtains can then be used on the other walls. Seats should always be well upholstered and comfortable. Few industrial theatres use cinema-style seats. Armchairs of different kinds are frequently found and the executive padded armchair is always popular. Ash trays should also be provided alongside every seat. It is also essential to have some method of communication between projection area and theatre. A simple two-way transistorised talkback will suffice, even a children's nursery type baby alarm! In a theatre used for production purposes, a separate volume control in the viewing area is a handy addition and a film footage counter can be a help, though, for normal industrial viewing purposes, neither of these items is essential.

I have already said that I feel it is better to project a small, well lit picture than attempt to produce one of greater dimensions. The screen size necessary in company cinemas depends on the focal length of the projection lens in use and the distance between projector and screen. The shorter the focal length of the lens, the larger the projected image and the further the projector is from the screen, the greater the picture size. So, on a 16-mm projector, a 2-in lens will give a larger picture than a 3-in lens and a smaller picture than a $1\frac{1}{2}$-in one. The practical screen size with a given projector can be best determined by testing image brightness from the projector position (which may be fixed by the dimensions of the room) with various lenses giving images of differing size and brightness. Manufacturers' literature will give advice on suggested throws with the particular equipment.

Previews

A well equipped company cinema can be used for presenting films to customers and staff. It can also be hired out to others, particularly if it is in a central area of town. Preview theatres are in great demand and if a theatre is really well equipped and efficiently run, it can be hired by people wishing to view their own films. The normal procedure is to charge a set sum per hour for the use of the theatre and the services of the projectionist. Several leading industrial groups have equipped theatres which are available for hire and able to run 16-mm and 35-mm film. Such theatres are to be found in many major cities throughout the world. They are frequently used for the presentation of new film previews.

The life of a new industrial film can be said to begin when the laboratories deliver the first satisfactory graded print. Release copies will follow and the film will go into use. Many sponsors like to arrange a preview to celebrate the completion of a film and to ensure that it starts life with as much publicity as possible. Previews can be very worthwhile. They can provide a lot of editorial press coverage and can also ensure there is a good demand for prints from the start, thus eliminating a build-up period waiting for the new film to become known. But previews must be planned and thoroughly organised if they are to be successful.

Every sponsor and producer has his own ideas about how to organise a preview. My ideas on the subject have been tested many times and may, perhaps, be of interest to anyone planning a show for the first time. Previews are not cheap and they need a lot of arranging. I always remember one very indignant producer friend of mine cornering me when I attended the preview of one of his latest films. It was a very lavish affair and my friend was fuming with rage as he whispered in my ear "They've spent more on this b—— preview than they gave me to make the film!" Costs can be high, but they should be kept in proportion to the production budget. Previews are often held in small private theatres seating between fifty and two hundred people. Some international companies launching major prestige films book a large cinema and invite far more people, but for most industrial launches, a gathering of between 50 and 200 people is about right. The sponsors plan the arrangements and this is what they have to plan.

The preview day must be fixed several weeks in advance and the theatre must be booked and the booking confirmed in writing. Theatre bookings made on the telephone must always be confirmed. The choice of date will depend on the sponsor's assessment of the availability of the people he wants to form his audience. Some sponsors feel that Monday is a dead day and Friday is no good because everyone is out of town. There is certainly something to be said for both these views. Late-night shopping nights can cause traffic congestion and delay people on their way to evening shows . . . and so the objections go on. The sponsor must pick a date and print the invitations. These should be sent out at least three weeks before the showing is due to take place. They should give the date, time and place of the showing and the briefest possible details of what is going to be shown. Here is a possible form of invitation.

"The Directors of Cornelders Travel invite

....

to attend a preview of their new film
"CRUISING ON THE RHINE"
at Sorel Films Theatre, 120 Long Acre, London W.C.2.

on ....   at ....
Refreshments   RSVP

You will note that the invitation lists refreshments. This is important, particularly for attracting the press. Sandwiches and drinks are often provided at these occasions and a full buffet meal may be laid on for full-scale previews. It is well worth making the occasion as memorable as possible and food is an excellent way of making an event worth remembering. A meal served after the film showing also gives the sponsor's representatives time to circulate among the guests and test their reactions. When a buffet meal is served after the showing, it is sometimes a good idea to provide an aperitif before the presentation.

The programme for the showing should be planned and rehearsed. Make sure the projectionist knows the right starting and stopping points and has the correct sound level for the print. Most sponsors like a company director or official to introduce the showing and it is important to arrange a cue with the projectionist so that he knows exactly when to start. Introductions should be kept short. Too many directors try to say what the film says for them. Just welcome the guests, introduce the film and then sit down. The film will do the rest. Some sponsors like to provide a little light relief before their directors introduce the main film. A cartoon may be projected first. This is a good idea, for someone always arrives late on these occasions and it is courteous to those who arrive on time if the performance is started promptly. A cartoon or short film enables the show to start as planned. After ten minutes of relief, when everyone is assembled the sponsor can introduce and show the new film. It is a good idea to provide a detailed synopsis of the film and a list of credits naming those taking part and responsible for production. The press always need this information. The sheets should include as much detail about the film as possible, in particular what size copies are being made available and where they can be obtained from. Some sponsors prepare a preview folder with stills, a synopsis and product details.

Who should be invited to a new industrial film preview? The answer to this question depends on the film. The press should be invited though few national daily newspaper reviewers attend industrial film showings. A few enlightened papers have industrial film correspondents who do an excellent job and who are always interested in new industrial films. If the film is specialised, or likely to appeal to a particular audience, the specialist press should be invited and representatives of trade organisations and company contacts. The Painton film attracted a good press turnout. As the film was about home decorating it appealed to many women's editors and do-it-yourself magazines. Representatives of the paint trade and building industries were also invited as well as agents and guests of the sponsoring firm. The forty copies of the film have been heavily booked up ever since. Previews can be expensive, though they need not be excessively costly. They should ensure a good demand for any good film.

Industrial film festivals and conventions are held from time to time. They offer another kind of audience for industrial film. Are they worth taking part in? Some producers and sponsors rave about film festivals.

Others say they are a complete waste of time. I would certainly never rave about a festival, though I do not think they are entirely a waste of time. They do help to raise standards and promote an interest in industrial film. They give a sponsor a chance to enter his film in competition with others and possibly win an award. Festivals provide an opportunity for sponsors to get together and discuss ideas, films and producers and they give producers a chance to show their latest work and discuss ideas, sponsors and films. Many poor films are entered for many film festivals. Fortunately selection committees weed out the worst but some poor films still slip through. Festivals can do an excellent job if they are well organised and if enough people take part but unfortunately, these two conditions are seldom met. In fact, festivals are often badly organised. Competitive festivals are often judged by the same people year after year so that results can almost be predicted in advance. Too many films are judged for what they appear to be and not for what they actually achieve. In my opinion, films should be judged for their technical excellence and for their ability to do the job they set out to do for the sponsor.

Industrial films can, and should, be a first class investment for the sponsor. A festival award or certificate is a welcome fringe benefit, but the real success of a film depends on other matters. Many potential sponsors are afraid to make films. They feel their money will be wasted. They may be right, for if a film is badly made or poorly distributed it may not be successful. We live in a world used to visual aids. Industrial films are popular and a well made film should have no difficulty at all in earning its keep. If it is well made and properly distributed it will prove to be a good investment.

Glossary

ACTION. When a film is edited with separate magnetic soundtracks the picture to which the tracks are matched is often simply called "the action".

ARRIFLEX. A range of cameras and allied film equipment produced in West Germany.

AUTOCUE. A prompting aid enabling performers appearing in front of a camera to read from a script while filming is going on.

A AND B ROLLS. A negative cutting system. Cut master material is assembled in two rolls. The system enables prints incorporating optical effects to be printed from original master material in one stage.

A AND B WINDINGS. Two forms of winding used for films which have only one edge perforated. Film wound emulsion in, and unwinding clockwise, is an "A" winding if the perforated edge is nearest the operator. If it is away from him the film is a "B" winding.

ANSWER PRINT. The first graded ('timed' in the USA) show print is often known as an answer print.

BIG CLOSE UP (Abbr. B.C.U.). Shot framing only a small part of a subject, closer than a close up (C.U.), part of a human face for example.

BLOW UP. The technique of making a larger picture copy of a film shot on a smaller gauge. A 35 mm copy of a 16 mm film is known as a "blow up".

CASSETTE. A film (or tape) magazine holding a length of film (or tape) which runs continuously between two spools or hubs enclosed in it.

COMMENTARY. Spoken words accompanying a film as distinct from those spoken by characters appearing in it. The speaker usually remains unseen. Also known as narration and "voice over" and "voice".

CLOSE UP. (Abbr. C.U.) A shot taken, in effect, close to a subject, revealing detail. In the case of a human subject, the face only or the hands only would be classified as close up.

CUTTING COPY. A film copy made for editing purposes. Also known as a work print.

CONTINUITY. The flow from one shot to another without breaks or discrepancies. Smoothness in the development of subject matter.

CUE SHEETS (DUBBING). When film soundtracks are being mixed together the points at which sounds start and end are plotted on a cue sheet. The sheet guides the dubbing mixer who mixes the tracks.

CUTAWAY. A shot showing something other than the main theme of the action. A cutaway is inserted between shots of the main action. Often used as a bridge of time or to avoid a jump cut.

COMBINED PRINT. A print where the soundtrack and action are printed together on one piece of film. Also known as a married print.

CROSS MIX. The dubbing technique of fading out one sound track and fading in another simultaneously.

CLAPPER BOARD. Two pieces of board hinged together in such a way that the two parts can be banged together at the start of a synchronised sound take. Scene and take number are written on the board and filmed at the start of the synchronised shot so that the action can be identified later by the editor. The editor matches the point where the board is banged together with the corresponding bang on a separate magnetic soundtrack and thus re-synchronises sound and picture.

CUTTING ROOM. The film editor's kingdom. It contains all the equipment needed for editing picture and sound.

DAILIES. The American name for rushes (q.v.).

DUPE. Duplicate. A dupe negative is a duplicate (copy) negative and not the actual film exposed in the camera.

DISSOLVE. An optical effect in which one scene gradually replaces another. In essence a fade out and fade in are superimposed. Also known as a mix.

DOUBLE SYSTEM. A system of sound recording for shooting synchronised sound takes. Sound is recorded on separate perforated magnetic film or on $\frac{1}{4}$ in tape for later transfer to perforated magnetic film, and not on the actual piece of film exposed in the camera as is the case when shooting single system sound.

DUBBING. The name given to the various processes involved in re-recording a number of separate magnetic soundtracks to make one final mixed soundtrack. Also the name given to re-voicing a film in another language.

EDGE NUMBERS. Also known as key numbers these are marked on the side of original film and thus on every copy made on a printer printing via a full gate. The numbers are used to match camera original material to an edited cutting copy when film editing work is complete. If edge numbers are missing or are indistinct ink numbers can be printed before editing starts.

EMULSION. The side of the film coated with a light sensitive emulsion in the case of picture stock. The side of a magnetic soundtrack coated with ferrous oxide. Easily identified as the least shiny of the two sides.

FADE IN. Gradual emergence of a shot from complete darkness.

FADE OUT. A shot which gradually disappears into darkness.

FAIRCHILD. The name of an American manufacturer of cassette film projectors which are very widely used.

FACILITIES FEES. Sum payable for the use of a location, or of facilities.

FINE CUT. The final edited version of the cutting copy. The last stage at which alterations can be made and the last stage before camera original and cutting copy are matched by the negative cutter.

FIRST ASSEMBLY. The first assembly of scenes is script order.

FINAL MIX. The final film soundtrack in which all the separate tracks prepared for dubbing are mixed together.

FINE GRAIN. Films stock with extremely fine grain emulsion. The term can apply to master films used in the camera but is often used to describe stocks employed by a laboratory for the intermediate states in the course of preparing duplicate master materials.

FRAME. A single picture on a length of cinematograph film or a corresponding amount of a perforated magnetic soundtrack.

GRADING. Estimating the amount of printer light that must be allowed to pass through scenes of an original film from which a copy is being produced. Colour correction for scene to scene colour balance is also worked out at the same time.

GAUGE. The width of a film. The largest in general use for commercial cinema work is 35 mm. 16 mm film also is used by professionals. Super 8 mm is principally an amateur gauge though it does have a limited industrial use.
Standard 8 mm and 9.5 mm are now both obsolete.

INTER-POSITIVE. A fine grain, low contrast colour print used in the course of making some duplicate colour negatives.

INTER-NEGATIVE. A duplicate colour negative. In the USA the term usually refers to a colour negative made from a reversal colour master and used for making release copies. Duplicate colour negatives of colour negative originals are there more widely known as colour dupe negs.

JUMP CUT. A cut from scene to scene which disturbs the continuity by omitting an interval of time revealing a person or object in a different position in two adjacent shots.

KEY NUMBERS. See EDGE NUMBERS.

LEADER. A piece of film attached to the beginning and/or end of a film. The head leader contains a start mark and numbers at each film foot down to 3. There then follows two feet of black to which the first frame of picture can be joined. Similar leaders should be used for all sound-tracks.

LIBRARY SHOT. Shot used in a film but not taken specially for it. A shot taken from an outside source—usually a film library—and not one provided by the unit shooting the film.

LABORATORY. The processing of ciné film is always handled by a specialist laboratory. Film production companies do not have their own laboratory facilities.

LOOP. A short length of film joined end to end to enable it to run continuously.

MOVIOLA. The trade name of a US editing machine. Sometimes used as a general term for all motorised editing machines, particularly in the USA.

M & E TRACKS. Music and effects soundtracks. A mixed track free of commentary. It is essential if foreign language versions are required. M & E tracks should contain all lip synchronised dialogue spoken by people in view of the camera but not words spoken by a narrator, as voice over.

MARRIED PRINT. See combined print.

MASTER. A camera master is the original film exposed in the camera. Also known as the "original". A master magnetic recording is the original sound recording.

MEDIUM SHOT. (Abbr. M.S.) A shot taken at normal viewing distance usually cutting actors at the waistline.

MUTE. A picture negative or positive without a combined soundtrack.

OPTICAL (EFFECT). A dissolve, fade in and fade out, wipe and other special effects are known as opticals.

OPTICAL (SOUNDTRACK). A soundtrack printed photographically alongside the picture. Sound modulations can be seen on a print with an optical track.

POSITIVE. Print.

RELEASE PRINT. A projection copy of the finished film.

RECCE. A visit made to locations at which filming could take place, and designed to find out what facilities are available and what equipment is needed.

RUSHES. Copies of the film exposed in the camera made immediately after the original has been processed. Designed principally for checking and editing, rush prints are usually ungraded. Also known in the USA as "dailies".

ROYALTIES. Payments due for the use of copyright library film material or music in a film made by someone other than the copyright owner.

SPONSOR. The organisation (or occasionally the individual) providing the financial backing for a film.

SPONSORS MESSAGE. The main point(s) the film is designed to explain to an audience.

SPONSORS BRIEF. A preliminary instruction given by a sponsor to a producer setting out guidelines for the film to be produced.

SLATE. See Clapper Board.

SHOW PRINT. Copy of the finished film for projection.

STOCK SHOT. See library film.

SYNCHRONISATION. The precise marriage of sound and picture so that the sounds heard on the soundtrack exactly compliment the pictures seen on the screen.

STILLS. Still photographs. Often taken while filming, as a continuity aid, and often for later use as press publicity.

STEENBECK. A West German make of editing equipment.

SHOOTING SCRIPT. A camera script listing precise details of what the camera films and what the soundtrack says.

TREATMENT. A draft script in which the way a film subject is developed from scene to scene is outlined.

TRIPACK FILM. A type of colour film with three light-sensitive emulsion layers.

UHER. A brand of tape recorder.

VIDEOTRONIC. A type of continuous loop film projector using super 8 mm sound film.

Index

A/B rolls 204, 223
Accident prevention 26, 28
Acmade equipment 194
Action cuts 198
Actors 94, 176
Aims of films 13, 17, 30
All Systems Go 100
Animated viewers 192
Answer prints 98, 224, 225
Arc lights 140
Arriflex camera 125, 130
Asbestos information committee 88
Audience executive 13
  interest 63
  for cassette presentation 13
  for internal shows 13
  for film library shows 11
  for television 12
  for size 30
  specialist 16
Autocue 181
Automatic exposure 129, 135

Batch numbers 117
Bell Howell printer 226
Blow ups 98, 120
Bolex cameras 130, 137
Brief 47
Budget 57, 60, 92, 95
Building tracks 210

Call sheets 105
Camera characteristics 123, 125
  hire 93, 95

movements 174, 202
  positions 25, 98
  (report) sheets 169
Cassette projectors 13, 16, 79, 97, 120, 238
Casting 176
Checkerboard 223
Cinema (see Preview theatre)
Clapper board 149, 151
Close ups 169
Colour balance 155
  stocks 112, 120, 122
  tests 191
Colortran 141, 146
Commentary 208, 213, 219
  soundtracks 25, 69, 96
Commentators 212
Continuity 150, 160, 163, 198, 201
Costs 11, 29, 31, 33, 92, 95, 103, 117, 154
Cross mix 219
Cue sheet (dubbing) 219
Cutaways 164, 207
Cut price filming 33, 54, 59
Cutting copy (see also Rushes) 95, 198, 190
  rooms 43m 193
  techniques (see Editing)
  to music 74, 208

Dailies (see Rushes)
Dating 30
Demonstrations on film 22
Depth of field 128

Directors 149, 158
Disasters 32
Discussion 24
Distribution by sponsors 13, 31, 234
  for television 12
  international 12, 15, 87
  to cinemas 230
  via film libraries 11, 31, 232
Dramatic sequences 90
Double takes 198
Dubbing 96, 219
Duplicate masters 114, 118, 227
Duration 33, 59

Eastman Double X 116
Eastmancolor 112, 115, 118, 155
Eclair cameras 136
Editing 51, 96, 98, 125, 153, 191, 196,
  207, 208
Edge fogging 118
Edge numbers 189, 206
Ektachrome 113, 115, 155
Equipment check list 186
  hire 40, 46, 93
  internal unit 40, 46
Exhibition stands 12, 240

Facilities fees 103
Failures 33
Fairchild projectors 13, 238
Film cassettes 239
  festivals 245
  life 30, 243
  projectors 241
  stock 93, 96, 110
Filters 155, 156
Fine cut 199
Final mix 219
Fire at Work 86
Fire Protection Association 87
First assembly 192, 197
Flue lining film 17
Focus 128
Foreign versions 220

Gauge 96
Grading 189, 225
Group PR film 29, 53
Guild Sound and Vision 238

Hand held shots 139

Hard selling 28, 77
Hiring equipment 40, 46, 93
Humour 25, 65, 80

Identifying a take 149
Incandescent lights 140
Insurance 94
Interchanging formats 97, 119
Inter departmental liaison 45
Intermittent movement 124
Internal film units 36, 174
Interviewing technical staff 47
Investment 30

Joiners 197
Joint sponsorship 87

Key numbers (see Edge numbers)

Laboratory processing (see Processing)
  sequences 72
Lenses 124, 127
Liaison for an international unit 45
  with sponsors 41, 86, 103
Library distribution 11
  film shots (see Stock shots)
  sound effects 214
Lifton film 79
Lighting 95, 129, 139, 146, 154
Location shooting 35, 103, 145, 153, 162,
  178
London Fire Brigade 87
Low budget films 33, 37, 57

Magnetic (sound) stripe 125, 224
M and E tracks 220
Minimax 88
Miniola 194
Mobile shows 12, 30, 236
Moviola 194

Nagra recorders 143
Narration (see Commentary)
Negative characteristics 110, 112
  cutting 96, 188, 205, 222
Neutral density filters 157
Non-theatric distribution 230

One light prints 190
One man bands 37, 55, 59
Opticals 203
Optical sound 224

Pace 168, 207
Painton film 58
Panchromatic stocks 118
Parallax 126
Picture synchroniser 195
Planning distribution 16
Polaroid camera 163
Premises for a film unit 42
Pre-production planning 40, 50, 56, 146
Prestige 28
Previews 243
   theatre 43, 96, 240
Prints 223
Processing 93, 94, 111, 117, 122, 170, 186
Producer-sponsor liaison 41, 78, 86, 103
Production team 38, 55
   time 108
Professionalism 34, 48, 52, 54, 152, 174, 212
Public relations 28

Quality of production 33, 48
Quartz lights 141

Reccy 35, 103
Reduction printing 97, 119
Rehearsals 35, 149, 160, 188
Research 61, 89
Reversal characteristics 112
Rock and roll 221
Royalties 108
Running speeds 124
Rushes 52, 118, 170, 186, 196

Safety films 26, 86
Saving money with film 21, 22
Security 183
Selling consumer products 14, 58
   delivery dates 20
   holidays 14, 31, 54
   plant 15
   services 19
   specialised subjects 16, 18, 79
   the unportable 16
   to trade audiences 17
Shooting script 34, 51, 89, 98
   schedule 103
   without a script 165
Single frame stop motion 172
Slate (see Clapper board)
Slow motion 171

Sound advance 125, 225
   creative use of 90
   effects 215, 216
   on prints 224
   preparation of 153, 192, 210, 213
   recording equipment 143
   shooting systems 125, 151
   transfers 95, 187
   two versions in some language 17
Splicers 197
Sponsor brief 57
   control 40, 86
   liaison with producer 78, 103
   message 33
Sponsorship joint 90
Spot effects 216
Staff for an internal unit 47
Staff training 23, 25
Stages of production 34
Standard of production 31
Steenbeck equipment 194
Stills 154
Stock shots 107
Storage space 43, 120
Studio for small film unit 44, 95
Study notes 24
Sub contracted filming 50
Success 87
Super 8 mm film 13, 97, 120, 239
Synch pulse 125
Synchroniser 195
Synchronising 191, 196
Synchronising sound shooting 151, 166

Talking to camera 181
Technical advice 42
Technicolor camera 121
   projectors 13, 238
Test shooting 117
35 mm film 96, 111, 119
Track laying 210
Trainees 48
Training films 23
Treatment for sales promotional films 14
   hard sell theme 58
   simple subjects 174
   specialised subjects 16, 78
   staff recruiting films 23
   training films 24
Tripack films 121
Tungsten halogen lights 141

T/V showing of industrial films 12, 87

Videotape 97, 163
Videotronic projector 13, 79, 238
Viewfinder systems 126, 138
Viewpoint 98

VIP visits 182

Wild tracks 153, 175, 213
Windings 123
Writing commentaries 209, 213

Zoom lenses 129